ONE WEEK
LOAN

Comedy

*An Introduction to Comedy
in Literature,
Drama, and Cinema*

T. G. A. NELSON

Oxford   New York
OXFORD UNIVERSITY PRESS
1990

Oxford University Press, Walton Street, Oxford OX2 6DP

Oxford New York Toronto
Delhi Bombay Calcutta Madras Karachi
Petaling Jaya Singapore Hong Kong Tokyo
Nairobi Dar es Salaam Cape Town
Melbourne Auckland

and associated companies in
Berlin Ibadan

Oxford is a trade mark of Oxford University Press

Published in the United States
by Oxford University Press, New York

First published 1990 as an Oxford University Press paperback
and simultaneously in a hardback edition

British Library Cataloguing in Publication Data
Nelson, T. G. A.
Comedy : an introduction to comedy in literature,
drama and cinema.—(OPUS)
1. Comedy
I. Title II. Series
791

ISBN 0–19–219241–8
ISBN 0–19–289220–7 (Pbk.)

Library of Congress Cataloging in Publication Data
Nelson, T. G. A.
Comedy : an introduction to comedy in literature,
drama, and cinema / T. G. A. Nelson.
p.   cm.—(An OPUS book)
Includes bibliographical references (p.   ).
1. Comedy. I. Title. II. Series: OPUS.
PN1922.N4 1990 809'.917—dc20 89–27901

ISBN 0–19–219241–8
ISBN 0–19–289220–7 (Pbk.)

Typeset by Colset Private Limited, Singapore
Printed in Great Britain by
Biddles Ltd, Guildford and King's Lynn

Acknowledgements

I am grateful to the University of New England, New South Wales, for granting me a period of sabbatical leave in which to write this book. Thanks are also due to Geoffrey Borny, Ian Campbell, Julian Croft, Ian Donaldson, Dennis Drummond, Hester Eisenstein, Bruno Ferraro, Michael Gregory, Graeme Hirsch, Alison Hoddinott, Gabrielle Hyslop, Michael Lee, William Mann, Elaine Moon, Helen Nelson, John Ryan, Helen Stokes, Elizabeth Teather, and Vanessa Todd, all of whom have given valuable help.

Contents

1

Laughter

In 1980 Umberto Eco published his mystery-novel *The Name of the Rose*. The setting was a medieval monastery. The motive for the murders was to keep secret the existence of a manuscript of Aristotle's supposedly lost treatise on comedy. Superficially, this sounds a slender motive for a series of brutal and bizarre killings. But to Eco's principal characters the great philosopher's attitude to comedy and laughter is of clamorous importance. The protagonist seeks Aristotle's authority to uphold his view that laughter is desperately needed in a world dominated by the spirit of seriousness, by fanaticism, intolerance, and fear. The antagonist wants to suppress Aristotle's treatise because he sees laughter as embodying all that is demeaning and trivial; as a threat to religious faith and to the dignity of human life. These contrasting views can be found not only in the fictional world of *The Name of the Rose* but in the writings of philosophers, theologians, social reformers, and imaginative writers from classical times to the present.

This book will consider the cases for and against comedy and laughter. But before an evaluation can begin we must be clear about what we are discussing. Today we sometimes speak as if laughter were all that is involved in comedy. But in the Middle Ages, as Nevill Coghill shows, harmony and reconciliation rather than wit or hilarity were considered the essence of comedy: comedies were tales which began with obstacles standing in the way of happiness but went on to show these obstacles being overcome. This view of comedy survived into the Renaissance period. Sir John Harington, a contemporary of Shakespeare, described as 'a pretty comical matter' a story in which an innocent woman narrowly escaped being burned for adultery. What he had in mind, presumably, was the neat plot and the eventual avoidance of disaster, for the tale in question is not rich in jokes. During the same period Sir Philip Sidney and Ben Jonson both warned against concepts of comedy which made it depend too heavily on laughter. Yet Harington, Sidney, and Jonson all enjoyed laughing and making others laugh.

I mention this older use of the word 'comedy' because it reminds us that the modern usage encompasses two concepts, not one. Laughter is the more obvious. The less obvious is that of a movement towards harmony, reconciliation, happiness: the medieval idea. It will be seen that these two elements are in conflict. Laughter is often discordant, malicious, or vindictive: it can disrupt harmony rather than promoting it. Thus Charles Mauron, a psychoanalyst, sees contradictory tendencies in comedy. The movement towards reconciliation, he argues, answers to the universal human longing for reunion with a lost mother; scornful laughter and comic rivalries express a wish for triumph over a repressive father. Whatever our feelings about psychoanalysis, we may agree that there is a potential for conflict between the subversiveness of comic action and dialogue, full of pratfalls, insults, ridicule, defiance, and irreverence, and the steady movement towards harmony in the comic plot.

The rest of this chapter will be devoted to a discussion of laughter: my second chapter will attempt a mapping of the territory of comedy in relation to some neighbouring modes and genres. To make this separation in the early stages is necessarily to postpone detailed discussion of the relationship between those two contradictory, yet equally fundamental, tendencies of comedy, the impulse to laughter and the movement towards harmony. That discussion will be found in the last chapter of this book. But it is important for us to bear in mind, from the outset, that any discussion of laughter in isolation from comic form, and any discussion of comic form in isolation from laughter, will be incomplete as a discussion of comedy. Bergson's *Laughter* (1900) and Freud's *Jokes and Their Relation to the Unconscious* (1905) are both important contributions to their subjects, but they fail to deal adequately with comedy because they consider only one of its main features. To a lesser extent Northrop Frye's criticism, which stresses that aspect of comedy which moves towards joy, reconciliation, and new beginnings, underplays the element of laughter in comedy: at times it seems to merge comedy into the related mode of romance.

Almost the first thing we notice about laughter is its problematic nature. Freud, who gave it an important place in psychic life, recognized that hostile and cynical jokes were more common, and usually more potent, than innocent ones. When we laugh, we usually laugh at someone or something: 'Nothing', Nell muses in Samuel Beckett's *Endgame*, 'is funnier than unhappiness.' It has often been observed that people enjoy laughing at other people's physical deformities and at the misfortunes, especially bodily misfortunes, which befall them. The narrator of *Gravity's Rainbow*, a grotesquely comic novel by the American writer Thomas Pynchon, remarks of one of the villains, 'Like Adolf Hitler, Springer is easily tickled by what the Germans call *Schadenfreude*, the feeling of joy at another's misfortune.' 'Joy' is, of course, too strong a word to cover all cases. In the eighteenth century the English philosopher Bernard Mandeville gave a less one-sided description of the emotions excited by another's misfortune:

At disasters, we either laugh, or pity those that befall them, according to the stock we are possessed of either malice or compassion. If a man falls and hurts himself so slightly that it moves not the latter, we laugh, and here our pity and malice shake us alternately: 'Indeed, sir, I am very sorry for it, I beg your pardon for laughing, I am the silliest creature in the world,' then laugh again and again, 'I am very sorry,' and so on.

This last example suggests that the same incident may arouse both a sense of pity and a sense of ridicule. Such mixed feelings are common. In Edward Albee's *Who's Afraid of Virginia Woolf* Martha, describing an incident in which her father playfully punched her husband and knocked him flat into a huckleberry bush, recalls: 'It was awful, really. It was funny, but it was awful.' Evidently many of the funniest moments in our lives have something awful about them. Aristotle noted that the mask worn by the comic actor was 'ugly and distorted' but did not 'imply pain', yet people sometimes laugh at ugliness and distortion which are real and which do involve pain. Bergson made the similar suggestion that people laugh at a hunchback because his deformity looks like one which has been put on to amuse us (like the comic mask) and can be corrected at will. Presumably compassion sets in when reason reminds us that in this case correction of the deformity is impossible. Most human beings have to be taught not to laugh at people who look or behave differently from themselves, and at dignity punctured by insult, mishap, or ridicule.

This may suggest a function for comedies and other artificial means of arousing laughter: they gratify impulses which we normally have to repress. Freud plausibly connects them with regression to an infantile state. Children and some adults enjoy *Two Thousand Insults for All Occasions* and *The Official Irish Joke Book*, without necessarily believing in the stupidity of Irishmen or intending to save up choice insults for use against acquaintances. Racist and sexist jokes are more likely to be told to people who share their underlying assumptions than to the people at whose expense the jokes are made. In such situations they may sometimes work as a safety-valve for aggressive impulses: they need not invariably act as a provocation to strife. However, there is no guarantee that jokes against (say) women or racial minorities will not, in the long run, contribute to their oppression: clearly there are, as Ronald de Sousa reminds us, occasions when it is wrong to laugh. Yet if I stop myself laughing at everything which might give pain to others, my life will be like Mr and Mrs Ramsbottom's dreary outing in the popular British comic monologue. The Ramsbottoms, on their trip to the seaside, were disappointed to see 'no wrecks, and nobody drownded—'fact, nothing to laugh at at all'.

The protagonist of Eco's *The Name of the Rose* invoked Aristotle in defence of his own favourable valuation of laughter. But comments on laughter in Aristotle's surviving work are rather guarded. (Generous quotations and detailed references will be found in Lane Cooper's book.) Aristotle certainly did not praise comedy or laughter in the extravagant tones adopted by more recent writers: he never anticipated the joyous invitation of the sage in Nietzsche's *Thus Spoke Zarathustra*, 'Come, let us kill the Spirit of Gravity!' Aristotle does remark in the fifth chapter of the *Poetics* that comedy was not at first taken seriously, which implies that it had begun to be so by his time. He also mentions it several times in conjunction with tragedy, without specifically implying that comedy is inferior. And he does state, in one of his books on animals (*De Partibus Animalium*, III. 10), that human beings are the only creatures that laugh. But this last comment comes in a chapter on the rib-cage and neighbouring regions of the body, and the mention of laughter arises from a discussion of tickling. At this point Aristotle is considering laughter chiefly as a physical phenomenon, and it is in any case marginal to his main discussion. Elsewhere Aristotle mentions several other human traits which animals do not share, such as the faculty of deliberation, the gift for political organization, and the ability to remember the past. So his statement that laughter occurs only in human beings carries, in context, no great philosophical weight. Overall, his utterances on laughter and comedy are descriptive and objective, not evaluative. There is nothing to suggest that he placed laughter very high on the list of those characteristics which distinguish human beings from animals.

While Aristotle is unlikely to have written a eulogy of laughter, other philosophers have treated it with outright distrust. One of the sharpest criticisms is expressed in a few sharp paragraphs by the seventeenth-century philosopher Thomas Hobbes. For Hobbes the cause of laughter is sudden exaltation at a triumph of our own or an indignity suffered by someone else: we laugh when we feel superior to others. More specifically, Hobbes seems to see laughter as an expression of unfounded pride: those who laugh most are those who are momentarily released by laughter from awareness of their own lack of ability. We laugh at those who have stood above us, but who gratify our wish for superiority by falling from their pedestals. Or we laugh at mistakes which we might once have made ourselves, but which we have now learned to avoid. Hobbes's theory of laughter has come to be described as the superiority theory. It can be widened into a malice theory: as Lady Sneerwell says in Sheridan's *The School for Scandal*, 'There's no possibility of being witty without a little ill nature.' Many attempts have been made to discredit the superiority theory, and we can see why. The suggestion that laughter, which may be specific to human beings, arises from malicious delight in superiority to others is not flattering to humanity. The point is brought out deftly in John Barth's modern comic fantasy *Giles*

Goat-Boy, whose central figure is a young man reared among goats. Seduced by the applause of people who come to the goat-farm to look over the fence, he starts competitive games such as King of the Castle. One day the spectators encourage him to taunt another goat, his friend, who cannot displace him from his perch: 'I found myself making the peculiar roaring noise I'd heard humans make. . . . The word *laughter* was not yet in my vocabulary; I'd often mimicked its sound, but now I understood its cause and use. Inspired, I made water upon my friend. "Ha ha ha!'' we all laughed as he sprang away.'

Laughter, then, is often rooted in malice. It is also treacherous: people laugh when they feel superior, but the tables may turn so that the laugher becomes the butt. This, in fact, is what happens in *Giles Goat-Boy*. The hero's triumph is followed by humiliation when he accidentally falls over the fence and finds himself among the human visitors: they strike him and jeer at him, partly because they are afraid. 'Why', the victim asks afterwards, 'had they cheered my stunt and then *ha-ha'd* all the time they kicked me? . . . What manner of beast was it that *laughed* at his victim's plight?' It is a fair question. We may not grant that all laughter is malicious. But it is a mistake to play down the importance of scornful laughter, as some philosophers have been inclined to do. In Bruce Mason's New Zealand play *The End of the Golden Weather* some youths challenge a mentally retarded man called Firpo to a race. The victim turns up at the appointed time and makes an unexpectedly good start which puts him ahead of the field. But he fails to last the distance: as the other runners begin to pass him, he falls flat on his face. The narrator's comment is revealing: 'There is a great shout of laughter. It is a comedy after all: the funny scene has just come later than usual. . . . I could feel relief in their laughter: the Comic Muse had done her stuff and they would not have to cope with a Firpo who had won. . . . Now they could enjoy the race.' Evidently dramatists and novelists, as well as certain philosophers, associate laughter and comedy with feelings of malicious superiority. Its favourite targets are those who look as if they may prove superior, but fail to live up to their promise.

The superiority theory is one of three which have dominated

discussions of laughter during the last few centuries: though applicable to many instances of laughter, it falls short of explaining all. Another is the incongruity theory, articulated in the nineteenth century by Schopenhauer. It is not absolutely incompatible with the superiority theory: indeed, the relation between all three main theories is best described as one of overlap rather than mutual exclusion. However, the incongruity theory is sometimes thought of (by John Morreal, for example) as a rival of the superiority theory: it is certainly a useful weapon in the hands of those who want to rescue laughter from any necessary association with malice. It also has a wider application in that it helps to explain the success of many jokes. But 'helps' is the operative word. Consider one of Schopenhauer's examples. An actor is forbidden to improvise during his act. Soon afterwards he is required to ride a horse on stage. The horse drops dung, to the amusement of the audience: the comedian reproves his mount for getting laughs from a joke which is not in the script. No doubt some of the humour of this story derives from incongruity. But victory over authority also contributes: comedian and audience triumph over the director or impresario who has tried to place checks on their enjoyment by forbidding improvisation. So in this example freedom, the sense of release, and even Hobbesian triumph, seem as important as incongruity. Nevertheless it would be foolish to dismiss the incongruity theory as trivial or marginal. It keeps cropping up in different forms: several ideas about laughter which we shall have cause to consider later turn out to be variants of it.

The third main theory of laughter is that it arises from psychic release, 'the arousal', as James Feibleman puts it, 'first of terrific fear, then of release, and finally of laughter at the needlessness of the fear'. This again seems helpful, not only to our conception of laughter but to our conception of comedy. It complements the medieval formula, where comedy begins with dangers or difficulties and ends with their resolution; it suggests that the structure of a comedy may be similar to the structure of a joke. We have all sat on the edge of our seats when some disaster threatened a comic character, only to laugh with relief when calamity was avoided. Take a recent example. The meek Professor

Petworth in Malcolm Bradbury's novel *Rates of Exchange* visits an East European country where he feels unsure of his welcome. He is intimidated by grim stewardesses on the flight, and by a succession of soldiers and security-men who examine him after the aircraft touches down. At last he is ushered into a room containing another enormous security-guard. He 'feels himself seized . . . his nose is being pushed hard into the leather cross-strap over the man's shoulders . . . his hands touch the cold metal of the machine gun on his back . . . His groin is being bored, his back being beaten.' But then the guard releases him from the clinch and cries, 'Cam'radaki! Velki in Slaka.' What seemed like the third degree was in reality a welcoming hug. Here the humour, for the sympathetic reader, consists partly of release from fear on Petworth's behalf.

A Freudian critic, Ernst Kris, notes that this sudden release from anxiety, leading to laughter, does not work for everybody, and our experience confirms this. Certain episodes in films (such as Harold Lloyd's terrifying climbing sequences) deliberately provoke fear in order to make the audience laugh with relief when the danger is ended. But some members of the audience, those who have been least successful in mastering this particular fear, may find it impossible to laugh. Kris cites Hobbes, who saw laughter as arising from 'some eminency in ourselves, by comparison with the inferiority of others, or *with our own formerly*' (Kris's emphasis). We laugh at dangers or difficulties which we once feared but now feel we have mastered. But if we are not confident of our mastery, we do not laugh. Kris cites the example of a teacher who was unable to laugh at children's mistakes because she had bad memories of being ridiculed as a child. This helps to explain why some people seem to have no sense of humour or to be insensitive to certain kinds of joke. Incidentally, Kris changes direction later in his essay, implying that laughter at something dangerous or frightening indicates, not a total, but only a partial, overcoming of anxiety. In a striking phrase he describes the human being as 'an eternal pleasure-seeker walking on a narrow ledge above an abyss of fear'.

It will be seen that, for Kris, the psychic release theory complements the superiority theory. However, a psychic release joke like the one Bradbury tells about Professor Petworth also owes much to reversal of expectation, to incongruity, and to our recognition of the fact that the same set of signs may bear diverse interpretations. It is not essential for readers, if they are to enjoy the passage, to feel superior to Petworth at this moment: his mistake is one that any of us might make. At times, then, there may be more empathy than superiority in our reaction to the plight of a comic character: we do not necessarily feel superior even to the weakling or fool. The French comic novelist Raymond Queneau was irritated by a comment that many of his characters were simpletons: he retorted that readers who let themselves despise such figures must be swollen headed.

Feelings of superiority may cause laughter, but there is room in comedy for more subtle effects. The notion of psychic release, too, while it helps to explain some occasions of laughter, cannot explain them all, nor is it prominent in all comedies. Morton Gurewitch, writing of Shakespeare's *Comedy of Errors*, notes that it offers 'small solvent for psychic repression' and notably fails to 'open the floodgates of carnival'. Yet this play is as rich in broad humour and farcical incident as any of Shakespeare's comedies. Even Freud, Gurewitch notes, 'nowhere suggests that "comedy" is an entity marked by a joyous insurrection against authority, . . . a gay dechristianization designed to recharge our enfeebled nature and purge us of guilt'. It begins to look as if laughter may often be, in the Freudian sense of the word, overdetermined. (Laplanche and Pontalis give as one meaning of overdetermination 'the fact that formations of the unconscious (symptoms, dreams, etc.) can be attributed to a plurality of determining factors'.) While Freud is clearly right to postulate a relationship between jokes and the unconscious, there are few jokes whose appeal can be confidently explained in terms of a single factor such as enjoyment of superiority, delight in incongruity, or psychic release. There even seem to be a few instances of laughter which have little to do with any of the stimuli or constraints mentioned so far. I may laugh when I am tickled. I may laugh from sheer pleasure, possibly at someone else's triumph rather than my own. I may laugh with other people rather than at them. I may laugh at myself.

Perhaps the most important distinction between writers on laughter is between those who emphasize its healthful and recreative aspects and those who find it predominantly derisive, aggressive, or objectionable. These rival attitudes emerge most clearly in discussions of jokes on controversial subjects, so we shall now examine the relation of laughter to two of these. The first is woman; the second religion. In both cases the temptation of some groups and individuals to indulge in offensive humour seems perennial, while those who object to their sallies have two possible strategies available. The first is simply to deplore the laughter and to reject the ridicule; the second is to appropriate laughter for the defence of what has seemed to be under attack.

According to George Meredith, in an essay on comedy published in 1897, a 'great comic poet' will always find 'a state of marked social inequality between the sexes' repellent. Susan Carlson, in an article published some nine decades later, finds this view unconvincing. 'Mention of comic heroines like Lysistrata, Rosalind, Viola, Beatrice, Millamant, and Anne Whitefield', she concedes, 'conjures up images of enviable and brilliant female power, freedom, and intelligence.' But recent feminist writing, as well as her own experience, convinces Carlson that 'comedy invariably limits its heroines': they are always reabsorbed into the male-dominated world at the end. In the past this has been generally true. In Aristophanes' *Lysistrata* women take over the most sacred shrine of Athenian religion, and withdraw sexual favours from their husbands until they agree to stop going to war. But there is no suggestion in the play that exercise of power by women could be permanent or even frequent. Indeed the fact that this play could be presented in a society in which women were so clearly subordinate to men was doubtless due to a conviction among male Athenians that no programme resembling Lysistrata's could ever be implemented by real Athenian women.

In comic drama and fiction of the Renaissance, which is full of clever and resourceful women, the heroine almost invariably accepts marriage and subordination in the final chapter or scene. In English Restoration comedy, which is sometimes represented as treating women and men on equal terms, the women are

expected to save their virginity until marriage, whereas their partners' licence to stray is taken for granted. Wycherley's Margery
Pinchwife is married off to an older man before she knows what
freedom is: after a tantalizingly short stay in London she is
whisked back to the country by her unbearable husband. In the
early years of our own century, as Walter Kerr remarks, the
female leads in Buster Keaton's films were 'merely there to be
rescued and as likely to foul up the rescue as anything else': they
sat 'at home reading letters' while Keaton did the work of the
film.

The obvious remedy for a comic tradition which laughs at or
patronizes women is to create a rival tradition in which women
laugh at or patronize men. While we can find instances of this
from quite early times, there has until recently been an air of
diffidence about most of them. Helena in Aphra Behn's Restoration comedy *The Rover* has some sharp satirical speeches on
cohabitation with that supposedly desirable creature, a husband:

The giant stretches itself, yawns, and sighs a belch or two loud as a
musket, throws himself into bed, and expects you in his foul sheets; and
ere you can get yourself undressed, calls you with a snore or two. . . .
And this man you must kiss, nay you must kiss none but him too, and
nuzzle through his beard to find his lips. And this you must submit to for
threescore years, and all for a jointure.

But in order to make such speeches acceptable Behn also has to
give Helena lines like, 'I love mischief strangely, as most of our
sex do who are come to love nothing else.' This reasserts the
conventional view that a woman needs a man to love: her preoccupation with her husband or intended husband will keep her
from other, more dangerous, involvements. The character is thus
pushed back towards a female stereotype which the men in the
audience know, and do not greatly fear.

In modern times, of course, female characters have become
more outspoken. The protagonist of Rose Macaulay's *The
Towers of Trebizond* speaks for many twentieth-century women
when she complains: 'Women get called rude names more than
men, because it is not expected that they will hit the people who
call them names, so they are called old trouts, old bags, cows,

tramps, bitches, whores, and many other things.' Yet even in modern comedy the independence of female characters tends to lapse towards the end of the novel or play. In *The Towers of Trebizond* the apparently emancipated Turkish woman doctor finally accepts marriage and reverts to the Muslim religion. The recent film comedy *Nine to Five*, where the female staff imprison an unpopular works manager in his house while they run the factory, ends with the rebels accepting forgiveness and praise from a man who stands a little higher on the ladder than the deposed tyrant.

More genuinely innovative, despite its conformity in other respects to the conventions of commercial film comedy, is *Outrageous Fortune*. Both leading roles go to women. The man whom both, at first, find attractive is soon unmasked as a villain, in league with the arrogant theatre director from whom the two aspiring actresses take lessons. Of these two male characters, the first belongs to the type whom women are supposed to idolize and the second to the type who think women need to be mastered. Both are soon cast off: the two leading characters show no sign of needing a replacement for either. At the end one of the women achieves, after the manner of Sarah Bernhardt, her ambition of playing Hamlet: the men are relegated to the position of spectators. In this comedy the laughter, though not bitter or searing, is unmistakably the laughter of superiority, for once directed against men as men rather than against women as women.

Higher intellectual pretensions characterize Beth Henley's American comedy *Crimes of the Heart*, originally a play but later filmed. This time the laughter is not that of superiority but of incongruity and psychic release. The main characters are three sisters living in a semi-rural part of the Southern United States. The real subject of the film is the warmth of their mutual relationship, and the naturalness with which childhood intimacy is resumed when the two who have left the family home return to it. Tension, unhappiness, and lack of fulfilment brood over the lives of all three women, but are repeatedly dissolved in laughter. When one sister is charged with shooting and seriously wounding her husband, it is agreed that she must be defended by the best lawyer in town. Unfortunately there is equal unanimity about the fact that the best lawyer in town is the stricken husband. Later, while one sister is downstairs making a telephone call which promises to change her whole life for the better, another is upstairs trying to hang herself from a light fitting. After the attempt fails, the would-be suicide trails distractedly downstairs, with the cord still around her neck, to try the gas oven. The incongruity is irresistible: it also encourages the audience to feel confident that the next suicide attempt will also fail.

The expectation is not disappointed: indeed, in both film and stage versions of *Crimes of the Heart* cheerfulness keeps on breaking through. The sisters repeatedly relapse into merriment, chiefly from simple pleasure in being together. The spectres of death, loneliness, and rejection are kept at bay by an underlying atmosphere of holiday and festivity. There is much drinking of lemonade, eating of ice-cream and chocolates, perusal of photograph albums. The film version ends with a freeze shot. In it the Cinderella figure among the three sisters, who was depressed at the beginning by the failure of the others to remember her birthday, stands radiant with pleasure between her two siblings in front of a large birthday cake. *Crimes of the Heart* goes far, then, towards refuting Susan Carlson's conclusion that comedy is inherently and necessarily sexist. It is a festive comedy with women at its centre: it sees no need to go out of its way to jeer at men. The laughter that it invites is a laughter of empathy rather than superiority.

Another area where comedy must tread carefully is that of the sacred. Spiritual leaders have sometimes expressed disapproval of comedy and laughter as such, consigning them to the realm of the body rather than that of the spirit, or to the devil rather than to God. The Buddha is said to have asked, 'How can there be mirth and laughter when the world is on fire?' The Bible, some Christian theologians observe, records that Jesus wept (John 11: 35) but not that he ever laughed. In Dante's paradise there is a 'riso dell' universo', a cosmic burst of joyful laughter; but Baudelaire and others have argued that this laughter of pure joy is something separate from the comic, and not to be confused with it. A German writer on aesthetics, J.P.F. Richter, took a different view, seeing the comic writer as aspiring 'to project the model of the divine image through the animal kingdom of fools'. However, Richter admitted that achievement of this ambition was dauntingly difficult. A few examples come to mind, such as the spectacle of earthy, ass-headed Bottom in *A Midsummer Night's Dream*, waking after a night of supernatural experiences in the forest and comically misquoting St Paul on divine rapture. But it has to be admitted that this kind of comic experience is rare. Morton Gurewitch points out that, 'For every comedy that hints at a blissful serenity beyond the grasp of reason and experience, there are hundreds that project not an iota of cosmic blitheness.'

There is, however, other evidence that laughter and the sacred are not incompatible. The diabolical Screwtape in C. S. Lewis's *Screwtape Letters* places no great faith in sexual humour as a means of temptation. For many humans, Screwtape warns his subordinate, the fun of an indecent story actually reduces its lasciviousness: obsessive seriousness about sex is of more use to the devil than laughing about it. And we are invited to infer that, in this instance, Screwtape's analysis is correct. The argument that gravity and humourlessness are the marks of false, rather than true, religion is an attractive one, often taken up by writers of comedy. Molière's Tartuffe, the solemn ascetic, is only the most outstanding example among many. In both Eastern and Western comic tradition those who claim to have renounced the flesh are suspected of indulging themselves in secret, or of using their gravity and the spiritual authority which springs from it for worldly ends. It is hard not to share Huck Finn's preference for laughter and adventure over 'soul-butter and hogwash' or Tom Sawyer's longing, during en epidemic of religion in his home town, for the sight of 'one blessed sinful face'. Yet there are occasions when even the most anarchic comic impulses seem to be enlisted on the side of religion, or at least spirituality. Lee Siegel shows that, in India, important deities are associated with mirth: Ganesh is born from Siva's laughter. Christ's forerunner, John the Baptist, was described as a voice crying in the wilderness: the comic dramatist George Bernard Shaw was flattered when someone referred to him as a man laughing in the wilderness.

However, the religion validated in comedy belongs to the

fringe, not the establishment. In the 1980 American film *The Blues Brothers* one brother sees the light at a religious service in a Negro quarter of town, where devotion is expressed in ecstatic rock-and-roll singing, dancing, and acrobatics. The scene is like a realization of Harvey Cox's vision of a comic, festive, celebratory Christianity, superseding the sour-faced kind. As a result of this experience the brothers plan a charity concert to save the Catholic orphanage where they were brought up. As they strive to put the concert together, hoping to pay the nuns' rates out of the takings, they leave a trail of unpaid debts, wrecked police cars, and criminal charges behind them. Throughout, they keep reminding one another that they are on a mission from God; predictably, they fulfil it with seconds to spare.

Another kind of religious humour is found in Tom Stoppard's *Jumpers*. The protagonist, George Moore (not the author of *Principia Ethica* though often, understandably, confused with him), is a university teacher of philosophy, described by his complacently positivist Vice-Chancellor as 'our tame believer, pointed out to visitors in much the same spirit as we point out the magnificent stained glass in what is now the gymnasium'. Living in a sceptical age, in which the Church is in the process of being 'rationalized', George locks himself in his study to prepare a defence of his continued belief in, or attempt to believe in, God. As he writes his lecture, which is destined never to be delivered, he remains oblivious to the murder, corruption, and crooked dealing going on outside his study door. To his wife, who asks impishly, 'Haven't you invented God yet?' he replies distractedly, 'I'm having him typed out.' Later, catching himself indulging in a piece of sentimental rhetoric, he mourns: 'The fact that I cut a ludicrous figure in the academic world is largely due to my aptitude for reducing a complex and logical thesis to a mysticism of staggering banality.' But it is language and logic that betray George, not the pre-linguistic and pre-logical thesis which he is struggling, vainly, to express. The play as a whole, though it laughs at the protagonist for his ineffectiveness and his misguided approach to his problem, never makes his search for God, as such, appear ridiculous. It ends with a dream sequence in which the Archbishop of Canterbury, a former veterinary surgeon who gained his ecclesiastical appointment as a reward for political services, emulates the medieval martyr Thomas Becket and begins to defend the Church: 'Surely', the archbishop pleads, 'belief in man could find room for man's beliefs?'

'The moral of [*Jumpers*], in so far as it has one,' wrote A. J. Ayer, 'seemed to be that George was humane, and therefore human, in a way the others were not. This could have been due to his beliefs, but it did not have to be.' Ayer, a logical positivist philosopher sent to review a play which was partly a satire on logical positivism, analysed the play's thesis correctly: his enjoyment of its comedy overrode his antipathy to its philosophy.

Raymond Queneau's comic novel *Zazie dans le Métro* resembles *The Blues Brothers* and *Jumpers* in that, while its unorthodox approach to the sacred might be disconcerting to a reader possessed by the spirit of seriousness, it adopts the traditional framework of a contest between angelic and diabolical forces. The youthful heroine's guardian angel, a night-club drag artist called Gabriel, is both more likeable and less ridiculous than the pathetic devil figure Trouscaillon. Trouscaillon pays for Zazie's French fries, her Coca Colas, and even her blue jeans, but fails to seduce her; nor can he defeat or capture Gabriel, even when backed by a paramilitary force with automatic weapons. Needless to say, the atmosphere of Queneau's novel is far from being smug or conformist: the 'good' characters are engagingly, unselfconsciously free from the prejudices of convention and respectability. The same is true of the protagonist of John Barth's *Giles Goat-Boy*, a beguiling New Messiah who is brought up among goats and uses a goatish (i.e. natural and uncorrupted) system of values to judge twentieth-century America. Barth's comic-epic fantasy is rich in grotesque realism, and his Messiah even shows an intuitive understanding of the virtues of the devil. Like Blake's poetry or Shaw's plays this novel uses comic incongruities to unsettle a rigid religious tradition and invite a new beginning. This, indeed, is the usual approach to the sacred in comedy. Those who seek to mock religion by associating it with the spirit of seriousness are answered by a systematic attempt to relocate laughter on the angels' side.

So far we have considered certain theories of laughter, and the relationship of laughter to certain controversial subjects. At this point, however, we need to allow for two likely objections. Why do we need theories of laughter and comedy? Aren't they both essentially freewheeling, multifarious, resistant to theory? For the Shakespearian critic L. C. Knights, 'The greatness of any comedy can only be determined by the inclusiveness, the coherence and stability of the resultant attitude; to define its method is the work of detailed and particular analysis, and abstract theories of comedy can at best only amuse.' W. D. Redfern makes a similar point less primly: 'The only generalization about comedy which has ever convinced me is that laughter is one of only three phenomena which occupy our *total* attention: the other two are the sneeze and the orgasm.' The second problem is that, as Francis Hutcheson noted in the eighteenth century, treating laughter gravely (and when has theory not been grave?) exposes us to the charge of writing 'in a manner very unsuitable to the subject'. Readers, expecting to enter a well-upholstered cinema, find themselves in the middle of a battlefield: the formidable names of Plato, Aristotle, Cicero, Horace, Hobbes, Kant, Schopenhauer, Kierkegaard, Nietzsche, Bergson, Freud, and Sartre burst around them like shells. Whatever happened to the Keystone Kops?

My answers to these objections are closely related. I agree that no single theory can explain all laughter or all comedy. The difficulty is that we all, consciously or unconsciously, uphold certain theories and resist others: before we can even identify our own assumptions we need to look at the range of possible attitudes. My own survey of laughter and comedy convinces me that significant recurring patterns do exist, and (to answer the Keystone Kops query) that the same patterns appear in commercial comedy and in what Knights calls 'great' comedy. So I shall not confine myself to 'detailed and particular analysis' of classics (as Knights would), nor shall I consider it beneath my dignity to refer to popular works or performers. There has always been interaction between popular and literary comedy: think of the exchanges between *commedia dell'arte* and *commedia erudita* in Renaissance Italy or, in more recent times, the influence exerted on Beckett and Queneau by music-hall and the silent screen. What is more, there is evidence that comic theory has actually influenced comic practice. The passage just quoted from *Giles Goat-Boy* is transparently a comment on Hobbes: philosophy is here incorporated into comic fiction. Take another example. The critic Georg Lukács remarks that Schopenhauer's philosophy is like a beautiful hotel where you dine on the edge of an abyss. It is tempting to speculate that this was the germ of Douglas Adams's comic/ cosmic fantasy *The Restaurant at the End of the Universe*, in which time-travellers journey to the end of time and have, as the accompaniment to their meal, the pleasure of watching the end of everything. Philosophy and theory are not necessarily at odds with comedy: they stimulate one another. In a few comedies, such as Tom Stoppard's *Jumpers* and *Professional Foul*, philosophy becomes an explicit and central concern. In a radio interview Stoppard remarked that philosophers' utterances often needed only minimal adaptation to become absorbed into comedy or farce, and Queneau seems to have shared this view. But the corollary is that, if some aspects of philosophy are farcical, some aspects of farce are philosophical. Their concerns overlap.

Those who remain impatient of theory are directed to the middle chapters of this book. They are devoted to marriage, birth, and death; to rogues, tricksters, dupes, and fools; to realism and its rivals (including reflexive comedy and absurd comedy). They concentrate on discussion of actual comedies and avoid pushing too much theory forward all at once. But particular theories of comedy do underlie them. Some examination of theory must after all be undertaken if our study of comedy is to go beyond a mere catalogue of jokes. The last two chapters consider the more radically theoretical question of the relation of festivity, play, and scapegoating to comedy. The chapter which immediately follows this introduction aims to place comedy in relation to some neighbouring literary genres such as tragedy, satire, and farce.

2

Comedy and Related Forms

Comedy, according to M.H. Abrams, is a word usually applied only to plays, though comic form also occurs in non-dramatic poetry and prose. In turning, as we now do, from laughter to comedy we shall give some degree of privilege to drama, since that is the medium for which the oldest surviving bodies of distinctively comic literature were written. Aristophanes was already writing dramatic comedies in Athens in the fifth century BC, in competition with other dramatists whose work has not survived. Aristophanic comedy is often referred to as Old Comedy, in contrast to the next important group of comic works, the New Comedy of Menander, another Attic Greek. Menander was born around the middle of the fourth century BC, about forty years after Aristophanes' death.

Aristophanic comedy had some regularly recurring formal features, particularly the *agon* or dispute between contesting parties, on which the play centred. But Aristophanes' plots were skeletal and his tone exuberant; the plays were full of fantastic and farcical incidents, slanging matches, cheerful obscenities, and uninhibited political satire. Menander's plays, or at least the parts of them which survive today, were more staid. Where Aristophanes had concerned himself with the community, Menander showed more interest in the family and in the individual family member. Despite the great and deserved prestige of Aristophanes, which has generally managed to triumph over his reputation for obscenity and scurrility, it is from Menander that the most notable continuous tradition of European comedy descends: it runs through the Roman dramatists Plautus (third and second centuries BC) and Terence (second century BC) to Italian and English Renaissance playwrights such as Machiavelli, Ariosto, Shakespeare, and Jonson. It influences Molière in seventeenth-century France, and from him passes to eighteenth-century figures such as Beaumarchais, Marivaux, Goldoni, Sheridan, and Goldsmith: its lineaments are still clearly discernible in Oscar Wilde's *The Importance of Being Earnest*, first performed in 1895. The New Comedy's most conspicuous contribution to later drama is the plot in which a young man and a young woman succeed in overcoming obstacles to their marriage. But other ingredients of New Comedy, such as comic servants and rogues, also achieved lasting popularity.

New Comedy is originally a scripted form of drama, though Menander's plays had interludes featuring a drunken chorus, which (since no scripts for them have come down to us) may have been improvised. Improvisation was much more fundamental to the Italian *commedia dell'arte*, an important and distinctive form (chiefly, but not exclusively, devoted to comedy in the modern sense of the word) which flourished in the sixteenth and seventeenth centuries. Just as New Comedy is contrasted with Old Comedy, so *commedia dell'arte* is contrasted with *commedia erudita*, or learned comedy. The learned comedy was so called because it derived, in the first place, fairly directly from the work of Plautus and Terence. The *commedia dell'arte* sometimes borrowed plots from the *commedia erudita*, and in this sense it too could be said to be descended from New Comedy. But for the *commedia dell'arte* the plots were written down in skeletal form only. There was no extended script: instead a brief scenario provided a vehicle for verbal and visual humour with a strong improvisational element. In general, the list of stock characters in the *commedia dell'arte* (many of them, such as the soldier or the old man, traceable ultimately to Roman Comedy) varied little from play to play; in a given company the same actor might continue playing the same role for many years on end.

Whereas New Comedy can be seen to possess a clear, though not absolutely continuous, tradition, the same cannot be said of Old Comedy. Comic works reminiscent of Aristophanic comedy appear in Western European literature from time to time, notably in the work of Rabelais in the early sixteenth century in France: Rabelais's linguistic inventiveness, love of fantasy, liking for political satire, and delight in cheerful obscenity all mark him as Aristophanes' heir. But Rabelais was a writer of prose fiction, not of drama; and indeed this turns out to be true of most works reminiscent of Old Comedy which have appeared since

Aristophanes' time. This in turn reminds us that drama holds no absolute predominance in the field of comedy. The work of such early prose writers as Petronius (Roman, first century AD), Lucian (Greek, second century AD), and Apuleius (Latin-speaking African, second century AD) contains strong comic elements. So does Cervantes' *Don Quixote*, which appeared at the beginning of the seventeenth century in Spain. Among English writers, Fielding in the eighteenth century began his career as a dramatist but owes his place in the history of comedy to his novels *Shamela*, *Joseph Andrews*, and *Tom Jones*. Comedy in drama and comedy in prose fiction have, of course, frequently nourished one another. The short stories in Boccaccio's *Decameron*, written in the mid-fourteenth century, influenced the revival of Italian comic drama which began just over a century and a half later. In England the comic drama of the Restoration period, which reached its peak in about 1676, lent plots and type-figures to the eighteenth-century English novel, a body of work which includes at least as many examples of comic as tragic writing.

Clearly, then, a study of comedy cannot restrict itself to a study of the drama. But having once passed beyond drama, we may find it difficult to know where to stop. To cover everything that makes people laugh we should need to consider more than half of all plays, novels, films, short stories, and half-hour television shows; nearly all cartoons (still and animated) and graffiti; many operas; some ballets and paintings; innumerable monologues on records and radio; revue-sketches, night-club acts, and clown interludes in the circus; a sprinkling of advertisements and news stories; a few sporting, social, and political events; countless laughable episodes in works which are not predominantly comic. Malcolm Bradbury, in his recent squib *Mensonge*, has even sought to make comedy out of literary criticism.

Since these cannot all be covered adequately in a short book, I shall concentrate on varieties such as drama, prose fiction, and film, which display what Abrams calls comic form. (This I take to denote a story or plot which moves towards a laughable or celebratory ending.) I shall, however, allude from time to time to works which do not display this form. In particular I shall consider novels and plays such as Cervantes' *Don Quixote* or Ionesco's *The Bald Prima Donna* which have strong comic elements though they are far from being unambiguously comic. Few good comedies are homogeneous in tone and content: in some cultures it is hard to find anything approaching pure comedy, as Lee Siegel found when he came to write his book *Laughing Matters: Comic Tradition in India*. Even in Western Europe, where the comic tradition stretches back over twenty-four centuries, many works traditionally referred to as comedies display marked serious or tragic elements; while in modern writing there are signs that pure comedy (in so far as there ever was such a thing) is losing ground to mixed forms in which tragedy and comedy combine.

In our first chapter we defined comedy as consisting of two conflicting elements, one being laughter (often mocking, derisive, or discordant), and the other being the movement of a story towards an ending characterized by harmony, festivity, and celebration. To reach a more exact definition is difficult, as Umberto Eco complains:

From antiquity to Freud or Bergson, every attempt to define comic seems to be jeopardized by the fact that this is an umbrella term (referring, in Wittgensteinian jargon, to a network of family resemblances), that gathers together a disturbing ensemble of diverse and not completely homogeneous phenomena, such as humor, comedy, grotesque, parody, satire, wit, and so on.

In our first chapter we suggested that the two fundamental elements of comedy were laughter, on the one hand, and a movement towards harmony on the other. We also saw that these elements were liable to conflict, and we should now add that there are many works in which one of them virtually submerges the other. Thus rather than seeking to evolve a rigorous definition of comedy, which, as Eco notes, is a perilous undertaking, we shall suggest that any work which shows either of the two fundamental characteristics just mentioned may qualify for consideration. In so far as a further definition will be attempted, it will be approached relationally. In what remains of this chapter we shall seek to draw a map of comedy in relation to some related modes or genres, which we shall regard as neighbouring territories. However, what has to be remembered is that all these territories overlap with comedy to some extent, just as minority ethnic groups are often to be found living in countries which border on their countries of origin. Some modes which we shall consider, such as the comedy of manners, obviously fall almost entirely within the territories of comedy as such. Others, such as tragedy, will seem to lie clearly outside. But in every case we must beware of trying to effect a clear division. It is characteristic of literary genres and modes that they constantly meet and blend.

Let us begin with satire. Satire has one obvious affinity with comedy: we think of it as intended to make us laugh. Yet at one end of its spectrum, satire approaches the condition of the denunciatory sermon: the call of the prophet Jeremiah to the backsliding Hebrews or of Bishop Wulfstan to the degenerate Anglo-Saxons. Such sermons may be vivid in their imagery and highly wrought in their style: what sets them off from satire is not any lack of literary qualities but their earnestness, their refusal of laughter. Satire sometimes justifies itself on the grounds that great offenders can safely ignore sermons: they are, as Pope put it in the eighteenth century, 'Safe from the bar, the pulpit, and the throne | But touched and shamed by ridicule alone.' In short, satire claims to discourage vice and folly by means of ridicule, which gives pain to the victim. But in some satire there is more earnestness than derision, a 'strong antipathy of good to bad' (to quote Pope again). At times, then, missionary zeal nearly overwhelms laughter: satire and Jeremiad almost blend. Further along the spectrum we find a different type of satire, less savage and superficially more tolerant. This satire is close to the type of comedy which Baudelaire called 'significative comedy', by which he seems to have meant comedy which carried a meaning or message as opposed to the comedy of pure play. Both satire and 'significative comedy' arouse laughter. Both are concerned with moral or social values. Both aspire to improve the quality of life by sharpening awareness of failings in people's dealings with each other. This may explain why theorists, both neo-classical and modern, sometimes write of comedy as if it were indistinguishable from satire: as if, in fact, its main function were corrective. The American critic James Feibleman can find, even in an apparently light-hearted spoof like Sellar and Yeatman's *1066 and All That*, 'a fierce attack' on British insularity and complacency, 'so fierce that the laughter which it at first occasions is pulled up short'. By contrast, many British readers find the book far from 'fierce'. They read it to bolster their conviction that they are capable of laughing at themselves: they do not see it as an attack or as a threat. In other words, they read it as comedy while Feibleman reads it as satire.

This difficulty arises constantly. How 'seriously' or playfully should we take a given joke? A mayor's wife in New Zealand once told Noel Coward that he must never sing 'Mad Dogs and Englishmen' again because it was an insult to the homeland. In this case we feel fairly confident that the criticism is misguided, but often the decision is more difficult. Are we to take Wilde's comedy *The Importance of Being Earnest* as a playful fantasy or as a sharp satire on the English upper classes? Critics sometimes warn that the brilliance of Wilde's dialogue should not blind us to the seriousness of the social criticism, but not all audiences would agree; for some people, the fantasy and playfulness rob the satire of its sting. Why, again, do so many modern readers find *Gulliver's Travels* unbearably bitter and misanthropic, whereas Swift's talented friend Dr Arbuthnot confidently labelled it 'a merry work'? When Voltaire in *Candide* comments on a British quarterdeck-execution ('In this country they shoot an admiral every so often, to encourage the rest') his satiric scorn is unmistakable. But it is hard to maintain rage about the manner of appointment of the First Lord of the Admiralty in W. S. Gilbert's *H.M.S. Pinafore* or the adulterous capers of the gods in Offenbach's *Orpheus in the Underworld*, though both originally referred to real contemporary scandals and both have parallels in our own social world.

Evidently many factors influence our unconscious decisions as to whether particular works are satiric or comic, so I shall not attempt any systematic exclusion of satire from this book. Instead, before leaving the topic, I shall offer two suggestions. The first is that the difference between satire and comedy is best described in terms of reader-response. If your laughter contains an element of anger or moral disgust, you are responding to the wit or humour as satire. If these elements are absent, you are responding to it as comedy. The second point is related. We have seen that in their urbane forms satire and comedy come close to one another. But when the laughter becomes harsher, a bifurcation takes place. As social or moral evaluation begins to sharpen, we enter the domain of satire. But while evaluation remains relatively unobtrusive, we remain in the realm of comedy.

Baudelaire and his modern follower Edith Kern have envisaged a type of comedy called 'absolute comedy' in which evaluation is avoided altogether. The form which comes closest to realizing this somewhat visionary idea is farce. The prestige of farce has generally been low; but in recent times it has found a champion in Eric Bentley, critic and man of the theatre. Irritated by a patronizing definition in a standard reference book, Bentley set out to show that farce, like dreams, allowed 'the disguised fulfilment of repressed wishes'. 'In all comedy', he declared, 'there remains something of destructive orgy, farce being the kind of comedy which disguises that fact least thoroughly.' One kind of farce, then, turns characters into caricatures, emphasizes the body at the expense of the spirit, and mocks altruism and morality. It deliberately dehumanizes its characters, or subordinates humans to objects. As the director of the farce-within-a-farce remarks in Michael Frayn's *Noises Off*, 'That's what it's all about. Doors and sardines. Getting on—getting off. Getting the sardines on—getting the sardines off. That's farce. That's the theatre. That's life.' Not only can people be subordinated to objects: they can also seem to change, or exchange, their personalities according to setting or circumstance. In *A Flea in Her Ear*, by the French *farceur* Georges Feydeau, all kinds of unexpected parallels emerge between the two locales, one the house of a wealthy married man and the other a brothel. Most of the characters, male and female, find their way readily from one to the other, and settle into the new environment with disconcerting ease; even more disturbingly, the master of the house turns out to have a double in the brothel in the shape of a feckless, alcoholic porter. Our faith in the uniqueness of the self, and in certain types of social distinction, is amusingly, but disturbingly, undermined.

In the world of harsh farce the qualities needed for survival are ready wit, a gift for improvisation, and something worse than indifference to the interests and feelings of others. In Alan Ayckbourn's *Living Together* a plodding male character, berated by a woman friend, turns for reassurance to another man:

TOM. Do you think I'm dim and dismal? I think that's what she said. Yes, that was it. Dim and dismal and stupid. Do I come across as that?
NORMAN. No. I'd say—you had the good fortune to be born without a single suspicious or malicious thought in your head.

Norman speaks ironically. In the world of ruthless farce 'dim and dismal' and 'born without a single suspicious or malicious thought' amount to the same thing.

A more benign type of farce is displayed in the coin-swallowing scene in Chaplin's film *The Great Dictator*. Several men sit down to eat their pudding, having agreed that whoever finds a coin in his portion shall assassinate Hitler. Unknown to them, the heroine, who disapproves of the assassination plot, has put coins in all the slices. Each man, as he finds his coin, slips it surreptitiously on to the next man's plate. The exception is the barber (Chaplin), who swallows his coin instead of passing it on. But, since the others keep passing theirs around, he keeps finding more coins on his plate: as he swallows more and more he begins to give off metallic sounds like a till or a slot-machine. Here, though the victim has little malice or suspicion in his nature, the audience is not tempted to think of him as dim or dismal. The laughter in the coin-swallowing scene is not malicious, nor is it as 'significative' in Baudelaire's sense as most other parts of the film, which merge comedy with passionate protest against Nazism. There is little leakage of this value-system into the coin-swallowing scene. We are not, for example, invited to click our tongues at the cowardice of the men, each anxious to saddle his neighbour with the heroic task of ridding the world of a tyrant. Nor, on the other hand, do we sneer at the victim for letting himself be tricked into accepting the other men's coins.

Farce has two faces, one harsh and one bland. The extreme of blandness is reached in Brandon Thomas's *Charley's Aunt*, with its harmless transvestism, ludicrous catch-phrases, and implausibly mistaken identities; the extreme of harshness is represented by Joe Orton's *Loot*, with its body-snatchings, bribery, and betrayals. These different types of farce are linked, however, by more than the use of a few shared devices such as slapstick, identity-confusion, and enjoyable improbabilities of plot. Often we can discern the skeleton of harsh farce beneath the plump figure of bland farce.

An intriguing recent development (perhaps traceable to Chaplin or even, ultimately, to Aristophanes) is the vogue for outright political farce or 'farce of ideas': this brings farce back, unexpectedly, within the boundaries of 'significative' comedy. The farcical episodes are not isolated from the political part but actually constitute it: politics and farce become synonymous. (Two accomplished pieces from different points on the political spectrum are Dario Fo's *Accidental Death of an Anarchist* and Tom Stoppard's *Travesties*.) Such blending and stretching of different comic and farcical forms will suggest why I have decided not to exclude farce from this book. Neither comedy nor farce can live for long without the other. And despite the militant tone of Eric Bentley, who writes as if he were the first critic to defend it, farce has always had its champions. As early as 1693 Nahum Tate, then Poet Laureate, spoke up for it in the preface to his own successful farce *A Duke and No Duke*. In ancient Athens Aristophanes, when jeering at rival playwrights, always targeted their use of farcical techniques; but the devices he mocked are all, as Douglas MacDowell shows, used in his own plays. In more recent times, both Shaw and Ionesco have claimed to find Feydeau's farces nauseating, yet both have borrowed from him. What seems to happen is that at a certain point audiences and dramatists tire of the currently fashionable brand of farce: suddenly it begins to appear repetitive, wearisome, even repugnant. Yet it is never long before farce is reintroduced in a new form, sometimes by the very writers who caused it to be tossed aside.

If farce has often stood low in critical esteem, comedy of all kinds has traditionally been placed lower than tragedy. At the end of Plato's *Symposium* Socrates is heard telling Agathon the tragedian and Aristophanes the comic dramatist that 'the genius of comedy' is 'the same as that of tragedy', and that 'the true artist in tragedy' is 'an artist in comedy also'. However, we do not learn what arguments Socrates used to prove his point: we are simply told that neither Agathon nor Aristophanes understood them, since both were fuddled by that time. (The *Symposium* itself, incidentally, has a strong comic and festive cast: the word 'symposium' means 'drinking party', and the setting for the dialogue is a convivial evening at Agathon's house.) Elsewhere, in the third book of Plato's *Republic*, it is contended that tragedy and comedy, while 'closely allied', cannot be successfully written by the same person or even successfully acted by the same performers.

This is more in accord with mainstream classical theory. Aristotle, as we have seen, implies that in his time comedy had only lately begun to be taken seriously. But it was not until the twentieth century that critics began to consider the two modes as equal and complementary, like yin and yang. Northrop Frye's influential essay 'The Argument of Comedy' presents tragedy as 'implicit or uncompleted comedy': tragedy and comedy, he argues, are both parts of a mythic ritual cycle based on the seasons, with comedy representing the resurrection of the god-hero and the triumph of spring over winter. Frye even shows signs of wanting to exalt comedy over tragedy. This subversive idea surfaces again in Thomas Pynchon's novel *Gravity's Rainbow*, where two characters squabble over the relative merits of the tragic Beethoven and the comic Rossini, with Rossini's champion getting somewhat the better of the argument. To the accusation that Rossini retired at thirty-six and got fat, while Beethoven lived a life full of tragedy and grandeur, he retorts: 'So? Which would you rather do? . . . A person feels *good* listening to Rossini. All you feel like listening to Beethoven is going out and invading Poland. Ode to Joy indeed!' Elsewhere the same character insists, 'I'm choosing *my* game, one full of light and kindness. You're stuck with that stratosphere stuff and rationalize its dullness away by calling it "enlightenment".' 'Your "light and kindness"', growls his rival, 'are the jigging of the doomed.'

Arguments about priority or superiority are, no doubt, sterile. But that tragedy and comedy can complement, and often interpenetrate, one another is hard to dispute. Shakespeare's comic *Midsummer Night's Dream* and his tragic *Romeo and Juliet* were written at almost the same time. The comedy has a play-within-a-play in which the love of two young people is opposed by their families: after a series of accidents the young man stabs himself, mistakenly believing that his sweetheart is dead. This plot closely resembles, and its handling riotously parodies, the tale of star-crossed lovers which forms the main plot of *Romeo and Juliet*. The tragedy of *Othello* is full of comic devices such as overheard (and misunderstood) conversations and a lost handkerchief. Brabantio and Othello behave, at times, like the deceived father and cuckolded husband so often encountered in comedy; Othello's greatest fear often seems to be that he will lose his status of heroic leader and be reduced to a comic butt. Iago, the villain, weirdly resembles the comic trickster and go-between, embezzling the money and presents sent by the foolish lover Roderigo to the unapproachable Desdemona. These comic elements, of course, only succeed in making the tragedy more painful: its dignity and splendour are threatened by the intrusion of the sordid and the everyday.

Shakespeare, of course, is well known for mingling tragedy and comedy: eighteenth-century French critics chided him for it. But French works have not been exempt from doubts about classification. Madame de Sévigné defiantly described Racine's *Bajazeth* as a comedy; Rousseau called Molière's *Misanthrope* a tragedy. Flaubert's *Madame Bovary* is usually thought of as tragic, but there is much that is comic in its evocation of provincial life. In Russia, at the beginning of this century, Chekhov found his masterpiece *The Cherry Orchard* turning, in the process of composition, into 'a comedy, in places even a farce': he was annoyed when the director, Stanislavski, pushed it back towards 'drama' or tragedy. Both possibilities are latent in the play. In Mark Twain's predominantly comic *Huckleberry Finn* the hero faces a tragic dilemma: whether to risk damnation by helping a runaway slave to escape (which is tantamount to robbing a respectable person of her property) or to betray friendship by peaching on Jim, the slave. William Faulkner's *As I Lay Dying*, with its epic-tragic journey across country to give decent burial to a mother's corpse, collapses into comedy in the closing moments: the widower takes advantage of the trip to acquire a new wife and a fresh set of dentures.

Most good comedies contain potentially tragic scenes. In *The Merchant of Venice* Shylock threatens to cut out Antonio's heart; in *Much Ado About Nothing* a guiltless woman is repudiated and disgraced at the altar. In these plays the colouring goes from light to dark to light again; there are, however, many fine comic works (especially modern ones) in which the return to happiness is never achieved. Rose Macaulay's *The Towers of Trebizond*, for example, begins with lively humour. There is an eccentric aunt who rides to and from church on a camel, a succession of Protestant clergymen with a taste for angling, and a car stolen by an Anglican bishop from outside an exclusive London club. But the tale lapses suddenly into one of sin and retribution; the early lightness never returns.

Tragedy and comedy may overlap at almost any point, including subject-matter, structure, and devices of plot. Shakespeare's comedy *As You Like It* and his tragedy *King Lear* both contrast the honest harshness of nature with the veiled cruelty of human beings. In the comedy the deposed duke reflects that the winter wind, when it 'bites and blows' on his body, reveals to him those human weaknesses which flattering courtiers did their best to conceal: the winds are 'counsellors | That feelingly persuade me what I am'. In the tragedy the protagonist, another deposed ruler, is granted a similar insight into the servility and mendacity of the underlings who flattered him in his days of power, as opposed to the cruel but salutary frankness of the elements, which reveal his frailty:

To say 'ay' and 'no' to everything I said was no good divinity. When the rain came to wet me once, and the thunder would not peace at my bidding, there I found them, there I smelt them out. . . . They told me I was everything; 'tis a lie, I am not ague-proof.

King Lear and *As You Like It* have more in common than the obsessive theme of the deviousness of man as compared with the straightforwardness of nature. They also share a common structure. In *A Natural Perspective*, a book specifically devoted to

Shakespearian comedy, Northrop Frye notes that comedies such as *As You Like It* and *A Midsummer Night's Dream* begin at court, in an atmosphere where the longings of the young people are repressed. The action then moves to the forest or 'green world', as Frye calls it, where the love-intrigues work themselves out in a setting where social pressures are at a minimum: finally, when the redemptive magic of the natural world has taken effect, the characters return to the social world with new hope. There is a weird parallel to this typically comic cycle in *King Lear*, where the action begins in the courts of princes, moves to the barren heath (a world of nature), and then moves back, in the last two acts, to the stratified social world.

In Aristotle's *Poetics*, two elements, recognition (*anagnorisis*) and reversal of fortune (*peripeteia*), are singled out as essential to the complex, as opposed to the simple, tragic plot. The most important kind of recognition is identified as the recognition of persons, as when a long-parted brother and sister are made known to one another in the *Libation Bearers* of Aeschylus or when Oedipus learns his true parentage in Sophocles' *Oedipus the King*. However, recognition scenes are almost equally fundamental to comic plotting: lost children and lost siblings are joyfully recognized in plays from Plautus' *The Rope* to Joe Orton's *What the Butler Saw*. Reversal of fortune, too, is as necessary in comedy, which traditionally moves from a situation of difficulty to one where difficulty is overcome, as in tragedy, where the plot moves in the reverse direction. Often, of course, the recognition or discovery of identity actually brings about the reversal of fortune: in *Twelfth Night* the reunion of the twins Viola and Sebastian removes most of the misunderstandings which have prevailed in the course of the play. Recognitions, then, can be used to bring about joyful, celebratory, comic endings just as easily as they can be used to precipitate disasters. So common is the recognition device in all forms of drama and fiction that comic characters sometimes make jokes about it. 'There, you see,' says a character in Sheridan's *The Critic* after a recognition-scene, 'Relationship, like murder, will out.'

The most famous recognition-scene of all occurs in *Oedipus the King*, where a man's discovery of his real parentage leads him to the knowledge that he has committed incest and parricide. But even this quintessentially tragic instance can be used to throw light on comedy. The recognition-scene in *Oedipus the King* is typical in an important respect: it involves discoveries about the family. Ludwig Jekels, noting the extent to which concern for the family dominates both tragic and comic plots, suggests that comedy effects a reversal of the Oedipal pattern so common in tragedy. In tragedy it is the son who is guilty; in comedy it is the father. The reversal is neatly illustrated in a seventeenth-century play by Sir William Davenant, *The Platonic Lovers*. Here a son lectures his father on the duties of parents to children. His father, he loftily insists, must supply him with armour, clothes, and jewels. His final demand is, 'When the time conspires with my necessities to call you to it, you must make haste and die.' Elaborating on Jekels's suggestion, we may note that where a recognition-scene in tragedy may reveal that incest has been committed, those in comedy often work to avert the threat of incest or to absolve one or more characters of the guilt of incestuous love. In Plautus' *The Rope* an old man finds himself stirred by the attractions of a young woman, but discovers in time that she is his daughter. In Fielding's *Joseph Andrews* the hero and heroine are alarmed, towards the end of the novel, by the news that they are brother and sister: later, a celebratory comic ending is made possible by the discovery that the story was not true.

So closely are tragedy and comedy linked that Norman Holland, another psychoanalytic theorist, can suggest that comedy is simply tragedy speeded up. In support of his point we may cite Walter Kerr, who records that comic effects in silent films were often achieved by shooting a sequence slowly and projecting it fast. The speeding up of an action creates a machine-like effect: the resulting emotional detachment enables the audience to take disasters (or near disasters) as jokes.

To say that comedy and tragedy are intertwined implies, among other things, that the atmosphere of comedy is never one of unalloyed happiness. Nietzsche, who through the mouth of the sage Zarathustra invited his readers to kill the spirit of gravity, was just as deeply opposed to the spirit of light comedy, or what he called (in one of his finest and most withering phrases), 'senile and slavish pleasure in existence and cheerfulness'. This last, as he explains in *The Birth of Tragedy*, was epitomized in the bourgeois comedies of Menander; in the repetitive, self-perpetuating nuclear family; in Christianity; in short, in everything that Nietzsche himself most despised. Bernard Shaw may have had Nietzsche in mind when he made Captain Shotover say in *Heartbreak House*: 'I tell you happiness is no good. You can be happy when you are only half alive. I am happier now I am half dead than ever I was in my prime. But there is no blessing on my happiness.' Comedy does not exalt what Shotover elsewhere calls 'The happiness that comes as life goes, the happiness of yielding and dreaming instead of resisting and doing, the sweetness of the fruit that is going rotten.' Contempt for this vegetable existence is characteristic of comedy in general. Rosalind in *As You Like It* is scornful of the 'priest that lacks Latin' and of the 'rich man that hath not the gout', since 'the one sleeps easily because he cannot study, and the other lives merrily because he feels no pain'. The essence of comedy is vitality, not swinish contentment. The philosopher Suzanne Langer characterizes comic vitality as 'a brainy opportunism in face of an essentially dreadful universe'.

If this sounds like an exaggeration, we may consider the temperament of the typical comic writer or performer. We all know the story of the man who goes to the doctor about his depression. The doctor advises him to see a show by a great comedian who is currently in town. 'I am the great comedian,' retorts the patient. Like so many jokes, this is too true to be entirely funny. The great British comedian Tony Hancock committed suicide while touring abroad. Georges Feydeau observed that he seldom laughed, either in the theatre or in private, being taciturn and rather unsociable by nature. Jaroslav Hašek in *The Good Soldier* Švejk has a vignette, presumably a self-portrait, of a writer called Hajek, 'a very cheery and nice man. He used to go to a pub and always read his stories there, which were so sad that everybody roared with laughter at them.' ('Nothing is funnier than unhappiness' again.) Noel Coward records an evening spent with Charlie Chaplin 'when at one point he played an accordion and at another a pipe-organ, and then suddenly became almost pathologically morose and discussed Sadism, Masochism,

Shakespeare, and the Infinite'. A heightened sensitivity to the potential dreadfulness of the universe seems to be characteristic of those who know how to make others laugh.

Intimations of tragedy can be found even in the predominantly genial comedy of manners, which arises out of people's ways of adjusting to social living. Among the favourite sources of humour in this type of comedy is the perception that the average person would rather tell others what they want to hear than give voice to his real thoughts: the logical extension of this is to flatter people to their faces while laughing at them behind their backs. The potentially tragic character is the one who cannot bring himself to obey this rule (Alceste in Molière's *Misanthrope* or Holden Caulfield in Salinger's *The Catcher in the Rye*) and who sees himself, with some justification, as a lonely truth-teller in a world of phonies. The lone campaigner who scorns compromise is a model of integrity but also of self-esteem: his intolerance of others' imperfections implies a denial of his own. At the other extreme stand characters like Célimène in Molière's play or Sally in Salinger's novel, who play the social game for all they are worth yet feel for it (in Célimène's case at least) a secret contempt, betrayed by their covert fascination with the misanthrope who rejects it.

Célimène takes pleasure in double-dealing: she confides her real opinion of each admirer to his rival, while flattering each to his face. The time must come when they will compare notes. Célimène, then, puts at risk the position in society on which so much of her life depends. She breaks the rule put into words by Lady Utterword in Shaw's *Heartbreak House*: 'Intelligent people can always manage, unless they are Bohemians. . . . If you will only take the trouble always to do the perfectly correct thing . . . you can do just what you like.' The comment does not come from one of the most admirable characters in the play, but it expresses a covert assumption of mannered comedy. A Bohemian puts herself outside society by defying the rules: a socialite remains in it by respecting them in word and in theory, while circumventing them in practice.

Society is hypocritical almost by definition: it offers us ways of masking (not extirpating) our antisocial desires. Célimène's mistake is carelessness: by letting her mask slip, she risks exchanging the security of the socialite for the exile of the Bohemian, which is not at all what she wants. Célimène, then, does not fit easily into society as the sensible Philinte and Éliante do. In a way her cynical involvement is just as powerful a criticism as Alceste's outright rejection. But while Célimène's enterprise in bending the rules displays a mischievous wit, there is something rigid, over-serious, in Alceste's solemn refusal to play the social game. Célimène is only taking to an extreme an activity in which all social beings must indulge. And it is an essentially playful, adaptive, laughter-loving activity. In mannered comedy society, though satirized, is accepted as a necessary mediating term between our animal and our moral nature. Because it exists to prevent clashes between them, to allow them to coexist, it is necessarily a thing of compromises and contradictions. The best way to deal with these is not to puzzle over them or rage against them, but to accept them and to laugh at their incongruity. The social game, played skilfully, can be fun.

It is often assumed that the comedy of manners is a distinctively urban mode. A tale like 'Was' in William Faulkner's *Go Down Moses* shows how easily it can be adapted to rural life. On the edge of Faulkner's tale there is a misanthrope 'who owned no property and never desired to since the earth was no man's but all men's'. Most of the other male characters, though not quite misanthropes, are misogynists: they choose to live in a place 'where ladies were so damn seldom thank God that a man could ride for days in a straight line without having to dodge a single one'. But despite the isolated locale and the tendency to opt out of society, the characters clearly live in a universe of social rules. Buck, one of the ageing McCaslin twins, has a necktie which he wears (albeit resentfully) if he has to go where he may meet a woman, though he knows that a tie marks its owner as someone who has not renounced the social law. An important article of this law is the rule that, if a man spends a night in the same house as an unchaperoned woman, or enters her bedroom while she is there, he must marry her. One of the story's climaxes comes when Buck is tricked into a bed which, unknown to him, is occupied by a maiden lady. As her screams echo through the house, her brother comments drily: 'Well, 'Filus, she's got you at last. . . . You come into bear-country of your own free will and accord . . . . You knew the way back out like you knew the way in and you had your chance to take it. But no. You had to crawl into the den and lay down by the bear.' The urban comedy of manners depends on topicality: it offers an alert critique of metropolitan society at a particular place and time. In the rural comedy of manners the fun lies in recalling or inferring the rules of a remote, outdated, or vanished world: Faulkner's tale comes to us 'out of the old time, the old days'.

The comedy of manners balances our animal against our moral nature: its near neighbour, sentimental comedy, comes near to denying our animal nature altogether. This may explain why it is so widely regarded as a self-contradictory or self-defeating mode. Not only is animality central to comedy: sentiment and fine feeling are often seen as inimical to it. Horace Walpole in the eighteenth century described life as a comedy to those that think, a tragedy to those that feel: Bergson, a century later, went further, suggesting that all feeling was fatal to laughter. Actually there is nothing inherently fatal about mingling feeling and laughter. The real risk run by sentimental comedy is that of centring on pseudo-conflicts rather than real ones. Typically, two young people have to decide whether to follow their impulses and marry without their parents' permission: after resolving to do so, they find that their parents had destined them for one another in the first place. There is something a little too convenient about this convergence of desire and social propriety. Nevertheless, it expresses a widespread longing. The anthropologist Claude Lévi-Strauss, certainly no sentimentalist, once composed a comedy along these very lines. The family of the woman loved by the male protagonist 'would have been delighted to give her to him', but 'it would have been intolerable for him to obtain her according to the rules of the social code; he had to win her in defiance of the established order, not through it.' The sentimental-comedy plot surrounds the desired union with a feeling of transgression; later it is revealed that no real transgression is involved. This desire for ultimate reconciliation with society is not necessarily or exclusively associated with soft-headed or conformist writers or works. Denis Diderot, whose novel *Jacques the Fatalist* is pungently satirical, also wrote sentimental comedies in which social and generational conflicts involving high-minded characters are implausibly resolved. On a cynical view such writing is calculated (in the words of Bertholt Brecht in the preface to *The Threepenny Opera*) to 'display the usefulness of bourgeois virtues and the intimate connection between emotion and crookery'. But others, apart from crooks, need emotion: their feelings must be allowed expression.

The phrase 'sentimental comedy' is commonly used to describe a group of plays originating in eighteenth-century England and France. Non-specialists know of them chiefly through Goldsmith and Sheridan, who announced their intention of laughing them off the stage. But John Modic, a modern critic, has traced the comedy of sympathy from Menander in late classical Greece to Cumberland in late eighteenth-century Britain, and it would be easy to extend the study to more recent writers such as the American playwright Neil Simon. It is true that the term 'sentimental comedy' has sometimes been used indiscriminately to cover any comedy that is not relentlessly ruthless in tone. But if we revise the terms (sympathy versus ridicule, humanity versus harshness) we arrive at a useful, though admittedly broad, distinction. And it should be obvious that neither kind of comedy is dispensable. Sympathy, sentiment, fine feeling: however often, however devastatingly they are mocked, they keep returning, even in works which overtly condemn them. Goldsmith offered *She Stoops to Conquer* to the eighteenth-century public as a revival of 'laughing comedy' in opposition to 'weeping comedy' or the comedy of sentiment. The play has a tavern scene (only one, however) with a bevy of agreeably low characters, and there is some satire on a young man who is shy with society women but forward with servant girls. But the youth who is mocked for sentimental hypocrisy succumbs, in the end, to genuine feeling, nerving himself to offer marriage to a poor woman instead of to the heiress whom his father wanted for him. 'My very pride begins to submit to my passion,' he announces, 'The disparity of education and fortune, the anger of a parent, and the contempt of my equals, begin to lose their weight. . . . I can have no happiness but what is in your power to grant me.' Finally he discovers what the audience has known all along: the supposedly dowerless girl is really the heiress. His desires, and his father's wishes for him, do not after all conflict. It is hard to regard this as anything but sentimental comedy.

Let us not conclude too readily that feeling is fatal to laughter. Modern, as well as ancient, examples tell against that view. We can hardly quarrel with Walter Kerr's description of Chaplin in his greatest film roles as 'the single character whose silhouette embraces both sentiment and comedy, and *both at the same time*'. And Raymond Queneau's writing, as W. D. Redfern contends, likewise undermines those theories which 'concentrate . . . on the violent aspects of comedy (which are undeniably basic to it) and overlook its gentler and more sociable functions'.

At the opposite end of the spectrum from mannered and sentimental comedy stands what the Russian critic Mikhail Bakhtin calls the comedy of grotesque realism, epitomized in the comic novels of Rabelais. Aristotle, in the *Poetics*, located the origins of comedy in phallic songs and fertility festivals. He also tentatively linked it with troupes of actors who wandered from village to village because they were banned from cities by municipal authorities. Bakhtin would agree about the rustic origins of comedy, but would not see it as pre-eminently phallic: for him it gives prominence to the whole bodily 'lower stratum'. The name of the comic peasant Sancho Panza in *Don Quixote* means 'belly', and food as well as sex has preoccupied comic characters from the time of Aristophanes to the present. But grotesque comedy does not stop at the paunch. In David Lodge's *Small World* the brilliant and elusive Angelica, asked at a literary conference to name the characteristic organ of comedy, replies instantly, 'The anus.' Anal and excremental comedy is enjoyed not only by Rabelais but by Alexander Pope, James Joyce, and Thomas Pynchon, among others.

It is a truism that comedy risks offending its audience by gross incidents and allusions, and that there is something slightly suspect about those comedies which keep such risks to a minimum. In seventeenth-century France Racine, best known for his decorous neo-classical tragedies, chose, when he came to write a comedy, to adapt the gusty Aristophanes rather than the inoffensive Terence. In *Les Plaideurs* (*Petty Sessions*) Racine borrows from his source, *The Wasps*, a scene in which a dog and a litter of puppies are brought into court. But in Racine's version they make water on the presiding judge: this detail, as Geoffrey Borny points out, is Racine's addition. In *Petty Sessions* the incident is an isolated one, but Bakhtin shows that in true grotesque comedy dismemberment and defecation have a positive value and a symbolic meaning: what passes into the earth to decompose will return at harvest time in the form of food. The emphasis is on the organic unity of all life: 'The material bodily principle is contained not in the biological individual, not in the bourgeois ego, but in the people, a people who are continually growing and renewed.' (By 'the people' Bakhtin seems to mean a kind of organic village community, self-sufficient and self-perpetuating, resistant to central authority.) The language of such comedy is full of joyous and inventive abuse, cursing, and insult. Its keynote is freedom from restraint; it rejects all that aspires to the self-sufficiency and completeness celebrated in classical art. Its movement is downward towards earth, not upwards towards heaven: it is antipathetic to all that is merely abstract and spiritual. In its scheme of things hell becomes a place of warmth, feasting, and celebration: the devils are jovial fellows.

Having absorbed Bakhtin's notion of grotesque realism, we find instances of it in unexpected places. In India and Nepal the wise elephant-headed god Ganesh is associated with urine, excrement, and broad humour. Among Western authors we find grotesque realism not only in Rabelais but in Aristophanes, in William Blake, even in Mark Twain. Twain's Huckleberry Finn thinks that heaven, as described by the widow, sounds boring: when assured that Tom Sawyer won't get there he feels relieved, because he wants himself and Tom to end up in the same place.

It will be seen from our discussion that some minor forms or modes which fall clearly within the boundaries of comedy (grotesque realism and sentimental comedy, for example) are more clearly exclusive of one another than such apparently antithetical major forms as comedy and tragedy. Indeed the most frustrating, and at the same time most fascinating, aspect of comedy and laughter is their paradoxical nature. Norman Holland, a writer cited earlier in this chapter, ends the first section of his book on laughter with a list of its contradictions. Humour may affirm life within society or seek to revolutionize society. It may affirm the value of existence as God's gift or reject life as sinful. It may accept life as low while aspiring to what is high. These and other paradoxes haunt comedy as well as humour. We shall find especially profound contradictions in the comic approach to the great human preoccupations of marriage, procreation, and death.

3

Marriage

'The great symbol of pure comedy', writes Helen Gardner, 'is marriage, by which the world is renewed, and its endings are always instinct with fresh beginnings. Its rhythm is the rhythm of the life of mankind, which goes on and renews itself as the life of nature does. . . . A comedy, which contrives an end which is not implicit in its beginning, . . . is an image of the flow of human life.' The belief that comedy celebrates marriage is still held by many theatre-goers; the view that it follows a cycle of renewal like that of the natural world is shared by Northrop Frye. But there are dissenting voices. 'Because a comedy by Shakespeare almost always ends with a marriage,' warns L. J. Potts, 'it is generally supposed that the purpose of comedy is to encourage optimism, or at least cheerfulness. The tradition of ending with a marriage was not invented by Shakespeare; but the popular view of comedy in England is no doubt based on a sentimental response to *As You Like It* . . . and other Shakespearian plays.' The essay in which Gardner made her pronouncement about marriage in comedy was an essay on *As You Like It*, and Frye's views seem likewise to have grown out of his passion for Shakespearian comedy and romance. Let us, then, try to evaluate the comic treatment of marriage without giving undue prominence to Shakespearian comedy.

In English medieval drama the comedy arises from marital quarrels rather than from domestic peace. A favourite character is Noah's wife, who brawls with her husband and endangers her family, delaying until the last moment before agreeing to enter the ark. In the *Second Shepherds' Play* of the Wakefield cycle there is a long, witty speech against wedlock, delivered not (as we might expect) by Mak the sheep-stealer but by one of the law-abiding shepherds. Later the comic oration against marriage becomes an established tradition: Sam Weller receives a solemn warning from his father in *Pickwick Papers*, and Captain Grimes utters a sad farewell to bachelorhood in Evelyn Waugh's *Decline and Fall.* In France Beaumarchais's *The Marriage of Figaro*, whose title seems to promise celebration of marriage, has the Count, who married Rosine for love in an earlier play, pursuing her maid Suzanne. 'I love her a lot,' he says of his wife, 'but after three years marriage gets so damned respectable!' (In the Mozart/Da Ponte operatic version, one of the finest arias is the Countess's song of slighted love at the opening of the second act.) When Marceline reproaches Bartolo for breaking a promise of marriage he retorts that he must have been mad to make it: 'If that sort of thing bound a man to marry, he'd have to marry everybody.' Bridoison adds, 'And if people looked into things really closely, they'd never marry at all.' Even Suzanne finds herself asking whether Figaro's devotion will survive the wedding.

In order to see whether valid generalizations can be drawn from these scattered examples, let us consider the treatment of marriage in Western European comedy in the early modern and modern periods, beginning with the revival of vernacular stage comedy in Italy in the early sixteenth century. Among the best-known examples is Machiavelli's Florentine comedy *Mandragora*, which centres not on a young couple scheming to overcome their elders' opposition but on a young woman married to an old man who wants her to have children. The old man, Nicia, refuses to admit that it is his infertility, not his wife's, which is keeping her childless. The obvious solution is for another man to give Lucrezia a child, but she is too virtuous to bed any man but her husband. Callimaco, an admirer of Lucrezia, poses as a doctor and announces that, if she is to conceive, she must drink the juice of the herb mandragora. But there is a catch. The first person who has intercourse with Lucrezia after she has taken the potion will die. This, of course, is a lie designed to persuade Lucrezia's husband to let someone else spend a night with her. He must seek out a filthy, drunken old vagabond to do the job and incur the penalty. As expected, the husband accepts this as the least unacceptable solution. Nobody will miss a tramp. He will not live to tell tales of bedding a social superior's wife, and if he did nobody would believe him. The husband will begin sleeping with his wife again, she will bear a child, and all will be well. What the cuckold does not realize is that the tramp will be Callimaco in a fresh disguise.

Lucrezia herself is not in the secret: indeed, when first told that she must give herself to another man, she is shocked. In the end she finds herself being successively urged to infidelity by her husband, her mother, and her confessor. When she finally agrees she learns that her companion is not an unsavoury vagabond but a young and vigorous man. A child is duly conceived and the deluded husband, in his gratitude to the supposed doctor, grants him unrestricted access to the house. The inference is that Callimaco and Lucrezia will continue indefinitely to make love, and children. An arid marriage will become the cloak for a satisfying extramarital relationship.

Mandragora, then, substitutes a rival ethos for the ethos of marriage. It is that of courtly love, which requires the lover of a beautiful and virtuous woman to make sacrifices for her sake, using time, energy, intelligence, and money unstintingly to win her. By these criteria the husband, Nicia, fails pathetically. He is not prepared to risk death for the woman he supposedly loves; in the last resort he is willing to expose her to the embraces of a loathsome vagabond rather than risk his own life or reputation.

Any definition of 'pure comedy' that excluded *Mandragora* would discredit itself, yet Machiavelli's play spectacularly fails to fulfil Gardner's prescription. It is true that its ending is (in Gardner's phrase) 'instinct with fresh beginnings', but they are hardly those that she had in mind. And the generation of children by Lucrezia and Callimaco sets up a contrast, not an equivalence, between the order of nature and the order of marriage. The effect is to remind us that marriage is not natural, though copulation is. If any cultural code is offered as a supplement to, or improvement on, nature it is the subversive code of courtly love, not the socially approved code of marriage. But Machiavelli's handling of marriage, though more daring than most, is no grotesque exception to some grand generic rule. The modern French playwright Jean Giraudoux called one of his plays *Amphitryon 38* because it was the thirty-eighth play to be based on the myth in which the king of the gods takes on the likeness of a mortal man, Amphitryon, and seduces his wife in his absence. The popularity of this story among European playwrights suggests that cuckold-comedy is at least as normal as courtship-comedy, in which a young man falls in love with a young, unmarried woman and eventually wins her as his wife.

Let us, then, look at cuckold-comedy more closely. What is the basis for its satire on marriage? From the comic viewpoint it is a scandal that the best wives often go to those who lack mental and sexual energy rather than to those who have them. Rescuing a desirable woman from a foolish, impotent husband is a service to her as well as a deserved put-down for him. It is especially enjoyable to see the foolish husband tricked into handing his wife over to his rival, thus meeting the very fate which he is neurotically anxious to avoid. This plot device, prominent in *Mandragora*, was also common in seventeenth-century English comedy (Ben Jonson's *Volpone*, Middleton's *A Chaste Maid in Cheapside*, and Wycherley's *The Country Wife*), and survives vestigially today. In Peter Carey's Australian novel *Illywhacker*, published in 1985 but set in the period following the First World War, the central character teaches his new bride to fly without realizing that she is becoming infatuated with the aeroplane:

When you hear what follows you will wonder at my blindness. How can the fellow not know? His wife is besotted with aviation. She spends her days with navigation and maintenance. He assists her in every way he can, and yet he says he never realized the thing was serious.

It is a sign of the times that by this date the woman is deemed capable of some passion that does not involve a rival male, but the wry allusion to the old plot is unmistakable. As usual the wife's desire carries her beyond what is thought permissible within marriage: this time, instead of bearing a child to another man, she tries to abort her husband's child, fearing that motherhood will interfere with her flying lessons. What persists from the Renaissance to the present is the motif of the blindness and self-delusion of the husband, vainly expecting to keep a desiring and desirable woman to himself.

It begins to seem as if empirical evidence may support, not Frye and Gardner, but Freud, who argued in his book on jokes that wit and humour were more likely to ridicule marriage than celebrate it:

Among the institutions which cynical jokes are in the habit of attacking none is more important or more strictly guarded bv moral regulations but at the same time more inviting to attack than the institution of marriage, at which, accordingly, most cynical jokes are aimed.

George Orwell, in his essay on the seaside-postcard humour of Donald McGill, likewise stressed the popularity of sexual and scatological jokes. So did Eric Bentley, whose essay on the psychology of farce suggests that 'gross wishes' (roughly equivalent to Freud's cynical jokes) 'are mainly, if not exclusively, desires to damage the family, to desecrate the household gods'. However, it is notable that none of these writers sees the subversion in antimarital humour as having revolutionary implications. Bentley is convinced that 'the marriage-joke . . . exists only for a culture that knows itself committed to marriage'. And Orwell judges that 'a dirty joke is not . . . a serious attack upon morality, but . . . a sort of mental rebellion, a momentary wish that things were otherwise . . . a harmless rebellion against virtue'. This is a version of the useful safety-valve theory of humour, which holds that festive desecration of necessary but irksome institutions, and defiance of conventional restraints, is not aimed at removing them but at making them easier to bear.

Cuckold-comedy is the most obvious repository of antimarital humour: courtship-comedy, which leads up to marriage, might be expected to treat it more reverently. But a degree of cynicism about marriage seems to be characteristic of comedy as such. Bentley, writing of Wilde's *The Importance of Being Earnest* (a classic courtship-comedy), remarks that the dialogue comments obsessively on all the themes of life which the plot suppresses, including unhappy marriage. Bentley uses this both-ways quality in the play to show that it is neither trivial nor derivative. But is not the same quality present in most courtship-comedies? This type of comedy conventionally moves towards the apparent harmony and closure of marriage, but both the harmony of the comic ending and that of marriage itself are under suspicion from the beginning. 'As the catastrophe of all tragedies is death,' muses the playwright Mr Lyric in Farquhar's *Love and a Bottle* (1699), 'so the end of all comedies is marriage.' His friend Lovewell ripostes, 'And some think that the most tragical conclusion of the two.' The joke was taken up by Byron in *Don Juan* and has often been repeated since. Even in Goethe's *Elective Affinities*, a serious novel whose ruling metaphor is that of the chemical affinity between one person and another, we find a character musing:

In a comedy we see a marriage as the final fulfilment of a desire which has been thwarted by the obstacles of several acts. The moment the desire is fulfilled the curtain falls, and this momentary satisfaction goes on echoing in our minds. . . . In the real world the play continues after the curtain has fallen, and when it is raised again there is not so much pleasure to be gained by seeing or hearing what is going on.

The pronouncement is made by a cynical Count, one of the shadier figures, but events prove him right.

What Goethe's Count does not mention is that awareness of the precariousness of marriage is present within comedy itself. Morton Gurewitch observes that though Italian *commedia dell'arte* scenarios 'celebrate amorous unions or reunions', the 'festive, conciliatory, nuptial last scenes . . . are sops to romantic or moral conventions which have already been hilariously annihilated.' Since the *commedia* was an irreverent, popular form of drama, this is not too surprising. More disconcerting is the discovery that even Shakespeare's superficially more decorous comedies are full of jests about marital infidelity. Even *As You Like It*, Helen Gardner's 'pure' comedy *par excellence*, has scenes (notably those between the disguised Rosalind and her lover Orlando) which bristle with antimarital jokes. The fact that Orlando is being prepared for a good marriage by being warned about bad ones does not quite cancel the destructive effect of the humour.

In *As You Like It*, and in many other comedies, there is a tension between the forward movement of the plot, which is usually towards marriage, and the backward pull of the dialogue, which ridicules it. In most of the world's best-known comedies, jokes against wedlock sparkle and crack like fireworks; the prospect of apparently auspicious marriages for the privileged characters is offset by the presence of other figures whose marriages have gone wrong, or look like doing so. The endings of a few comedies, such as Farquhar's *Beaux' Stratagem* and Coward's *Design for Living*, actually celebrate the dissolution of marriage. Elsewhere, grand eccentrics like Shakespeare's Jacques, Dickens's Pickwick, and Gilbert's Bunthorne remain unmarried, some of them happily or even defiantly so: indeed, in the pairing off and consignment to married happiness that is customary at the end of a comic novel or play, it is the rule rather than the exception for some characters to be left unwed and for some marriages to be seen as heading for trouble. At the end of *Pickwick Papers* Dickens, deferring with ill grace to the 'unquestionably bad' custom of pigeon-holing all the characters at the end, leaves not only Pickwick but also Tupman and the elder Weller in a contentedly single state. In the course of the novel Sam Weller tells a gruesome story of a butcher who threw himself into his own sausage-machine to escape his wife's nagging; while the editor of the *Eatanswill Gazette*, hearing of the marriage of a professional rival, alternates between horror and delight: ' "Married!" exclaimed Pott, with frightful vehemence. He stopped, smiled darkly, and added, in a low, vindictive tone: "It serves him right!" ' Mr Pickwick is not tempted by wedlock, even when engaged in smoothing other people's paths to it: his worst ordeal is the breach-of-promise action *Bardell* v. *Pickwick*, brought on when his landlady interprets his talk about hiring a servant as a statement of intention to take her as his wife. After this ordeal, a mere offer of tea from a female can sound threatening:

'You'll take some tea, Mr. Pickwick?' said the old lady, with irresistible sweetness.
'Thank you, I would rather not,' replied that gentleman. The truth is, the old lady's evidently increasing admiration, was Mr. Pickwick's principal inducement for going away. He thought of Mrs. Bardell; and every glance of the old lady's eyes threw him into a cold perspiration.

Marital comedy has traditionally offered its readers and audiences two complementary, almost contradictory, kinds of pleasure. One is delight in the prospect of successful marriages for characters with whom readers identify. The other is laughter at disastrous or unsuccessful marriages, arising either from epigrams against wedlock in general or from particular disastrous unions which develop near the periphery of the plot. It is one of the paradoxes of traditional comedy that the leading characters, though confronted with a world filled with unfaithful, embittered, or desiccated married people, by those in short whose flame has been dimmed by marriage, still persist in their joint search for a paradise which they know to be elusive and perhaps illusory.

It is worth asking whether this situation has changed in the century or so since Wilde's *The Importance of Being Earnest*, perhaps the last important exemplar of the Menandrian tradition in European comedy. A suitably modern work with which to begin the enquiry is Donald Barthelme's short novel *Snow White* (ably discussed by George McFadden in his book on comedy):

The psychology of Snow White: What does she hope for? 'Some day my prince will come.' By this Snow White means that she lives her own being as incomplete, pending the arrival of one who will 'complete' her. That is, she lives her own being as 'not-with'. . . . But the 'not-with' is experienced as stronger, more real, at this particular instant in time, than the 'being-with'.

For a novel published in 1967 *Snow White* comes surprisingly close to the psychological theories of Jacques Lacan, for whom 'completion-by-the-other' is a delusion. For Lacan, indeed, the notion of fulfilment of desire is self-contradictory: when one wish is fulfilled we begin to yearn for something else. However, these insights are not altogether new: they have been anticipated by many writers of comedy. In *The Importance of Being Earnest* Algernon declares: 'It is very romantic to be in love. But there is nothing romantic in a definite proposal. Why, one may be accepted. One usually is, I believe. Then the excitement is all over. The essence of romance is uncertainty.' In the closing moments, when Jack is hunting frantically for the evidence which will prove whether he is a fit person to marry Gwendolen, the latter breathes: 'This suspense is terrible. I hope it will last.' The difference between Wilde and Barthelme is that Wilde makes the paradox seem amusing rather than depressing, whereas in Barthelme there is a real sense of forlornness. In *Snow White* the protagonist can dwell, as Gwendolen does, on the pleasures of suspense; but then, unlike Gwendolen, she finds herself brooding on the sombreness of waiting, which is suspense's reverse image:

'Well it is terrific to be anticipating a prince—to be waiting and knowing that what you are waiting for is a prince, packed with grace—but it is still waiting, and waiting as a mode of existence is, as Brack has noted, a darksome mode. I would rather be doing a hundred other things. But slash me if I will let it, this waiting, bring down my lofty feelings of anticipation from the bedroom ceiling. . . .'

Snow White's prince never does come. Instead of climbing through the window he is content to wait and watch, suffering from mild jealousy of the laundry delivery-boy; moments after he finally meets Snow White he dies from a poisoned drink which he took away from her because it might prove too exciting.

Snow White, then, confronts and sadly accepts the evanescence of our Western myth of completion by the other through marriage. In earlier comedy the myth is at some level seen to be a myth, but oddly fails to dissolve. Despite evidence of the devastation that marriage can inflict by failing to fulfil the promise of completion, characters and audiences retain a residual faith in the good marriage as a worthwhile goal and an object of celebration.

'Psychology', hazarded Wilde, 'is in its infancy as a science. In the interests of art, it is to be hoped that it will always remain so.' Since his time our consciousness has been increasingly infiltrated by the theories of Freud and Lacan and other writers of similar persuasion who work, with varying degrees of reluctance or glum satisfaction, to undermine the myths of oneness, harmony, and mutual completion on which the traditional comic synthesis depended. It is strange indeed that Frye and Gardner could evolve a theory of comedy as validation of the natural cycle at a moment in history when 'the literature of exhaustion' was in the ascendant: much of this literature is preoccupied with entropy, etiolation, purposelessness, and the running down of man's desire to participate in the processes of nature. Yet the literature of exhaustion is not all we have; and in other reaches of our culture we find evidence to suggest that Frye and Gardner are not entirely wrong.

Consider the frequency, in later twentieth-century American cinema, of the scene in which a disastrous marriage is avoided in the nick of time. In *I Love You, Alice B. Toklas* the audience is indulged, both at the beginning and end of the film, with a resplendent wedding. True, we are not invited to share a feeling of celebration: the bridegroom's first sight of the well-dressed, well-greased, burgeoning congregation presages the imminent loss of his selfhood. On each occasion his cowardice (or courage) gives him the strength to run away; he leaves behind him a festive gathering whose pretext for celebration has evaporated. Here the joke is at the expense of the opulence and display surrounding the wedding, which represents an assertion of the wealth and status of the group rather than the personal aspirations of the individuals. Much the same thing happens at the end of *The Graduate*, where a young woman whose family have forced her to the church to marry the father of her unborn child is rescued at the altar by the man who really loves her. A more recent comedy, *Blind Date*, uses a similar device. Examples of last-minute rescue from an unsuitable marriage occur both in films of real sophistication and in those designed frankly as popular entertainment.

Many film comedies do, of course, end with marriage: thus the film which ends with the prevention of a marriage, not with its celebration, gives its audience an exhilarating sense of independence from an established tradition. Yet what is rejected is not union as such but the unacceptable union which threatens to smother or degrade desire. To insist that such a wedding must be stopped is, in a backhanded way, to reaffirm the importance of a better marriage, and (significantly enough in a world in which divorce is readily obtainable) the determination to get it right first time. These films treat marriage as a rite of passage: the first experience of it is unrepeatable and must not be undertaken lightly. In many comedies, from Coward's *Private Lives* to the popular 1950s film *High Society*, the main function of divorce is the renewal of the original marriage-relationship. Even this, of course, need not bring fertility or harmony in any conventional sense: Coward's play ends, not with serenity and celebration, but with a torrent of joyous abuse, the legacy of Amanda and Elyot to the more conventional Sibyl and Victor. 'It's a tremendous relief to me to have an excuse to insult you,' Victor screams at Sibyl: soon his verbal lashings give way to physical violence, and it is at this moment that Amanda and Elyot 'go smilingly out of the door'. This ending does not teach us to expect serenity. But then the ending of Sheridan's eighteenth-century comedy *The School for Scandal* did not encourage audiences to expect serenity in future relations between Sir Peter Teazle and his wife, and many less genial comedies leave their audiences with even stronger intimations of future marital brawls.

In earlier comedy antimarital satire coexisted with, and threatened to subvert, an apparently celebratory attitude towards marriage. It could fairly be said that in today's comedy the roles have been reversed: while disenchantment with marriage seems to predominate, revalidation of marriage (or of completion-by-the-other) may almost perversely occur. In Harold Pinter's play *The Lover*, for example, a husband plays an elaborate game of visiting his wife in the guise of her lover on certain afternoons in each week. It is accurate, though trite, to say that the play is about role-playing: the same woman can play wife and whore; the same man can play rapist and rescuer, husband and lover, at will. But how do we see this role-playing? The play could be read as satirizing the couple's mania for privacy. They have chosen a sequestered country house and have constructed a life there which, with its endlessly proliferating games and ever-evolving rules, abolishes the need for other people. (The wife firmly rejects the overtures of the milkman, conceivably the only outsider who ever calls). Yet the aloneness of the couple is weirdly reminiscent of the solitary life of the holy hermit or dedicated artist. Their games are imaginative and creative; they bring a welcome uncertainty to what might otherwise become tedious. Much the same is true of the main relationship in Albee's *Who's Afraid of Virginia Woolf*, which elaborates Coward's solution while anticipating Pinter's. Once again two characters renew their relationship through endlessly inventive abuse, and through games in which either party is entitled, at any point, to effect a viciously destabilizing change in the rules.

Modern comedy has not broken as cleanly as it pretends with the longings of earlier times. (Coward's 'Some Day I'll Find You' is as much a dream of completion-by-the-other as 'Some Day My Prince Will Come'.) Recent comic writers have sought renewal through heterodoxy: cruelty as love, change as continuity, division as completion, marriage as transgression. It is Martha in Albee's play who delivers a tribute to her husband such as few men in earlier comedy ever called forth:

There is only one man in my life who has ever . . . made me happy . . . George, my husband . . . George who is good to me, and whom I revile; who understands me, and whom I push off; who can make me laugh, and I choke it back in my throat; who can hold me, at night, so that it's warm, and whom I will bite so there's blood; who keeps learning the games we play as quickly as I change the rules . . . George and Martha: sad, sad, sad.

That Martha does not merely hate George is as obvious as that Beatrice does not hate Benedick in *Much Ado About Nothing*: if either relationship were informed only by love or only by contempt, it would hold no dramatic interest. Where earlier comedy sought serenity through an ideal of marital harmony, but always seemed penetrated with the potential for discord, modern comedy makes a show of rejecting the traditional ideals but often finds itself thrown back on them. Admittedly Martha's encomium on George is uttered at a moment when George himself is preparing his most deeply destructive attack on her, but the attack does not erase Martha's feeling. The play ends in a deep stillness with Martha and George together, their ghost exorcised, the witches' sabbath over: 'Just us'. It is not a peace that passes all understanding; it is not a peace without fear. But it is a kind of peace, and one which comes to audience and characters as an immense, almost unbearable, relief.

Having begun by surveying the relatively familiar territory of early modern and modern Europe, we now need to test our generalizations about the treatment of marriage in comedy by taking a longer perspective. Following the example of Michel Foucault in his *History of Sexuality* we shall, then, move backwards in time to classical Greece and Rome, beginning with the Old Comedy of Aristophanes. Two of the plays, *Peace* and *The Birds*, end with celebratory marriages, but in each case the protagonist marries a goddess rather than a mortal woman. In *Peace*, as J.K. Dover notes, the hero who marries the goddess at the end already has a wife and children at home: one of his reasons for wanting peace is to ensure that his mortal family will have enough to eat. The celestial marriage seems, then, to be used as a symbol of fertility, celebration, consummation, happiness; this larger meaning is independent of any evaluation of married life as it is lived from day to day. In *Peace*, the 'joys of home and wife' are associated with rich harvests and tireless eating; but who should marry whom, and how they should go about preserving good relations with one another, are non-questions. In *Lysistrata* it is part of the fictional hypothesis that men need love and sexual satisfaction from their wives and that their wives need it from them; both will suffer if these privileges are withdrawn. But in *Clouds* the central character, dissatisfied with his idle grown-up son, wishes he could strangle the man who first persuaded him to marry the boy's mother: when he was a bachelor he lived contentedly among his bees, his olive-trees, and his sheep. Overall, however, jokes against marriage are less prominent in Aristophanes than those against politicians, pederasts, litigants, informers, and warmongers.

With the New Comedy of Menander we encounter the familiar comic plot in which a young man schemes to marry a particular young woman in the face of social or parental opposition. The emphasis is on reconciliation and harmony: a family unit or units will be formed, augmented, or united by marriage. In *The Bad-Tempered Man*, the only play of Menander's that has come down to us complete, the main plot consists of a steady movement towards marriage between a rich youth who has never had to work and the daughter of a misanthropic old farmer. The well-born youth, like Ferdinand in *The Tempest*, has to work to win his bride; he also has to win the confidence of his prospective brother-in-law, who is at first suspicious of the other's intentions towards his sister and later becomes worried about his own inability to provide a dowry. (The same problem will perplex the protagonist of Dickens's *Nicholas Nickleby* two millennia later.) Both boys are rather high-minded for young men in comedy, and the play as a whole is closer to what we know as sentimental comedy or *comédie larmoyante* than to riotous, uproarious, or harsh comedy. As if to compensate for this, Menander provides a closing scene which has nothing to do with the plot and, indeed, takes place after all the knots have been tied: in it, the misanthrope of the title is baited by a cook and another slave. The choric interludes in the plays, which are indicated in the main dialogue but have not been preserved, might have tipped the balance further towards riot and subversion.

Two plots which recur in the comedies of Menander and his Roman imitators, Plautus and Terence, are that of the young man who violates a free woman in a fit of drunkenness at a festival and that of the youth who loves a slave-girl, flute-girl, or courtesan whom he cannot marry. Both lead to reconciliation between individual desires and the established social order. The violator of a free woman is sorry afterwards and is anxious to right the wrong by offering marriage; the lover of a slave is enraptured to discover that she is free-born, and therefore entitled to marry him. The lovely young woman, though she sometimes gives her name to the comedy, often fails to appear on stage. This is due not merely to the convention by which female parts had to be taken by male actors (after all, female tragic roles such as Antigone's were created to be played by men) but also to social conditions. In life, little in the way of character could be expected from brides who were very young at the time of marriage and whose experience was confined to home and family. Foucault has taught us that more than rudimentary ideas of companionate marriage existed in the ancient world, but they do not find much expression in Greek and Roman comedy. The courtesans, the madams, and the rather rare mothers in New Comedy are more interesting than the potential wives.

Plautus, Menander's Roman adapter, showed much less respect for marriage than Menander had done. In his plays it is assumed that fathers want their sons to marry eligible girls and settle, whereas their sons want to marry ineligible girls or to pursue courtesans. The danger of the courtesan is obvious. Unlike a wife, she has no interest in preserving the family fortune, since she can have no title to inherit that fortune or to pass it on to her children. If anything it is in her interest to wheedle the young man into spending his money (and his father's money) outside the family: it is of no concern to her if the money runs out, since she can always look for another lover to be milked in his turn. Thus comic courtesans wheedle young men into treating them to lavish feasts and drinking parties: a woman who cannot qualify for the relative security of marriage must enjoy herself while she can. Usually it is assumed that the courtesan's interests are best served by preventing new marriages and disrupting existing ones, and that she will behave accordingly.

Some of the comedies of Plautus and Terence, however, endow individual harlots with good qualities such as altruism, and others countenance the respectable male citizen's desire to pursue them. In *Asinaria* a father expresses sympathy for his son's desire to rent a particular girl for a year, remarking that his own father showed a similar indulgence in his case. The old man even asks his son to let him have a turn with the girl: the son, though not enthusiastic, agrees. In this comedy it is the shrewish mother who is the blocking character, seeking to spoil the men's pleasures. The play takes to an extreme the suggestion sometimes made in other Plautine comedies, namely that fathers should remember what it was like to be young and should not punish their sons' follies too severely. The plot does not move towards marriage, and the family ethos is defied with impunity: this makes the play daring and exhilarating.

Another instructive example is *Casina*, which inspired a Renaissance Italian imitation by Machiavelli. The Prologue promises a traditional ending; the slave-girl for whom all the men are competing will be found to be free-born and will marry the son of the household. But this return to harmony is never presented on stage, and there is a suspicion that Plautus only mentions it to impart a spurious respectability to his play. The main plot is a straight intrafamilial contest for the slave-girl's favours. The master of the house desires her; to gain regular access he schemes to marry her to another slave who manages one of his farms. The old man's wife, getting wind of the plot, seeks to give her instead to a different slave, a toady of her own. The contest is complicated by the fact that the old man's candidate for the role of straw husband desires Casina as much as everyone else does, and would rather not let his master have the first fling. In the meantime the other servant, loyal to the mistress of the household rather than to the master, dresses up to impersonate the bride: when the supposed bridegroom retires to bed he finds himself kissing a bearded face instead of a beardless one. The play displays no faith in marital harmony: the plot germinates from the notion of a family riven by competing interests and longings. The husband's sexual ambitions are resented and frustrated by the wife; husband and wife have their respective partisans among the servants; the wife will try to snatch a desirable concubine from her husband, passing the girl on first to a trusted servant and then to her son.

These farce elements reappear in later European comedy from Aretino to Fielding and beyond: they are calculated to 'damage the family' because they show marriage being used as a front for unfamilial, indeed antifamilial, activities. However, the Plautine examples are especially enlightening because they contain no element of sexual puritanism or distrust of sexual promiscuity as such. Illicit affairs are a threat because they may drain the family fortune or threaten the harmony between family members.

From Menander onwards, a powerful and resilient mode of comedy has celebrated the progress of young people towards a (usually) auspicious marriage, resisting riotous and anarchic tendencies of the kind just described. But even this type of comedy has taken delight in displaying, side by side with the rapture of young people who overcome obstacles to their love, the plight of the married man or woman who is moved to wish for a younger, richer, more handsome, or better-natured partner, or for no partner at all. In *The Importance of Being Earnest* Algernon opines that divorces are made in heaven; in Gabriel Garcia Marquez's *Love in the Time of Cholera* a widow remarks that at last she no longer has to worry about where her husband is when he is out of the house. The protagonist of Kleist's *The Broken Jug* praises the comforts of bachelorhood; Lillyvick the rate-collector in Dickens's *Nicholas Nickleby* is used as an example of the havoc wrought by marriage on a man's appearance and morale. Happy marriages, it is true, are encountered from time to time: in Jane Austen's *Persuasion* the married life of Admiral and Mrs Croft is a long and cheerful collaboration. But this unusual marriage is balanced by that of Mr and Mrs Bennet in the same author's *Pride and Prejudice*. Mrs Bennet's obstinacy and stupidity have caused her weak but witty husband to despair of ever influencing anything that happens in his family: he has to content himself with sarcasms about his wife's conduct and character which she, fortunately for her own peace of mind, only partly understands.

Jane Austen draws attention to the imperfections of this marriage by having the younger, marriageable people (especially Darcy) contemplate it with dismay. Yet the plot moves steadily towards further marriages, most of which we are invited to accept as destined for success. The exception, the union of silly Lydia Bennet with vain and deceitful Captain Wickham, seems to be offered, like the inauspicious wedding of Touchstone and Audrey in *As You Like It*, as a defence against the incredulity of sceptical readers: if we are presented with some marriages which seem likely to turn sour, we will be less likely to reject the inference that the others will go well. There is no doubt that the happy ending is meant, at some level, to renew our faith in the possibility of good marriages; but the comic artist is aware that credulity will not accept too many of these without some sort of acknowledgement of their opposite. Yet while antimarital humour is endemic to Western comedy, the possibility of a good marriage never quite disappears from view. Comedy's verdict on marriage is best summed up in the words of a despairing lover in Sir John Vanbrugh's Restoration play *The Provoked Wife*: 'Though marriage be a lottery, in which there are wondrous many blanks, yet there's one inestimable lot in which the only heaven on earth is written.'

4

Procreation

At the beginning of the last chapter I quoted Helen Gardner on the positive valuation of marriage in comedy. In Gardner's view comedy is equally positive in its approach to procreation. 'A comedy,' she writes, 'which contrives an end which is not implicit in its beginning, . . . is an image of the flow of human life. The young wed, so that they may become in turn the older generation, whose children will wed, and so on, as long as the world lasts.' It is to a scrutiny of this statement that we now turn.

'So that' in Gardner's formulation looks implausible. Do we really see comic characters marrying 'so that' their offspring may supplant them? In comedy the sexual urge usually prevails over the social, and a succession of philosophers and psychologists from Locke to Lacan have suggested that erotic pleasure, not desire for children, predominates in the real-life sexual act.

To mention this disparity between the motivation of the act and its consequence is scandalous: in Shadwell's seventeenth-century comic melodrama *The Libertine* it is the impious Don John who claims to owe his father nothing for begetting him, since the begetter had only his own pleasure in mind at the time. But in comedy there is always a measure of sympathy for the Don Juan figure, including those maxims of his which deride the mutual obligations between children and parents. Denying any debt to the father who begot him, while refusing responsibility for the offspring of his own amorous couplings, is a means by which the comic scapegrace asserts his treasured freedom.

The prospect of parenthood likewise threatens the young woman's vision of herself as young, glittering, energetic, full of romance and promise. 'A heroine of romance with a big belly, or lying in, is a strange image,' wrote Bayle in his influential *Historical and Critical Dictionary*, published at the end of the seventeenth century; and Biddy Tipkin, the romance-struck country girl in Steele's comedy *The Tender Husband*, echoes Bayle almost word for word. On stage, the pregnant woman is an irresistibly comic figure; nature has caught her out. Characters in comedy anticipate Simone de Beauvoir's view that, while pregnancy and motherhood can be exciting and moving experiences, they must not be presented to all women as their inescapable destiny or as the only means of fulfilment available. In Menander's *Epitrepontes* a courtesan mocks a male character who thinks he knows what women want: 'Do you think I want children? I only want my freedom.' Protests against motherhood are common, too, in eighteenth-century English comedy. Lady Rodomont in Thomas Baker's *The Fine Lady's Airs* protests against giving birth to 'abundance of children' and being 'mewed up in a nursery'; in Mary Pix's *The Different Widows* Lady Gaylove protests that no topic of conversation could be more unfashionable than one's children. In a representative modern comedy, Noel Coward's *Design for Living*, the volatile Gilda is moved at one point to wish that she were 'a nice-minded British matron with a husband, a cook, and a baby'. But the outburst is uncharacteristic. Elsewhere Gilda declares, 'I don't like children' and 'I shouldn't feel cosy, married! It would upset my moral principles.' Her lover sees it as a point in favour of their relationship that 'We aren't peppering the world with illegitimate children.' (But if comedy is really so philoprogenitive, why aren't they?) In the third act a stuffy woman is chided for her childlessness by another of Gilda's lovers: 'That's what's wrong with this century. If you were living in Renaissance Italy you'd have been married at fourteen and by now you'd have masses of children and they'd be fashioning things of great beauty.' But Leo would tease this particular woman whether she had children or not. Besides, what he sees as the aim and culmination of the reproductive cycle is the exceptional individual who produces nothing but works of art.

W.C. Fields's epigram, 'I love children—parboiled' is not as alien to the spirit of comedy as it might appear. Jacques in *As You Like It* visualizes the infant 'mewling and puking in the nurse's arms'. In a modern comedy, *Dogg's Hamlet*, Tom Stoppard plays joyous variations on the theme: 'Sad fact, brats pule puke crap-pot stink, spit; grow up dunces crooks; rank socks dank snotrags, conkers, ticks; crib books, cock snooks, block bogs, jack off, catch pox pick spots, scabs, padlocks, seek kicks, kinks, slack; nick swag, swig coke, bank kickbacks; . . . frankly can't stick kids.' The play, of course, is chiefly about language-games, not family life. But the straightforward, socially unacceptable, misoprogenitive meaning of the speech is responsible for much of the humour.

The nausea of parenthood, the longing not to be responsible for the child in its more repellent aspects, is one of many antisocial emotions which comedy allows itself to express. Yet frequently it simultaneously suggests another, almost opposite, idea: what Ronald Paulson, writing of the treatment of children in the paintings of Hogarth, means when he describes the young as a source of needed disorder, associated with 'liveliness, comedy, the natural, the instinctual'. Considered in this light the child acquires many of the positive comic connotations of the rogue. Its untamed energy, unashamed selfishness, and resistance to that 'civilizing' process which the widow tries to impose on Huck Finn, all work to disrupt the ordered lives of complacent, well-to-do adults. And we admire them for it. The comic response to children is, clearly, two-faced.

In comic terms the worst humiliation associated with children is that of being tricked into taking responsibility for someone else's. It is a situation which can make even St Joseph feel foolish; in the medieval English play *The Annunciation* (from Coventry) he shows, on hearing that Mary is with child, all the symptoms of distress that the cuckold displays in secular drama. In the latter, typically, the trickster schemes to have the fun without paying for the consequences, while the husband strives to protect his 'property' from encroachments. In Greek and Roman comedy this motif is already well established: in Menander's *Epitrepontes* and Terence's *Hecyra* men indignantly repudiate wives or potential wives who have allegedly borne children to others. The same is true of English Renaissance comedy. In Marston's *The Fawn* a character remarks that the man who has no children 'shall be sure not to cherish another's blood, nor toil to advance peradventure another's lust'. The same thought troubles jealous husbands in Restoration plays such as Congreve's *The Old Bachelor* and Vanbrugh's *The Provoked Wife*. If taking on another's children is a defeat, success in transferring responsibility for one's own is valued as a sign of wit and resourcefulness. In Middleton's *A Chaste Maid in Cheapside* and Crowne's *The Country Wit* artful women dump tempting packages in the street: the men who go to investigate, hoping to find money or food, discover babies instead and are faced with the prospect of providing for their upbringing. In Diderot's *Jacques the Fatalist* the disreputable Chevalier de Saint-Ouin is glad to transfer to Jacques's master the cost of raising his child. He arranges for the dupe to be caught in a compromising situation with the Chevalier's mistress: when she gives birth, the dupe has to pay to board out the baby with a country family.

It may be objected that such incidents are rare. But this argument is two-edged: the fact that we do not think of them as frequent reminds us that, considering the amount of love-intrigue that takes place in comedy, the incidence of pregnancy and childbirth is suspiciously low. And it is indisputable that, when pregnancy or parenthood do occur or are mentioned, those characters who let themselves be landed with children are shown as losers in the comic *agon*. Such attitudes are especially common in works whose characters live close to the poverty-line. Mak the sheep-stealer in the medieval English *Second Shepherds' Play* resents his wife's inconvenient fertility; in *Jacques the Fatalist*, a peasant and his wife lament that in hard times sex is the only pleasure that costs nothing, so hardship is soon aggravated by an untimely rise in the birth-rate. However, similar comments are not unknown in comedies of high life: in Jane Austen's *Emma* the narrator observes that Mr Weston lost overall on his first marriage, since the death of his wife left him with a child to maintain. But to be presented with a fine grown-up child whom one has never had to maintain is to draw a winning ticket. When Figaro is revealed as Bartolo's long-lost son, the parent is reminded: 'He has wit, talent, good looks . . . and his upbringing never cost you a cent.' This same feeling may lie behind some of the lost-and-found child sequences of classical comedy, such as Plautus' *The Rope*: a child, even a girl child, may be welcomed by prosperous older people who need someone younger to love, and can receive her or him full-grown without the tedium and expense of upbringing.

Even rearing children can be made satisfying in comic terms, provided that it is shown as an assertion of vitality rather than a check on it. In some comedies, such as Charlie Chaplin's *The Kid* and the more recent *Three Men and a Baby*, the embarrassed males who find themselves saddled with infants gradually come to love them, showing unexpected skill and pleasure in bringing them up. Here the humour is partly generated by the paradoxical power of the baby's helplessness: deprived even of the fundamental resource of language, it still manages to command sympathy and assistance.

Wayland Young once wrote that there are two kinds of society: one, when it sees a baby, says, 'Let's bring it up'; the other says disapprovingly, 'Whose baby is that?' In fact most societies, and most literary works, display both responses. Approaches like that of Lloyd deMause in his volume *The History of Childhood* are too simplistic. Of the handling of children in Menander deMause has this to say: 'In Menander's *Girl from Samos*, much fun is made of a man trying to chop up and roast a baby. In his comedy *The Arbitrants*, a shepherd picks up an exposed infant, considers raising it, then changes his mind, saying, "What have I to do with the rearing of children and the trouble?" He gives it to another man, but has a fight over who got the baby's necklace.'

Menander is indeed an instructive example for those who know how to read him. In his time unwanted children were often exposed; exposure is mentioned, and sometimes resorted to, in his plays. But the examples cited by deMause need to be considered in context. That the poor shepherd in *The Arbitrants* should reconsider an impulsive decision to raise a foundling is not strange: stranger, if anything, is the idea that he might consider raising it in the first place. In *The Girl from Samos* the man who threatens to chop up the child speaks in a moment of uncharacteristic anger, not in a spirit of 'fun'. Everyone else in the play shows concern for the baby. The nurse, for example, chatters fondly to it in 'the language that nurses use'. Even the angry old man accepts the child when he learns who its real parents are. At first he thinks it has been begotten on his concubine, in his absence, by his own legitimate son: this if anything would give him reason to feel vindictive. In reality, the young man begot the child during a drunken spree, on the daughter of a neighbouring family. The concubine, a kindly soul, agreed to look after it until the son could confess his crime to his father and ask permission to marry the baby's mother. The child, then, is carefully fostered and protected by the other characters: moreover, its birth is what generates the plot. By the end of the play a new family has been formed around it.

The great age of writing about children was the Romantic age, the age of Wordsworth. What is most significant about Romanticism for our purposes is that it and comedy are almost mutually exclusive. There is incidental humour in Wordsworth's child-poems when adults are disconcerted by children's innocently brilliant insights. But a Romantic writer who embarks on a more radically comic work, as Byron does in *Don Juan*, proves thereby that he has deserted the Romantic cause. Byron's protagonist first appears as 'A little curly-headed, good-for-nothing, And mischief-making monkey from his birth': the promise of a comic portrayal of childhood seems about to be honoured when little Juan pours 'a pail of housemaid's water' over the narrator when he comes to call. But in practice few other details of Juan's childhood are given: Byron seems impatient for the moment when his hero will experience 'first and passionate love'.

The other significant child figure in the poem is Leila, the little Turkish girl whom Juan saves at the siege of Ismail. Leila is not a figure of comedy but a Romantic innocent in the corrupt adult world. Her best moment comes when she admires Canterbury Cathedral as a house worthy of God, but cannot understand why infidels are allowed in. But this is exceptional: elsewhere, Byron fails to give Leila an active role, and eventually he phases her out of the narrative. In the eighth canto there is a rhapsody on the natural innocence of Daniel Boon's children, brought up in the Kentucky backwoods far from European civilization. And we are also told that Juan himself 'upon woman's breast | Even from a child felt like a child'. But these validations of childhood are among the least comic elements in Byron's comic poem: more convincing as well as more amusing are the evocations of breeding as a manifestation of sexual vigour. Juan's mother is mocked for trying to shelter him from books that 'hint continuation of

the species'; Malthus is chided for 'turning marriage into arith-
metic' by warning people not to have children whom they cannot
afford to support. Yet there is also satire on 'regularly peopling
earth, | Of which your lawful awful wedlock fount is,' and over-
population is described wittily as 'the sad result of passions and
potatoes' (potatoes being credited with aphrodisiac properties).

Jane Austen, like Byron in his more sardonic moods, treats
children not with Romantic reverence but with a comic awareness
that responsibility for them threatens the selfhood of adults.
Emma's and Anne Elliot's married sisters are merged, or submerged, in their families: their children are over-indulged and
over-protected. Aunts are expected to show affection and tolerance towards nephews and nieces, and generally do so; but the
narrator's portrayal of family life has a waspishness which we
recognize as typical of comedy. The work of Dickens betrays a
conflict of impulses. His most purely comic novel is *Pickwick
Papers*. In Mr Pickwick's bachelor apartment there are, blessedly, 'no children, no servants, no fowls'. But there is in the
house 'a production of Mrs. Bardell's', an 'interesting boy' who
has to be taken away 'screaming and struggling' after attacking
Mr Pickwick for supposedly upsetting his mother. A candidate at
the Eatanswill election is reluctant to kiss a baby in public, but to
impress the constituents he brings himself to kiss half a dozen:
here the cult of childhood is shown as a piece of humbug,
exploited by hypocrites for purposes of display. By contrast,
expressions of hostility to children carry a genial sincerity: 'Business first, pleasure afterwards, as King Richard the Third said
when he stabbed the 'tother king in the Tower, afore he
smothered the babbies.' Such jokes lie well within the boundaries
of comedy.

Nicholas Nickleby, another early novel, sometimes reads like
pro-child propaganda. It makes a villain of Ralph Nickleby, who
loves money more than he loves his brother's offspring, and of
the schoolmaster Squeers, who starves and maltreats the boys at
Dotheboys Hall. Yet it is constantly infiltrated by antifamilial
humour, and by the acknowledgement that children are a source
of cares as well as blessings. Even Mrs Nickleby admits that it
is 'a hard thing to have to keep other people's children', not

recalling that she came to London to ask her brother-in-law to provide for hers. Her husband, she recalls, disliked roast pig because the sight of piglets in butchers' shops 'put him in mind of very little babies, only the pigs had much fairer complexions; and he had a horror of little babies, too, because he couldn't very well afford any increase to his family, and had a natural dislike to the subject'. The hint at cannibalism, the dread of expense, and the suggestion that piglets may be prettier than babies are not accidental pieces of grotesquerie: they point towards the centre of a novel obsessed with the fear of poverty and with the mingled longing for, and terror of, family life. At the beginning of Chapter Fifty there is a brief rhapsody on the life led by gipsy children, but the passage is atypical: most evocations of childhood in *Nickleby* dwell on the anxieties of parenthood and the precariousness of young life in the so-called civilized world. When a jovial guest at an inn offers a comic story to balance someone else's tragic one, the tale centres on the genial Baron Grogzwig, whose bachelor idyll was ruined by a nagging wife and twelve noisy, costly brats.

In the main narrative of *Nicholas Nickleby* the upwardly mobile Mr and Mrs Kenwigs have four annoyingly well-groomed little girls with blonde pigtails. Much of the laughter at the Kenwigs' expense comes from the conflict between their usual show of family feeling and the hostility which breaks out in moments of stress. Half-way through the book there is a poignant passage where the news of the rich uncle's marriage, presumed fatal to the expectations of the Kenwigs children, coincides with the birth of a sixth baby. The doctor has just finished pooh-poohing Mr Kenwigs's declaration that 'six is almost enough' when Nicholas appears with the news of Mr Lillyvick's marriage:

'My children, my defrauded, swindled infants!' cried Mr. Kenwigs, pulling so hard, in his vehemence, at the flaxen tail of his second daughter, that he lifted her up on tiptoe, and kept her, for some seconds, in that attitude. 'Villain, ass, traitor!'

    'Drat the man!' cried the nurse, looking angrily round. 'What does he mean by making that noise here?'

    'Silence, woman!' said Mr. Kenwigs fiercely.

'I won't be silent,' returned the nurse. 'Be silent yourself, you wretch. Have you no regard for your baby?'

'No!' returned Mr. Kenwigs.

'More shame for you,' retorted the nurse. 'Ugh! you unnatural monster.'

'Let him die', cried Mr. Kenwigs, in the torrent of his wrath. 'Let him die! He has no expectations, no property to come into. We want no babies here,' said Mr. Kenwigs recklessly. 'Take 'em away, take 'em away to the Fondling.'

With these awful remarks, Mr. Kenwigs sat himself down in a chair, and defied the nurse, who made the best of her way into the adjoining room, and returned with a stream of matrons, declaring that Mr. Kenwigs had spoken blasphemy against his family, and must be raving mad.

There is more than a suspicion, though, that Mr Kenwigs may be raving sane. Under the stress of events, the mask of the loving father of his family has cracked, and feelings of resentment at the burdens of paternity have been revealed. The scene could easily have been given tragic treatment (we might compare, for example, some of the scenes of poverty in the Marmeladov family in *Crime and Punishment*) but Dickens prefers to use Mr Kenwigs's defiance of family loyalties for comic effect.

Victorian novels, according to Baruch Hochman, are all obsessed with the conflict between 'finished', 'static' adult life and 'open', 'fluid' childhood. That laughter should be used to ease this tension was natural: jokes about the clash of interests between parents and children offered relief from the atmosphere of reverence which had surrounded childhood since the Romantic period. The joke about cannibalism proved especially popular. It is worth noting, though, that this joke can be enjoyed by children themselves: when a child laughs at the idea of a child being eaten he has overcome his fear that he might actually suffer this fate.

Consider Thackeray's version of the ballad 'Little Billee'. Billy is the youngest of three sailors who run out of food on a voyage. His shipmates Gorging Jack and Guzzling Jimmy threaten to eat him: Billy quick-wittedly appeals for time to say his catechism, and is rewarded by the miraculous appearance of the British fleet.

Jack and Jimmy are hanged, and Billy is made captain of a frigate. The threat of cannibalism is obviously the main point of the song, but the grisly humour is acceptable because it is so carefully distanced from reality. Billy's execution is delayed by a catechism artificially lengthened so as to contain twelve commandments instead of ten. And from the mast-head Billy can see, simultaneously, 'Jerusalem and Madagascar, | And North and South Amerikee'. Finally the hero passes abruptly from childish helplessness to an age where he is able to command a ship. Thackeray's ballad looks forward to Hilaire Belloc's cautionary tales, much enjoyed by children, in which disobedient boys meet dreadful fates. It seems pointless to accuse the authors of such poems of sadism. Humour of this kind is a safety-valve whereby the pressure of aggressive, dismissive, or annihilatory feelings is released.

Crucial in all writing about children is the question of viewpoint. To move rapidly from the child's viewpoint to the adult's is to reveal a potential for conflict and rivalry. Freud and several neo-Freudians have noted that sexual activity is mostly controlled by the pleasure principle, whereas parenthood requires acceptance of the reality principle. As we have already seen, this conflict between pleasure and duty is not experienced exclusively by men. In the chapter on motherhood in Simone de Beauvoir's *The Second Sex* it is argued that, while the man 'is resentful of the woman's too fertile body', the woman for her part 'dreads the germs of life that he risks placing within her'. De Beauvoir shows that, for many women, pregnancy and motherhood arouse ambivalent feelings, not feelings of unqualified acceptance; and that a wife and mother who is confined to home duties 'lacks the means requisite for self-affirmation'. Comedy emphasizes the impulse to reject parenthood rather than the impulse to accept it, attributing the former impulse to women as well as men.

As moralists, educators, or citizens we insist on the child's need for love and fostering, and resent dismissive remarks about children. Yet such remarks still come to be made: the impulse which prompts them has not lost its force. In literature, some fine effects can be achieved by clashing the two possible responses. In Nancy Mitford's *Love in a Cold Climate* there is a simultaneously comic and chilling moment when a society woman observes vaguely to her daughter: 'So the poor little baby died, I expect it was just as well, children are such an awful expense, nowadays.' The attendant nurse is horrified to hear a mother say such a thing to her own child. But in comedy, ancient or modern, the ageing aristocrat's response is almost normal. Her insensitivity towards her dead grandchild is in proportion to her capacity for self-fulfilment: 'The great flame of happiness' that an attentive young man has lit in her heart has 'long burnt up all emotions which did not directly relate to him'. The odd result is that the rich society woman, who cannot be bothered to conceal her indifference to the death of a baby, comes off better than the self-righteous nurse who is shocked by it. Lady Mountdore is herself a child, one whose energy and self-absorption are envied by more responsible people. She is too caught up in her own life to care about the loss of a baby who died too soon to know what life was.

Peter Coveney has detected in the work of Dickens 'an amazing inconsistency. . . . The child is now a symbol of growth and development, and now a symbol of retreat into personal regression and self-pity.' What this leaves out is the comic symbolization of childhood, which shows children as a burden or a nuisance. Dickens, like other comic writers, senses the adult's nostalgia for what Brown calls the 'privileged irresponsibility and freedom' of childhood. Being a child is in this respect greatly preferable to having one. Comedy seeks to fulfil, vicariously, our longing for a return, not to childhood innocence but to a childish freedom from obligations. The comic character wants to enjoy, simultaneously, the power and social standing of the adult and the carefree freedom of the child. It is true that comedy can revel in fertility and thus, to an extent, in the birth of new life. (In Mitford's novel there are several likeable, if bumptious, children, and the wish to breed is attributed from time to time to several childless characters.) But new arrivals are welcomed on condition that they do not interfere with adults' self-expression. The comic hero or heroine is a spoilt but lovable child whose aim is to win more than its fair share of pleasure of privilege. He or she will resent rivals of any age.

Oscar Wilde's *The Importance of Being Earnest* shows a more than intuitive grasp of these issues. In the second act the play moves, as a Shakespearian comedy might do, from the sophistication of the city to the relative naturalness of the countryside. The atmosphere is one of growth and proliferation: even the Rector and the spinster governess speak in unintentionally suggestive metaphors relating to bees, fruit, and pollen. But there is no carefree celebration of fertility. Miss Prism remarks disapprovingly that christening babies is 'one of the Rector's most constant duties. I have often spoken to the poorer classes on the subject. But they don't seem to know what thrift is.' For thrift, we may read 'abstinence': since the governess is forced to abstain, she resents her social inferiors' indulgence. But in a sense Prism is right: poor people can ill afford fertility. Older children may provide labour, but younger ones are a source of expense. Canon Chasuble describes the father of newborn twins as 'poor Jenkins the carter, a most hard-working man'. 'Hard-working' refers both to fulfilment of conjugal duties and to the toil needed to maintain the resulting brood. Chasuble's comment is made, significantly, in connection with a request from the young sparks, Jack and Algernon, for rechristening, which in their case is jokingly linked with a return to childhood. This recovery of privileged irresponsibility contrasts powerfully with Jenkins's commitment to manual labour, family duties, and biological reproduction. The rich youth's wish to have the best of both adult and childhood worlds underlies Jack's response to the Vicar's idea that he and the Jenkins twins be christened at the same time: 'Oh! I don't see much fun in being christened along with other babies. It would be childish.' This is amusing because it points both ways. On the one hand, Jack accepts the child-status that christening confers upon him, but resents the presence of possible rivals: on the other, he refuses all that is 'childish' in favour of the freedom he enjoys as a young adult. Jack's situation is thus, in the Freudian sense, overdetermined. He is simultaneously a child, a young bachelor, and even (in his guise as guardian of Cecily Cardew) a father.

A frequent impulse of comic characters is to reject children as an unwelcome burden. But that rejection operates within the limits of the genre, which delights in irresponsibility and represents selfishness as vigour. The fact that we laugh, perhaps guiltily, at anti-child jokes on the page or in the theatre does not mean that we will acquire a greater tolerance for cruelty, neglect, or rejection of children in everyday life. This, we may suspect, has always been true. In the late nineteenth and twentieth centuries, however, some schools of philosophy and psychology have advanced the comic arguments in a spirit of seriousness. It is odd that, in a period when many educationists and psychologists are still at work on a sanctification of childhood, and when adults in the wider community are being adjured to give more time and attention to children's needs, a minority group of thinkers should have stamped biological reproduction as enslavement to meaningless repetition, representing all that is most objectionable in the nuclear family.

Others, more impishly, have remarked how procreation threatens to upset the calculations of the respectable bourgeois couple. Here is Baudelaire tilting happily at 'Virtuous Plays and Novels':

Listen to Gabrielle, the virtuous Gabrielle, reckoning with her virtuous spouse how long a spell of virtuous avarice they will need to undergo, at compound interest on their money, for them to enjoy an investment income of ten to twenty thousand francs a year. . . . 'Then,' exclaim the virtuous pair, 'WE SHALL BE ABLE TO AFFORD THE LUXURY OF A SON'!

Baudelaire goes on to invoke the Marquis de Sade and the more notorious Roman Emperors, gleefully hinting that bourgeois marriage has revived their most unnatural practices. And there is indeed something chilling about a sexual life regulated by economic needs and calculations. A new melancholy descends over marriage, sex, and the family: are love and procreation within wedlock doomed to inauthenticity?

Thoughts like these have had their effects on comedy: it has become hard to treat the old problems with the same cheerful insouciance. In Barthelme's *Snow White* Prince Paul is wary of the cascade of jet-black hair which he sees hanging from a window: 'There is probably some girl attached to the top, and with

her responsibilities of various sorts . . . teeth . . . piano lessons.'
There may be a reminiscence here of a Li'l Abner cartoon where a
passing nymphet provocatively waves her pigtail, while the
grown man warns the boy not to pull it. But Barthelme's characters are acquainted with post-existentialist philosophy as well
as with Al Capp; even the fairy-tale heroine is moved to chide one
of the dwarfs for his 'Western confusion between the concept
"pleasure" and the concept "increasing the size of the herd" '.
Where Rabelais's Grandgousier and Gargamelle 'did oftentimes
do the two-backed beast together, joyfully rubbing their bacon
against one another', and rejoiced when Gargamelle conceived
(now, there *is* a comic fable that validates procreation),
Barthelme's heroine disdains such simplicity. Still more omi-
nously the head dwarf Bill, 'obviously chosen to be the darling of
the life principle', refuses the sexual routine in the shower which
so excites the others, finding that it grows monotonous. Yet part
of what disturbs the characters is that only a tiny percentage of
people have been affected by the malaise which they themselves
feel: 'Oh it is killing me', wails Clem, 'the way they walk down
the street together, laughing and talking, those men and women.
Pushing the pram too, whether the man is doing it, or the woman
is doing it. Normal life. And a fine October chill in the air. It
is unbearable, this consensus, this damned felicity.'

Barthelme's dwarfs earn their living tending the vats in a baby-
food factory. Towards the end of the book they go to a party,
presumably connected with their business since it is a 'howling
party', full of mothers who insist on discussing 'the bat theory of
child-raising': 'Spare the bat and the child rots. . . . We have a
book which tells us such things. . . . On page 331 begins a twelve-
page discussion of batting the baby. A well-worn page.' The
discussion upsets the dwarfs and they escape as fast as they can:
authority-figures (scoutmasters, mothers, nuns) reawaken their
childish fears. The dwarfs' stunted physical growth is a metaphor
for their failure to grow emotionally. They drink to assert their
adulthood: a vat of rum, which they eye longingly at the party
while the mothers are talking, makes for them an alluring contrast to a vat of baby food. Their energy and resourcefulness are
increasingly directed to irresponsible ends: latterly they neglect

the food-vats, and Bill is hanged for 'vaticide and failure'. But in the world of *Snow White* the dwarfs are not the only ones who have failed to grow up. Prince Paul is weak, indecisive, a voyeur. The rock star who loves Snow White, and should take over Paul's function as saviour and completing-other, is despised by his band because he is still possessed by a Northrop Frye-style myth of spring, love, and renewal. Snow White will not consider any lover who is not royal: her approach to life (based on romance) is no more promising than that of the dwarfs (derived from comedy). It is an entropic world, where those who have most individuality have least energy, least will to renew the species. In modern comedy and tragicomedy this refusal of issue is a commonplace. In Ionesco's *Rhinoceros* one of two surviving humans suggests renewing the human race; the other replies, 'I don't want to have children. It's a bore.' In Albee's *Who's Afraid of Virginia Woolf* Martha can't have children and Honey won't.

The comic attitude to children and childbirth has always been ambivalent. Comic celebration is directed towards irresponsible energy and fun rather than towards biological renewal. Babies in comedy are left on mountainsides, in baskets, on doorsteps, or even in the left-luggage compartments of railway stations; but the assumption, in all but the darkest works, is that they will turn up again when they are old enough to be interesting. Aristophanes, in *The Frogs*, chides Euripides for dwelling too much on domestic things in his tragedies, but the rule against cooing over children applies just as strongly to comedy: children restrict freedom, and freedom is one of the defining characteristics of the comic hero and heroine. 'Can't have a lot of kids complicating the clean exit with suitcase,' says Charlotte in Stoppard's *The Real Thing*; later, quizzing another couple on the reason for their childlessness, she asks, 'Is yours a case of sperm count or twisted tubes? Or is it that you just can't stand the little buggers?' Misoprogenitive utterances are not, even in comedy, received with unmixed pleasure and approval; comedy is, nevertheless, one of the few forms of discourse that takes for granted the human impulse to postpone or reject breeding in order to prolong and extend freedom, selfhood, and youth.

5

Death

Of the three great themes of human life—birth, marriage, and death—the last-named may seem the least promising as material for comedy. But this first impression proves misleading. It is nearly two centuries since Hazlitt remarked how hard it sometimes is to keep one's countenance at a funeral. In a funeral poem by E. E. Cummings, a man who in life failed repeatedly at different kinds of farming lurches down in his coffin to start a worm farm. Behind the laughter lies the notion that the dead person is somehow, somewhere, obstinately alive: after death he will simply continue in his old ways. The same feeling informs a modern television sketch in which, during a requiem mass for a comic actor, the dead man lifts his coffin lid during the eulogy to begin an 'Oh, no I didn't!' 'Oh, yes you did!' routine with the priest and congregation. The protagonist of Kurt Vonnegut's *Slaughterhouse Five* has some imaginary friends from the planet Tralfamadore who, when they see a corpse, think that the deceased is in a bad state at that moment but still exists in good states at many other moments. (They believe in the simultaneity of all moments in time.)

One of comedy's responses to death is a Tralfamadorian denial of its power or right to extinguish human personalities. At the end of Brendan Behan's *The Hostage* the slaughtered soldier rises and leads the cast in a chorus which parodies 'Abide with Me', a hymn which recognizes the transience and unimportance of the human individual in a way that Behan's play seems determined not to do. The corpse which refuses to lie down, the coffin which opens to reveal a living person, are among the oldest resources of comedy, from Middleton's Renaissance play *A Chaste Maid in Cheapside* to Pam Gems's semi-documentary about the singer Edith Piaf, where the protagonist rises from her death-bed to sing one of her great numbers, 'Je ne regrette rien'.

Baudelaire, in nineteenth-century France, particularly enjoyed a scene from a visiting English pantomime where a rogue-character, realistically guillotined on stage, got up after the execution and stole back his own severed head. A romantic variant of this motif appears in one of the incidental tales in *Don Quixote*. Basilio loves Quiteria, who has been persuaded to marry a wealthier man. On the day of the wedding Basilio appears and stabs himself. As he lies weltering in his blood, he begs to be allowed to say the marriage ceremony through with Quiteria: he wants to die knowing that he has been her husband, if only for a few moments. When his request has been fulfilled, with the somewhat grudging consent of the prospective husband, Basilio revives; his 'death' was staged by means of an old fair-ground trick involving a fake stab-wound and a hidden store of animal's blood. Basilio is now Quiteria's husband for life. Scapin plays a similar trick in Molière's *Les Fourberies de Scapin*, gaining forgiveness for his deceits on his 'death-bed'; in Uncle Remus's tales Brer Bear feigns dead in an attempt to catch the slippery Brer Rabbit. Usually the supposed deaths are treated seriously until the trickery is unmasked, but not always. Shakespeare's Prince Hal, standing over the enormous bulk of the 'slain' Falstaff on the battlefield at Shrewsbury, is no more able to refrain from mixing jests with his tears than was the narrator of Cummings's poem about the failed farmer. Hal's farewell is, of course, premature. Falstaff not only rises to protest against the disembowelment Hal has planned for him but lifts the body of Hotspur, the heroic rebel, on to his shoulders. The spirit of humour and festivity seems to assist survival: it is certainly a better talisman against death than Hotspur's heroics.

So common is the stage device of death followed by resurrection that the figure of the actor becomes associated with immortality. In Tom Stoppard's *Rosencrantz and Guildenstern are Dead* the Chief Player asks the riddle, 'What happens to old actors?' to which the answer is, 'Nothing. They're still acting.' The play's two anti-heroes are irritated by the Players' belief that they can act death convincingly, and that their 'experience' gives them a special insight into the nature and significance of death: they almost seem to be claiming that they can keep death at bay. At last, to disprove the actors' point, Guildenstern snatches a dagger from the Chief Player's belt and stabs him with it. When the victim has fallen and lain still for a moment the other players begin to applaud and the supposedly dead man gets up, dusting himself. To the astonished Rosencrantz and Guildenstern he observes coolly, 'For a moment you thought I'd—cheated.' In his world, paradoxically, what constitutes 'cheating' is tawdry realism: carrying a real dagger instead of a false one, dying in reality instead of acting it out. The actors explain to Rosencrantz and Guildenstern that they once got a condemned criminal to act in a play and performed a real execution on stage: the effect was thoroughly unconvincing. Heidegger once wrote that authentic existence consisted in the ability to launch oneself towards one's own death. Stoppard's Players, who are thoroughly inauthentic ('We're *actors*—we're the opposite of people'), find a kind of immunity from the thought of death in the practice of their art. Death for them is something that you experience many times; you always get up afterwards.

Often comedy presents premature death as the lot of those who are overcome with the spirit of seriousness. In Evelyn Waugh's *Decline and Fall* the solemn Prendergast is installed as chaplain of Egdon Heath prison. But he soon succumbs to the Governor's schemes for prison reform: a lunatic prisoner uses carpentry tools, issued in an attempt to foster the prisoners' creativity, to dismember him. The news of his death is passed around during the singing of a hymn in the prison chapel: the words of 'O God our help in ages past' are adapted to convey the news of the chaplain's fate. Once more, as in Behan's *The Hostage*, the stately language of the hymn-book is submerged in the rawer register of everyday life, as if in defiance of the Church's message that awareness of death must brood constantly over existence. For while death catches up with the serious Prendergast (the rogue, Captain Grimes, remarks that Prendy 'wasn't cut out for the happy life'), the comic characters elude it. After Grimes's escape from prison his hat is found floating in a treacherous bog. But his friend Pennyfeather senses that Grimes is 'of the immortals': 'He was a life force. Sentenced to death in Flanders, he popped up in Wales; drowned in Wales, he emerged in South America; engulfed in the dark mystery of Egdon Mire, he would rise again somewhere at some time, shaking from his limbs the musty integuments of the tomb.'

In contrast to the situation where the person marked out to die refuses to do so is that in which the body, which should be treated with reverence, is treated as an object. An extreme example is Joe Orton's *Loot*, where the body of someone's mother (surely the paradigmatic instance of the sacredness of the dead) is tossed from cupboard to coffin and back again, its claim to a peaceful resting-place repeatedly subordinated to that of a hoard of stolen money. The same motif appears, in milder form, in less ruthless comedies. Huck Finn hides money which belongs to living friends, and is in danger of being stolen, in their dead relative's coffin: he justifies his choice of hiding place by reminding himself that 'there warn't nobody there but the remainders of Peter'. This refusal to treat the body as anything other than an object is responsible for many of the visual jokes about death that pervade stage comedy and farce. In Stoppard's *Jumpers* the body of a dead professor hangs tantalizingly behind the door of the heroine's bedroom, swinging in and out of sight as people enter or leave. The body behind the door has become something of a stock device, as Stoppard himself acknowledges, but *Jumpers* is exceptional in its exploration of the possible implications. The hero, unaware that the corpse of a murdered colleague has been hidden in his wife's bedchamber, remarks that modern philosophy sees no problem as insoluble given a big enough plastic bag. His wife, preoccupied with the problem of getting rid of the body, asks wistfully: 'You don't happen to *have* a large plastic bag, do you?' At the climax of the first act of the play this verbal gag becomes visual: the villain appears carrying 'a small square of material' which unfolds into a plastic bag of impressive size. His underlings stuff the body into it and vanish. The disposal of the corpse thus becomes a virtuoso performance, a kind of cross between a ballet and a conjuring act. Later Archie, the magician-logician, will offer the police the convenient hypothesis that the murder victim 'left here last night in a mood of deep depression, and wandered into the park, where he crawled into a large plastic bag and shot himself'.

In *Jumpers* (in contrast to, say, *Loot*) the villains' refusal to treat the body as any more than an object is at odds with the ethical bias of the play: it epitomizes the pragmatism and materialism which distress Stoppard's hero and also, of course, Stoppard himself. Yet some of the best jokes in *Jumpers* come from this source: the play even draws attention to the fact that the morally fastidious protagonist, George Moore, fails his wife in her time of need, while the cool, body-snatching villain has the panache to rescue her. And even George has to admit that 'conditions of group survival or the notion of filial homage' make ways of behaving towards the dead which would be anathema in some cultures perfectly acceptable in others. 'A tribe which believes it confers honour on its elders by eating them' will, he points out, be 'viewed askance by another which prefers to buy them a little bungalow somewhere'. This might seem to offer an indirect justification of Archie's treatment of the corpse of McFee. However, what strikes George most forcibly, validating the ethical argument in his eyes, is 'not . . . that the notion of honour should manifest itself so differently in peoples so far removed in clime and culture. What is surely more surprising is that notions such as honour should manifest themselves at all.' Archie, however, will cheerfully desecrate a dead body if doing so furthers the pragmatic interests of the living. *Jumpers*, then, not only arouses laughter at irreverent behaviour but also seeks to explore its ethical implications.

The raising of ethical questions about the treatment of the dead is not, then, necessarily alien to comedy. Nevertheless, one typical comic response to death is that of the carefree child, for whom the selfhood of one who is not a close friend or relative is pleasingly vague, its extinction of small concern. The cartoon character Barry Mackenzie, an Australian expatriate living in London, is disturbed to receive an overseas telegram: has something happened to his mother? When he reads the cable he capers with joy because his aunt has died, leaving him enough money to prolong his stay abroad. A similar effect is achieved in *Tom Sawyer* when Tom, a Cadet of Temperance, longs for an opportunity to wear the red sash he has earned by his abstention from swearing and drinking. He fixes his hopes on the funeral of an old judge who is apparently on his death-bed. But the judge perversely recovers, and Tom resigns from the cadets in disgust. The next night the judge suffers a relapse and dies: Tom resolves never to trust a man like that again. Here, as in *Jumpers*, the effect is not to make someone's death seem inherently trivial: rather, it is to make a joke of the way that others respond to it.

Such effects are frequent in comedy. Wilde's Algernon has a fictitious friend called Bunbury whose illnesses give him excuses for avoiding inconvenient engagements. His aunt, finding Algernon flirting with a pretty woman at a country house, asks sceptically whether it is here that Bunbury resides. Algernon replies, 'Oh! No! Bunbury doesn't live here. Bunbury is somewhere else at present. In fact, Bunbury is dead. . . . I killed Bunbury this afternoon. I mean poor Bunbury died this afternoon.' Though Bunbury is imaginary the notion of him being casually killed, for the convenience of the youthful hero, is bracing and shocking in the same way that the deaths of Tom Sawyer's judge and Barry Mackenzie's auntie are. Confronted with a death which does not touch us deeply, our first, childlike, response is to wonder how it will bear on our own day-to-day concerns. Our social training teaches us to conceal this reaction, but we still experience it: to hear comic characters expressing it gives us an agreeable sense of vicarious transgression.

The supreme instance in comedy of the needs of the living overriding the rights of the dead is the tale of the Ephesian matron in Petronius' *Satyricon* (Roman, first century AD). I call it the supreme instance because, while in a modern translation it takes up less than three pages, its influence on later writers has been spectacular. Its paradigmatic quality comes from its deployment of two opposite responses to mortality. The first is extreme reverence and extravagant sorrow: the widow follows her husband into the tomb, 'torturing herself and trying to starve to death'. The second is irreverent use of the dead body for the convenience of the living. A soldier guarding the bodies of some criminals crucified near the dead man's tomb sees a light coming from underground and goes to investigate. With difficulty he persuades the widow and her maid to eat. Soon he is spending all his pay on food to share with them. Nourishment brings the widow back to life and health, so much so that she and the soldier become lovers. In the meantime the relatives of the crucified man steal the corpse and bury it: the soldier, whose duty it was to prevent this, resolves to kill himself rather than wait for punishment. But the widow persuades him to save himself by placing her husband's body on the cross in place of that of the criminal.

Let us note how significant burial is in the world of the tale. Part of the punishment for the criminal and his family is the knowledge that nobody will be allowed to inter him: the authorities think this so important that they post a guard to enforce it. Thus the widow's action in substituting her husband's body for that of the crucified man seems, not casually disrespectful, but sacrilegious in the highest degree. Yet when she commits the sacrilege to save the soldier, the reader experiences a sense of exhilaration which overrides any sense of shock.

What other inferences can be drawn from the tale? In Petronius' original, Eumolpus tells it as an illustration of woman's fickleness. But it can be read differently. In Christopher Fry's modern adaptation *A Phoenix too Frequent* the widow claims that in using her husband's body to save the soldier she is making him live again, this time as a saver of another's life. Though we may take this as special pleading, our comic, life-accepting impulses urge us to uphold the plea. It is tragedy (*Antigone* or *Hamlet*) that validates the impulse to lavish attention on the dead: comedy exalts the opposite feeling. In the *Satyricon*, it is the rich and vulgar Trimalchio who shows most concern for the fate of his body and the design of his last resting place. At the other pole stands the roguish Eumolpus, who in the last surviving section of the novel poses as a rich man in a town full of legacy-hunters: he hopes to feed on their expectations of gain after his death. He has no concern for his mortal remains, which will presumably get short shrift from the disappointed legatees.

There is a Petronian air about Evelyn Waugh's modern comical satire *The Loved One*, set among the dubious splendours of Whispering Glades funeral park in California. The modern Trimalchio is Kaiser of Kaiser's Stoneless Peaches, his family burial plot prepared in advance and already occupied by his wife and aunt. The Englishmen in the American East Coast community resemble the raffish-genteel Eumolpus and Encolpius in the *Satyricon*: like the born citizens among the freed slaves they feel superior, but are really parasites on the commercial prosperity of the rest. Where the decayed patrician Eumolpus tells a tale of a widow making love in her husband's tomb, the expatriate Dennis Barlow on his tour of Whispering Glades encounters lovers 'emerging from their nether world in an incandescent envelope' of sensual pleasure: once again a place dedicated to death has come to serve as a sanctuary for love. Perhaps it is this that imparts a strange poetry to Whispering Glades and its priestess, the apprentice mortician Aimée Thanatogenos.

The book revives several favourite comic devices, most of which make capital out of pseudo-reverential attitudes to Loved Ones. The standard shroud turns out to be a backless suit of clothes, the idea for which (as the receptionist admits) 'came from the quick-change artists in vaudeville'. The Petronian motif of lovers using bodies to further amorous purposes reappears when the master mortician Mr Joyboy gives corpses the Radiant Childhood smile when his courtship of Aimée is progressing and an expression of bottomless woe when it is broken off. The frigidity behind the apparently caring attitude of the staff is revealed in a 'disconcerting lapse from high diction' suffered by one of the hostesses: 'They fixed that stiff . . . so he looked like it was his wedding day.' Disappointingly, though, the opportunity for a Jonsonian comic celebration of wit and ingenuity, with rogues getting rich through unashamed exploitation of the customers, is refused. Indeed, Mr Joyboy and Aimée seem to be rejected by the novelist precisely because they cannot take the step of turning themselves into exuberant comic scoundrels. They espouse neither the defiant insistence that the vitality of the deceased is still lurking somewhere nor the pragmatic treatment of the corpse as if it were an object in the service of the living.

Instead they aim to restore to all Loved Ones the aspect they wore at the blandest moments of their lives. When Dennis sees his friend Sir Francis, whose face has been reconstituted after the distortion it suffered when he hanged himself, the result seems 'entirely horrible; . . . a painted and smirking obscene travesty by comparison with which the devil-mask Dennis had found in the noose was a festive adornment'. The bad faith of Joyboy and Aimée is such that they prefer death and dead people to life and living people. Joyboy pays more attention to his own status as high priest in the mortuary than to the needs of his lonely old mother. Aimée welcomes the change from beautician to mortician because she can now exercise the same skills on people who are mercifully unable to talk. Nothing is more alien to the spirit of Whispering Glades than the old life-accepting, death-accepting, comic American tradition of 'unceremonious manners and frank speech'. Before the Joyboy era there was 'some decline of gentility in the ascent from show-room to workshop. There had been talk of "bodies" and "cadavers"; one jaunty young embalmer from Texas had even spoken of "the meat". That young man had gone within a week of Mr. Joyboy's appointment.'

The Loved One wavers between what Baudelaire would call 'significative comedy' and 'absolute comedy'. Sometimes evaluative judgements are made. Aimée is dismissed as mad: she commits suicide when a drunken journalist, whose advice column she has been following, becomes impatient with her problems and advises her to jump off a tall building. Her actual means of self-disposal is to poison herself in the funeral parlour at Whispering Glades, in the hope that Mr Joyboy will perform a reverential operation on her corpse. But Joyboy is afraid of falling under suspicion. He begs Dennis to perform a cremation at the Happier Hunting Ground, which deals in funerals for pets, and which Aimée always regarded as a blasphemous travesty of Whispering Glades. As the price of his services Dennis extorts from Joyboy the money he needs to return to England. Before leaving he arranges to have Joyboy sent, on each anniversary of Aimée's death, a card with the inscription, 'Your little Aimée is wagging her tail in heaven tonight, thinking of you.' The last sentence of the book has him settling down with a novel 'to await his loved one's final combustion'.

Death, it seems, can be treated comically when the character responding to the death is childlike, or when the dead person is not one in whom reader or central character have much reason to be interested. It is the non-fulfilment of these two conditions that makes the ending of *The Loved One* so distressing. Neither narrator, reader, nor protagonist has reason to feel detached from Aimée, however much all three may feel irritated by her: all have felt the strange poetry of this fictional being, which makes the narrator, towards the end of the book, characterize her as a failed Antigone. And though Dennis, who has been 'half in love with easeful death' (that is, with Aimée and Whispering Glades), has something of th child about him, it is the irresponsibility of childhood he possesses, not the zest for life. If we are to judge Aimée and Joyboy, why not Dennis too? Yet the novel ends on an odd note of indecision as to whether Dennis is to be congratulated on his escape from a mad delusion or condemned for a failure of love.

More satisfyingly comic than Dennis are the drinkers at the Southern Cross Hotel in David Ireland's Australian novel *The Glass Canoe*. A tension is felt in the bar when a local boy, Sibley, who always tried hard at school and 'had strong healthy views on drinking too much piss . . . and dying at fifty', comes back from university to carry out a survey among his former companions. The implied question behind his research is how the drinkers can bear to be failures and misfits in a world which gives thrusting people like Sibley so many opportunities. Sibley's opinion of the drinkers is half-affectionate but it is also fatally patronizing: drinkers have 'always been considered treacherous in their dealings with . . . non-drinkers. After they leave school, they return to the natural surroundings of their fathers. A sort of homing instinct, as in birds. Drinkers can survive in conditions where the non-drinker would perish.'

Sibley's description of the difference between drinkers and non-drinkers unconsciously duplicates last century's orthodoxies about the differences between Aboriginals and whites. The sinister corollary is that Sibley does not understand the drinkers' mentality; he has no inkling that they see and resent his attitude towards them: 'They think I'm harmless. They know I'm harmless. I might have gone on to university, but they don't grudge me that.' He buys them beers in the same spirit in which 'colonizers all over the world' used to give 'beads and pretty nothings' to natives of newly encountered countries: 'His coloured pens were stuck neatly in his pocket, his face lit with missionary zeal; he looked so alive and alert and cheerful it was hard to believe he was real.'

About the time when Sibley disappears the pub acquires a new doorstop, an aluminium barrel that has been cut across the top and welded together again. It does not give a hollow sound when kicked. Soon it begins to change shape, shortening and swelling in the middle. Finally it goes off like a bomb. A smell of putrefaction percolates through the bar. To get rid of the stench, someone takes the keg outside and ties it to the pub sign: 'In the next months you could see a thin line going up the outside wall of the pub where the ants made a highway.' When the procession of ants ceases, the barrel is taken down and the pieces welded together once more. It resumes its old function as a doorstop. No more sociological surveys are conducted in the bar.

The death of Sibley is an example (an unusually clear one for modern literature) of the casting out of an agelast or opponent of laughter, someone who cannot or will not share in the comic and festive spirit of the group. The most obvious parallel is with Rabelais, especially the aspects of his work discussed by Mikhail Bakhtin and Edith Kern. Rabelais's world is one of drinking and carnival; it is also one of peasant life. Ireland's novel is set in the city, but is full of reminders of the rural origins of urban culture. At one point in *The Glass Canoe* a Rabelaisian battle is fought with smashed bottles and broken billiard cues: the opposing armies are the local drinkers and a group from a country pub who are visiting the city. Though many on both sides are injured and have to be taken to hospital, the encounter ends with friendly drinking among the survivors and the promise of a return match as soon as the city men can visit the country pub. The crunching and cracking of bones, the bleeding, the wounds, and the partial dismemberments recall the equally ferocious festivities at the castle of the Lord of Basché in Rabelais's *Gargantua*, where some visiting representatives of the central government suffer fearful mutilations. The death of Sibley, likewise, recalls the death of Tappecoue in *Gargantua*. Tappecoue refuses to lend a costume for a play: a religious play, but one which features a riotous chorus of devils. The devil/actors, having made merry at an inn before the performance, waylay Tappecoue and frighten his horse with fireworks: he falls, catches his foot in a stirrup, and is dragged along until he is dead. His mutilation is described in grotesque detail. Among modern critics both Mikhail Bakhtin and Edith Kern see the incident in terms of comedy, though they also see the analogy with the death and dismemberment of Pentheus in Euripides' tragedy *The Bacchae*. (Pentheus suffers for his defiance of Dionysus, the god of drunken inspiration and festivity.) The problem of festive excess and victimization will be dealt with more fully in later chapters. For the moment let us note that Bakhtin and Kern offer another pretext for the ferocity of Rabelaisian deaths and mutilations apart from festive licence, namely the necessary subordination of individuals to groups. Each member of a group will eventually die; the group itself will endure. The individual body is from this point of view insignificant, destined as it is to be reabsorbed sooner or later into the natural cycle. (Ireland's Sibley fulfils this requirement through the good offices of the ants.) Ireland's thematizations of death and dismemberment in *The Glass Canoe* represent a revival of Rabelaisian themes in modern imaginative writing.

In most of the comedies so far considered, the bodies which are treated disrespectfully are those of outcasts, nonentities, or strangers. But in some recent works the protagonist shows equal insouciance about the mortal remains of his closest relatives, and even about his own. Monk O'Neill in Jack Hibberd's Australian stage monologue *A Stretch of the Imagination* recalls that when his first wife died, 'The chief pathologist, an old Xaverian like myself, was kind enough to forward me a few of her things. . . . Gallstone. . . . Dentures. . . . There used to be a painted toe-nail . . . Gone.' (But the toe-nail later turns up: Monk has used it as a bookmark for his copy of Plato.) The play is full of references to ants, decomposition, and the merit of the decaying human body as a natural fertilizer. In his more ebullient moments (and he has many) Monk sees death itself as festive. 'A man should hurdle and pole-vault to his coffin': the last moments should be 'full of rhetoric and joy'. In many respects, then, Monk is a Bakhtinian–Rabelaisian character. What he lacks is the Rabelaisian sense of community. He lives alone by his own choice. His reminiscences are full of people whom he would rather call to mind than re-encounter in the flesh: 'Hector de Pilo . . . interred [*sic*] during the war on account of his salami extraction. Never saw him again.' The living beings who once surrounded Monk have vanished one by one: he has killed his horse and his dog, and severed all human contacts. But he is as cheerfully casual about his own death as about other people's. It is a characteristic he shares with other figures in modern literature, notably Samuel Beckett's Murphy.

When Murphy dies in an explosion caused by a leaking gas pipe, his will is found to contain careful instructions for the disposal of his remains:

> With regard to the disposal of these my body, mind and soul, I desire that they be burnt and placed in a paper bag and brought to the Abbey Theatre, Lr. Abbey Street, Dublin, and without pause into what the great and good Lord Chesterfield calls the necessary house, where their happiest hours have been spent, . . . and I desire that the chain be there pulled upon them, if possible during the performance of a piece, the whole to be executed without ceremony or show of grief.

Murphy's will is not executed in quite the intended manner. The bag containing his ashes bursts in a bar-room brawl, and by closing time 'the body, mind, and soul of Murphy' are 'freely distributed over the floor of the saloon' and among 'the sand, the beer, the butts, the glass, the matches, the spits, the vomit'. The joke is not on Murphy but on the world he leaves behind. The muck of the bar-room floor is a better setting for his ashes than the antiseptic chill of the mortuary, a place of 'immense double-decker refrigerators' with an 'unbroken bay of glass frosted to a height of five feet from the floor,' an 'aluminium tray,' a 'slab of ruin marble'. Murphy's funeral is comic and celebratory in so far as it denies the dualism which regards the body as somehow separable from the soul, and derides the scientist's vision of a 'glorious world of discrete particles.'

The idea that death may in some circumstances be a triumph, or that some people may be better off dead, can be encountered not only in the austere comedy of Beckett but also in popular farces like Joseph Kesselring's *Arsenic and Old Lace*:

ABBY. And then when his heart attack came—and he sat dead in that chair looking so peaceful—remember, Martha—we made up our minds then and there that if we could help other lonely old men to that same peace—we would!

In this play, admittedly, the dominant attitude of the old aunts towards the deaths of other people is the childlike insouciance which we have already encountered so often. The sisters seek single male lodgers of a certain age: instead of caring for 'their' gentlemen in conventional ways they poison them and bury them in the cellar. The notion that death will actually make the victims happier is transparently a pretext: the real motive is the fun of conducting funeral services. The whole exercise is a game, a contest even: the sisters are distressed when their nephew, a gangster, claims to have killed more people than they have. But the notion of using death to bring happiness is present in the play, and remains in the auditor's mind.

It reappears in a more recent comedy, the 1985 film *The Ultimate Solution of Grace Quigley*. Quigley is poor, well-bred, genteel, ageing, alone, and worried about her rent: she accidentally witnesses a murder carried out by a professional hit man. It occurs to her that the murderer might be blackmailed into using his skills for the benefit of old people who have nothing left to live for, starting with herself.

Quigley's own extinction quickly recedes into the background in the excitement of providing a service for others. But this film, unlike Kesselring's play, does not show the protagonist making decisions on the victims' behalf: this time the old people themselves make the request for 'treatment'. The difficulty which, predictably, arises is that the hit man, who has killed a succession of other criminals, finds it hard to nerve himself to administer euthanasia to lovable old people, however earnestly they themselves beg him to do so.

The Ultimate Solution of Grace Quigley makes little attempt to play down the despair and loneliness of old age; there is more than one sourly funny scene where groups of old people loiter furtively, like addicts of drugs or pornography, in hopes of buying the forbidden quietus. Perhaps the most successful strategy by which this longing for death is assimilated to comedy is that of making the decision to die into a paradoxical affirmation of life. A message from one of the victims, read out by request at his funeral, runs: 'Life is too beautiful to go around dying, and when dying is all you think about you are better off dead.' Some clients are told to stand around the piano singing 'When Irish eyes are smiling': the hit man goes into the garage, turns on the engines of the host's two vintage cars, and pumps exhaust fumes into the room. As he and Quigley listen, the music stops. 'But, Seymour!' protests Quigley, 'There's another verse!' Seymour replies curtly, 'Not this time, Mom!' Death has come to the clients at a time when their enjoyment of life, in the form of music and companionship, was at its height.

In its deft way, the film does offer a comment on life: its comedy is, to a degree, significative. But it does not make the mistake of offering direct propaganda for euthanasia. Part of its fable is the gradual maturing of the hit man and his mentor, Mrs Quigley. When they realize that power over life and death is beginning to corrupt them, they decide to renounce it. In the last sequence they come home to find a crowd of clients waiting at the door: to avoid meeting them they hail a taxi and drive away.

The joke on which the film centres, and the principle on which it turns, is freedom: freedom to terminate one's life or to help someone else to do so. Somehow it is finely comical to see splendid old people humbly, but with utter certainty, opting for death. Here, as in all comedy that concerns itself with mortality, the joke is on our pretence that there is only one permissible, or even possible, attitude to death: *The Ultimate Solution of Grace Quigley* presents us, among other things, with the hypothesis that death may come to seem an adventure, a supreme gift, a passionate experience like love.

If laughter returns us to childishness it can often do so in a way that leads to a new maturity and responsibility. At first it seems that the adolescent attitude to death, that it is amusing provided that it does not happen to me or to someone dear to me, is the only one which will allow death to be made laughable. But there can also be a gaiety and irreverence about ways of facing the fact of death, including one's own death: its forms range from the full-scale moral comedy of *Jumpers* or *Grace Quigley* to the bleakly farcical ending of *Monty Python's Life of Brian*, where the crucified men break into the song 'Always Look on the Bright Side of Death', or the sardonic graffito, 'You're being reincarnated as a mayfly. Have a nice day.' The same is true of comic attitudes to marriage and childbirth. It is exciting to cast off, for a while, our adult, mature attitudes to these eternal human concerns. But somehow the temporary release leads to a new acceptance. It helps us to understand the need for a reconciliation between the adult and the infantile, the serious and the comic, the communal, the familial, and the individual.

6

Rogue and Trickster

According to Umberto Eco, the comic effect is realized when a rule is violated by 'an ignoble, inferior, and repulsive (animal-like) character'. We feel 'superior to his misbehaviour and to his sorrow for having broken the rule' but we 'in some way welcome the violation; we are, so to speak, revenged by the comic character who has challenged the repressive power of the rule'. It is true that transgression is central to comedy. But do audiences feel superior to transgressors? Aren't we more likely to feel superior to the dupe than to the knave who dupes him? It is true that rogues may seem animal-like (Ben Jonson's Volpone comes to mind) but audiences cannot be relied on to dislike them, nor will their transgressions always be punished. In Jonson's best-known comedies there is a steady move away from the tendency to punish rogues: in *Bartholomew Fair*, which is full of them, no thief or swindler is punished or forced to disgorge. In Rostand's *Cyrano de Bergerac*, which ends tragically but has a strong comic strand, the swaggering Gascon soldiers proclaim themselves 'shameless brawlers and liars, who cuckold all jealous husbands': the boast contributes immensely to their appeal. In Gilbert and Sullivan's *The Pirates of Penzance* the policemen sing a sentimental-comic song about the essential humanity of the criminal, which proves unexpectedly convincing though the singers' motives are dubious. Damon Runyan, during the twenties and thirties of this century, revived the figure of the beguiling rogue in his tales of New York gangsters. These last examples stand even further from reality than most comedy, but that does not render them inadmissible as evidence of the magnetism of sensitive or enterprising villains.

However, sensitivity, though sometimes present in literary examples, is no essential constituent of the rogue's appeal. Gines de Pasamonte in *Don Quixote*, for example, has little of it. The Don, repining at the use of coercion on men who were born free, releases Gines and his fellow-criminals from a chain-gang, but

Gines's gratitude soon wears thin and he sets his fellows to stoning and stripping the knight and his luckless squire. Gines impresses us by his single-minded egotism—he has written a spirited autobiography, which he pawned while in prison but is determined to redeem—and by his instinct for self-preservation: the fascination he exerts is measured by the number of occasions when the characters and narrator feel impelled to mention him. But his actual appearances are few: it is as if Cervantes feared that Gines might take over the story from Quixote.

The inherent appeal of subversive, as opposed to law-abiding, behaviour is sometimes revealed in the idioms of popular speech. In Chaucer the expression 'good felawe' denotes, not a virtuous or trustworthy person, but a genial knave. (In the Prologue to *The Canterbury Tales* it is used to describe the Shipman, a smuggler and pirate.) Modern comedy has not lost sight of the fascination exerted by knavery over virtuous people. In Evelyn Waugh's *Decline and Fall* it is the mild-mannered Prendergast who, in a rare moment of drunken excitement, pleads the cause of the cad: 'Bounders can be capital fellows, don't you agree, Colonel Slidebottom? In fact, I'd go further and say that capital fellows *are* bounders.' It is a Chaucerian insight: the Chaucerian 'good felawe' is a bounder who is a capital fellow, at least from the roisterer's point of view. The feeling clearly extends, at times, from fictional rogues and knaves to those in real life. J. M. Synge, in a gloss on *The Playboy of the Western World*, wrote that the 'impulse to protect the criminal' was universal in the West of Ireland: it stemmed partly from 'the association between justice and the hated English jurisdiction, but more directly from the primitive feeling of these people, who are never criminals yet always capable of crime, that a man will not do wrong unless he is under the influence of a passion which is as irresponsible as a storm on the sea'. Not all the rogues and knaves we shall consider act under the influence of irresistible passion. But the prevalence in any culture of people who 'are never criminals but always capable of crime' helps explain the allure of the real as well as the fictional rogue. In Britain, an undeniable glamour surrounded the perpetrators of the Great Train Robbery. In Italy, according to Michael Sheridan (*Times Literary Supplement*, 5 February

1988), 'Columnists in Milan and Turin fulminate about social ills, while the dailies' news pages carry affectionate accounts of this or that idiosyncrasy of a known gangster, the current favourite being Luciano Liggio's penchant for landscape-painting.' In eighteenth-century England Richard Steele observed that the virtuous Cato had proved less attractive to posterity than the vicious Caesar. In the same century Henry Fielding, in a pamphlet on the increase of robbers, noted with reluctant admiration that, while the helpless poor begged, those with more 'art and courage' stole.

There is an obvious connection between tolerance or admiration for real-life villains and indulgent laughter over fictional rogues. Both the real and fictional transgressor appeal to us by virtue of their audacity and their ability to improvise. We admire and laugh with the two fast-talkers in Aristophanes' *The Birds* because their skill in smelling out frauds comes from their being such experienced frauds themselves. In Plautus the clever, articulate, deceitful, resourceful slave is invariably the most interesting and likeable character in the play. Similar characteristics attach to the legendary figure of Don Juan. These last examples suggest that plausible lying is endowed with the same comic appeal as theft. Hazlitt, at the beginning of the nineteenth century, called lying 'a species of wit and humour' which showed 'spirit and effrontery': the more stupefying the effrontery, the greater the fun. Few of us, perhaps, can resist the lure of the demonic in comedy, but we recognize that it can reach a point where it transforms itself into something that is not comical at all.

What is it, then, that distinguishes a likeable comic rogue? In the eighteenth century the philosopher Frances Hutcheson suggested that crimes and misfortunes made people laugh when attended by fantastic circumstances, but not when they consisted of sheer barbarity. The comic response is made possible partly by elements of fantasy, inventiveness, humour, cheerful audacity, and subtle trickery which keep 'barbarity' at bay. Trickery, perhaps the most important, can of course be repudiated in other contexts. In *Don Quixote* a romantic lover who has become a hermit proclaims that fraud and deceit are the worst crimes of all. But this view prevails within certain restricted genres of literature, in this case romantic pastoral, and corresponds with only some of our real-life moods. Deceits, most of them more amusing than abominable, are frequent in *Don Quixote*, even in the pastoral episodes. Some are practised for gain, some to bring the Don back to sanity, many for fun. Especially excusable is the deceit practised on those who deceive themselves. The knight errant is the self-deceiver *par excellence*: Don Quixote often takes what he wants by violence and then justifies himself by rules of chivalry which he seems to make up as he goes along.

When confronted with a character like Gines we are, then, tempted to infer that his roguery is knight-errantry minus the delusions. This notion entered the literature of chivalry, and discussions of it, even before the publication of Cervantes' satire on knights-errant. In Malory's *Morte d'Arthur* the evil Sir Breuse Sans Pité is pursued by one of King Arthur's knights: when he meets three other knights in the forest he begs them to rescue him from 'the most pitiless and treacherous knight living, Sir Breuse Sans Pité'. By the time the Arthurian knights have finished unhorsing each other, and have sorted out the misunderstanding, Sir Breuse has escaped. There is a disturbing feeling that he deserves his success, since the fellowship of the Round Table is itself tainted: the Renaissance humanist Roger Ascham commented that the most esteemed knights were those who slew most men without any quarrel, and committed 'foulest adulteries by subtlest shifts'.

In more recent literature the rogue's function has been to undermine, not aristocratic extravagancies, but bourgeois respectability and order. Brecht, in his notes to *The Threepenny Opera*, observes that there is a 'predilection for gangsters' among the bourgeois: 'Is there then no difference between them? Yes: a gangster is often no coward.' (However, Brecht presents the gangster figure less admiringly in *The Resistible Rise of Arturo Ui*, where the central character is a composite creation owing something to Hitler and something to Al Capone.) Mark Twain's Tom and Huck play at pirates rather than hermits because they likewise sense that 'a pirate's always respected'. The boys are forces of disorder which the ordered community needs if it is to survive. (Baudelaire alludes approvingly to the doctrine that 'between "disorderliness" and "genius" a necessary link exists'.)

But Tom, at least, arises out of the settled community, and both he and Huck appear likely to settle into it: they stand apart from Injun Joe, a grave-robber and murderer, and even from confidence-men like the 'Duke' and the 'King' in the book that bears Huck's name. Both boys break the rules of their settled and tranquil elders, but both respect the code and can at times be brought to square their impulses with it.

Mention of Tom and Huck raises the question of definition. Is it helpful to broaden the term 'rogue' to include such figures as these? 'Rogue' is often used in English as a rough translation of the Spanish *picaro*, which describes someone of low social status who lives on his wits, wanders from place to place, and attains a wide experience of the world. I shall use the term fairly loosely to indicate any character who is detached from a settled mode of existence, depends on his wit and ruthlessness for his survival, and perpetrates crimes rather than mere practical jokes. The term trickster I shall use to denote a more settled, less subversive variant of the rogue: this makes my usage narrower than that of Jung in his essay on the trickster figure.

Tom Sawyer, for example, is a trickster, not a rogue. He has a settled home by right of birth, and never looks like deserting it permanently. He does not depend on his deceits for survival; he practises them for the love of jesting, adventure, or fantasy rather than for gain. But Tom's friend Huck is in some respects a rogue. To survive or to maintain his freedom, which for Huck amounts almost to the same thing, he will lie fluently and steal deftly. Much of his early life is spent sleeping on doorsteps or in barrels; he has no family; when adopted he feels an irresistible urge to 'light out'. However, Twain keeps open Huck's as well as Tom's option to rejoin society; in *Huckleberry Finn*, as we shall see, he draws ever more careful distinctions between Huck and the hardened criminals.

This example shows that, though rogue and trickster differ, the line between them can never be sharp. Both share a restless creativity, a delight in plots and stratagems, a way with words. Pegeen in Synge's *Playboy*, where the word 'playboy' in the title means something like 'roistering rogue', resists the idea of marrying a 'middling kind of scarecrow, with no savagery or fine words in him at all': evidently 'savagery' and 'fine words' go together, constituting the rogue's glamour. Cervantes' Gines de Pasamonte, who has his share of 'savagery', is also endowed with a gift for languages, for writing, for drama; in the Second Part of *Don Quixote* he is found in charge of a puppet show. Trickery, improvisation, fast talking, deft plotting, perfect timing, prestidigitation, a sense of the dramatic: all these characteristics, shared by the rogue and trickster, link them not only to one another but to the artist, actor, and illusionist. Sheridan's Mr Snake uses a revealing form of words to assure Lady Sneerwell that she is still the queen of malicious innuendo: her rival Mrs Clackitt 'generally designs well, has a free tongue and a bold invention; but her colouring is too dark and her outlines often extravagant. She wants that delicacy of tint and mellowness of sneer which distinguish your ladyship's scandal.' The scandal-mongers are, of course, the villains of the play, but it is hard not to admire the dedication and discrimination with which they seek to elevate malicious gossip into an art form. This warns us once more against rigid distinctions. Just as, at one end of the scale, the rogue shades into the trickster, so at the other he merges with the villain, while all three can boast an affinity with the creative artist.

The rogue, even the comic rogue, is to some degree a representative of the devil in man. (Some writers, notably Baudelaire, would contend that comedy is essentially demonic.) Like the tragic hero, the rogue often finds himself at odds with divine authority: the difference is that the comic scapegrace seldom takes either himself or his antagonist completely seriously. In medieval religious drama, Cain, the first criminal, rarely appears as a repulsive and callous murderer: often he is endowed by the dramatists with a sense of humour and a gift for satire. When he hears the voice of God, he asks cheekily, 'Who was that that piped so small?' and assures Abel that 'God is out of his wit.' He chides his brother, who insists on giving his best produce to God, as a fool: we all know, he argues, that God doesn't eat or drink, so it won't harm him to be given the worst rather than the best. Cain and Abel are seen, then, partly in terms of an archetypal comic antithesis: the earthy, commonsensical, self-interested rogue and the gentle, accepting fool. However, it is only in the early stages of a play that Cain's irreverence and exuberance are permitted to appear comic and appealing. And Abel, in so far as he is a fool, is a wise fool: he does the right thing without being able to refute the worldly wisdom which mocks him for doing it.

We find the same kind of antithesis in *King Lear*: it is hard at first not to admire the audacious Edmund, with his roistering speech 'Now gods, stand up for bastards', and to pity the Fool, who warns against following a great wheel that runs downhill but is unable to take his own advice. By the end we have learned to admire the Fool more and Edmund less. Clearly there are limits to our admiration for the rogue's demonic energy. Indeed some tragedies disturb us by presenting villains whom we at first admire as comic tricksters: later we are forced to revise our estimates, rejecting the figures whom at first we had been half-inclined to accept. In Max Frisch's modern satiric tragedy *The Fire Raisers* the arsonists are brazen, plausible, and clever at playing on the guilt and weakness of the solid citizens. Yet interpreters of the play have seen them as representing the Nazis, or the subverters of Czech democracy after the Second World War.

Ambivalence of feeling about the rogue is conspicuous in earlier periods also. It pervades the coney-catching pamphlets of Robert Greene, a contemporary of Shakespeare, who wrote (as he claimed) to warn honest citizens against the wiles of rogues. The word 'coney' means, literally, a rabbit, but in rogues' slang it means a sucker or potential victim: the coney-catchers were thieves and confidence-tricksters. Greene's claim to special knowledge of coney-catching is based, he maintains, on intimate acquaintance with the rogues themselves: 'The odd madcaps I have been mate to, not as a companion, but as a spy to have an insight into their knaveries, . . . I learned at last to loathe . . . What I saw in them to their confusion I can forewarn others to my country's commodity.' Greene's claim that he joined the rogue-fraternities as a spy sounds spurious: his announcement that he learned to loathe the rogues 'at last' shows that he liked them at first. His anecdotes are advertised as 'merry tales'. Even sober readers are expected to laugh at the skill with which people with money are robbed or cheated; the comic discourse struggles successfully for mastery over the discourses of investigative journalism, morality, and law.

The affinity of Greene's tales with the world of comedy was recognized at once by his contemporaries, who lifted his material directly into their plays. Many of the knaveries in Ben Jonson's *Bartholomew Fair*, for example, come straight out of Greene. The Fair is a place where well-off people come to relax and enjoy themselves, and where less well-off people come to pander to the revellers' tastes. More bluntly, it is where gulls come to be relieved of their money and rogues come to relieve them of it. Edgeworth, a thief, is in league with Nightingale, a ballad-singer: it is Nightingale's task, when he sees Edgeworth hovering over a prospective victim, to make a sign with his head to show whereabouts on his person the coney keeps his money. Edgeworth then picks the pocket or cuts the purse, and hands the loot to Nightingale while pretending to buy a copy of a ballad. When the theft is discovered, and the bystanders demand that everyone be searched, Edgeworth will have nothing incriminating on his person; Nightingale will escape being searched since he has been holding his pedlar's tray, and has had no hand free to pick pockets. One of Edgeworth's deftest sleights is to filch a purse from a dim youth who has already been robbed once and is stoutly keeping his hand on the fresh hoard which he has sent for from home. But the position of his hand simply calls attention to the location of his purse. The cutpurse, knowing where the money is, tickles the victim's ear with a straw to make him scratch himself, and picks his pocket while the protecting hand is out of it.

Edgeworth delights not only in loot but in his own dexterity in obtaining it: he also enjoys making fools of the champions of law and order. Quarlous and Winwife, two witty gentlemen who look in on the criminal world from outside, seem to admire the rogues' dexterity more than they deplore their depravity: they even blackmail Edgeworth into doing a piece of dirty work for them. But they withdraw with prim distaste when Edgeworth suggests that they share a girl at a pig-woman's tent which doubles as a brothel: it looks too like a bid on the thief's part to draw the gentlemen into his ambience.

It is probably true that, in tragedy, most readers and auditors expect and demand the villain's eventual downfall; even in comedy the rogue or knave often comes to grief in the end. But here even the most respectable audience may, as in the classic case of Shakespeare's Falstaff, be mesmerized by the rogue's audacity and charm to the extent of resisting the 'poetic justice' of the punishment. In Jonson's *Volpone* the central figure coaxes money from rich men by posing as an invalid and promising each benefactor, separately, the inheritance of his fortune when he dies. When his trickery is exposed he is condemned to lie in prison until he really suffers from the diseases he pretended to have. We might expect that Renaissance audiences, endowed evidently with a harsher sense of humour than our own, would have applauded this ending for turning the rogue's deceits against himself. However, Jonson found to his annoyance that some playgoers thought Volpone's punishment too harsh for a comedy. Their rejection of the play's ending was presumably due partly to admiration for the daring and panache of the rogue.

Eco suggests that tragedy from an alien culture is more easily understood than comedy, because in tragedy the cultural norm is spelt out: we are thus able to understand the rules which the protagonist is breaking, even though they may be alien to those under which we live. In comedy, Eco believes, the rule is not spelt out but implicit: this explains why comedy does not travel well from one culture to another. However, in *Volpone* and many other comedies the rules are either spelt out or easily inferred. We can admire Volpone so long as we can accept his claim that the exercise of his cunning means more to him than the wealth it brings. At first he disdains to prey on the innocent and helpless: he accepts the challenge of cheating rich, greedy, powerful old men who, if they scented trickery, would take swift revenge. Latterly, though, Volpone loses both his caution and his scruples. First he schemes to ruin Bonario and Celia, two innocent young people; then his love of 'rare ingenious knavery' leads him to overreach himself, exposing him to unnecessary risk. So on two separate counts he 'deserves' to be caught and punished. If the Jacobean audience did not respond as expected, this was not due to the play's failure to spell out its rules: it was more a matter of the audience's refusal to accept the reimposition of norms on this particular comic scamp. Jonson succeeded better in other comedies, such as *Bartholomew Fair*, where the appeal of goodness and innocence was not used as a means of discrediting the rogue: where, indeed, the 'good' are simply the unwary, the less cunning, and the rogues incur no punishment for exploiting them. The same thing happens in modern comedies and farces such as Joe Orton's *Loot*.

Volpone shows that the comic writer may feel scruples about exalting rogues, and may try to detach his audience's sympathies from the rogue or deceiver at a crucial point. Another great comedy in which this principle operates is Twain's *Huckleberry Finn*. Consider the figure of Huck's father, in some respects a typical comic rogue. Pap is a homeless wanderer, the delight and despair of bourgeois society. (Huck notices that 'rapscallions and deadbeats is the kind the widow and good people takes the most interest in'.) Pap's relapse after swearing off drink is a fine comic escapade:

The judge said it was the holiest time on record, or something like that. Then they tucked the old man into a beautiful room, which was the spare room, and in the night some time he got powerful thirsty and clumb out on to the porch-roof and slid down a stanchion and traded his new coat for a jug of forty-rod, and clumb back again and had a good old time; and toward daylight he crawled out again, drunk as a fiddler, and rolled off the porch and broke his left arm in two places, and was most froze to death when somebody found him after sunup. And when they come to look at that spare room they had to take soundings before they could navigate it.

Huck sounds amused at the discomfiture of the Judge and the good people, and gives his father credit for having 'a good old time' at their expense. But this simply adds force to his admissions in other places that his own freedom and, at times, his life were placed at risk by his father.

Equally useful to Twain in his evaluation of roguery are those finely raffish figures the bogus king and duke, whom Huck meets and saves from pursuit about half-way through the book. These are more creative villains than Pap. They have histrionic talent, a gift for lying (itself, perhaps, a branch of histrionics), and a repertoire of deceits and crooked pranks. (The device of hiring a theatre, publicizing a show, and absconding with the takings when the audience is inside goes back to Elizabethan times, though the King and Duke refine considerably on the old version.) When they pose as English relatives on a visit of condolence to a bereaved family, they use the classic confidence-trick of giving away money: the Duke announces that he will surrender 'his' share of the legacy to the dead man's daughters. Sacrificing a smaller sum now may increase his chances of scooping a larger one later.

The Duke's audacity, like Volpone's, is monumental. Yet Twain, like Jonson, will seek to detach our sympathy from his villains; like Jonson's rogues they will become, simultaneously, more callous and less wary. Early on they help save Jim, the runaway slave, from capture; later they lose patience and betray Jim for a small reward. Earlier, they were prepared to cheat some country folk out of the price of admission to a show; now they prepare to rob an amiable family of everything it has.

The main difference between Twain's fable and Jonson's lies in the portrayal of those innocents whom the rogues plan to swindle or dupe. The 'good' characters in *Volpone* are often, and rightly, criticized as wooden: Jonson does not seem able to warm to, or even believe in, simple goodness as a positive value. But Twain, using the all-important mediating figure of Huck, succeeds in establishing the sacredness of goodness and innocence within his fiction. Though Huck, as we have seen, is something of a rogue himself, he cannot feel comfortable about helping his companions to cheat a family which opens its arms to them. He not only admires the beautiful sister but feels sympathy for the ugly one; and when the King and Duke plot to steal the family fortune, Huck betrays them, fearful though he is of their revenge. When Mary Jane receives Huck's warning, she offers to pray for him, and readily forgives him for not betraying his accomplices earlier. Huck is enraptured: 'She had the grit to pray for Judas if she took the notion—there warn't no backdown to her, I judge. You may say what you want to, but in my opinion she had more sand in her than any girl I ever see; in my opinion she was just full of sand. . . . And when it comes to beauty—and goodness, too—she lays over them all.'

Mary Jane's goodness, openness, and impulsiveness sometimes lead her into sheer folly, as when she voluntarily hands over
her whole fortune to the swindlers. In Jonson's comic world such
unwariness would lead to disaster, but in *Huckleberry Finn* it is
the essential complement to a group of virtues which attract loyalty, admiration, and love. The rogues who are ruthless enough
to exploit it, as the King and Duke are, will be punished, and
the inner laws of this comic fable will persuade most readers to
welcome their punishment. Crucial to Twain's manipulation of
reader-response is the fact that Huck, the trickster who is almost
a rogue, the figure with whom the reader is invited to identify,
will be too moved by Mary Jane's virtues to let others take advantage of her folly.

The contrast between the two types of comic world may be
finally established by one more comparison. In Jonson's
Alchemist an honest character called Surly decides to warn the
dupes against the swindlers; but when he tells his story they refuse
to believe him, and even abuse him for his pains. They do not
want to be undeceived: the delusion into which they have been
lured, the hope of limitless wealth, plays too skilfully on their
dreams. Surly is left to wonder why he bothered trying to help
them: 'Must I needs cheat myself | With that same foolish vice
of honesty?' he growls in disgust. In *Huckleberry Finn* there is an
uncannily similar incident: a local doctor detects the Duke and
the King as frauds because their imitation of an English accent is
so poor, and because they ignorantly refer to 'funeral orgies'
instead of 'obsequies'. But the King improvises excuses for these
blunders; his panache is such that the family believe the rogue
and chide the honest man for his suspicions. In Twain's fable, as
in Jonson's, there is admiration for the deceivers' skill and sang-
froid: when Huck sees the Duke's coolness in facing the doctor's
accusation he exclaims, half in disgust and half in awe, 'He was
the *worst* I ever struck.' But when Huck has to decide between the
clever but ruthless rogues and the rash but loving Mary Jane, he
chooses the latter: his affection for the prospective victim overrides his admiration for a skilful cheat.

This is what Eco calls humour as opposed to the comic.
'Humour', Eco writes, 'attempts to re-establish and reassert the

broken frame.' Often the frame in question is the law of loyalty, goodness, even innocence. In the world of the 'comic', as defined by Eco, all goodness is weakness or hypocrisy and the supreme virtue is quickness of wit: this is the world in which Jonson's characters live. But in Twain's world even a half-roguish figure like Huck can appreciate other qualities apart from quick-wittedness, and feel compassion for those whose innocence makes them vulnerable. He can even feel sorry for the King and the Duke when he sees them for the last time: they have been tarred and feathered, and are being ridden on a rail by an angry crowd. Bergson argued that feeling and compassion were fatal to laughter. Eco's notion of a realm of 'humour' bordering on, but distinct from, 'the comic' lets feeling in again by the side door. It validates a whole series of fictions which in this sense are 'humorous' but not 'comic', such as *Tom Sawyer* and *Huckleberry Finn*.

Twain manipulates his readers' responses to the rogue. Modern plays and novels seldom offer any explicit judgement, any decisive put-down or punishment which would bring the scoundrel to his knees. One of the most beguiling scoundrels in modern fiction is Evelyn Waugh's Basil Seal. In *Black Mischief* Seal turns up at a cocktail party to which the hostess 'particularly didn't ask' him. Dirty and unshaven, he demands Pernod or whisky instead of the cocktails that are being offered, and retires almost at once to use the telephone without asking permission. The remarks passed about him by the guests tend to polarize: 'Such a lovely person.' 'Horrible clothes, black hair all over his face.' 'My dear, he's enchanting. . . . He's been in hot water lately.' 'The truth about Basil is just that he's a *bore*.' Basil's schemes are grandiose, but the rogueries that subsidize them are amazingly small-time. In *Black Mischief* he steals his mother's emeralds to finance his African expedition; the theft seems unnecessary as well as mean since his devoted, neglected mistress is prepared to sign a large cheque for the same purpose. In Egypt Basil sells the emeralds for a fifth of their value. And when he leaves his ship at the next port his companion misses 'his shaving soap, bedroom slippers, and the fine topee he had bought a few days earlier at Port Said'. In spite of this pettiness Basil continues to exercise the allure that clung to him at the beginning of the novel:

Presently Basil came back from telephoning. He stood in the doorway, a glass of whisky in one hand, looking insolently round the room, his head back, chin forward, shoulders rounded, dark hair over his forehead, contemptuous grey eyes over grey pouches, a proud, rather childish mouth, a scar on one cheek.

'My word, he is a corker,' remarked one of the girls.

The technique is simple but effective. Endow your imagined character with as many repulsive characteristics as possible, and then keep saying that he is irresistibly attractive: the result will be a unique and complex creation. By refusing to judge Seal, Waugh implicitly dares the reader to do so: Seal is more energetic and imaginative, no more foolish or immoral or misguided, than most others in Waugh's fictional world. We seem to be back with Ben Jonson: in a universe where goodness seems feeble, pointless, or lacking in vitality there is an unmistakable allure about a life lived intensely, selfishly, for its own sake.

7

Dupers and Duped

Our last chapter, while concentrating on tricksters and rogues in their own right, necessarily glanced at their relationships with their victims. It is now time to consider this topic in more detail, concentrating on the gulling of the dupe and gross fool. An obvious starting-point is a group of tales in Boccaccio's *Decameron* called the *facezie* in which, as Tzvetan Todorov observes, one or more characters seem to be motivated chiefly by the desire to make someone else unhappy. The reason, Todorov believes, why such tales can seem comic is that, within the frame of the fiction, stupidity is shown as a fault so grave that it deserves to be treated as a crime. We are cajoled into suspending normal ideas of justice, not abandoning them; we are persuaded to accept a more ruthless code for the purposes of the tale.

To learn more about the code we must turn to those stories from the *Decameron* which centre on Calandrino, the most egregious fool of all. Calandrino will believe any story provided that the teller keeps a straight face. His so-called friends, notably Bruno and Buffalmacco, have the art of keeping countenance while telling the most fantastic lies. One tall story tells of a magic stone called heliotrope which will make the bearer invisible. Of course it is partly Calandrino's stupidity in believing this story that makes him vulnerable to his later punishment and humiliation, but there is also another factor which will be developed in the later stories: the ease with which the victim can be manipulated by appeals to his selfishness and greed.

Yet in this first tale Calandrino is not consistently selfish or greedy. Before going to search for heliotrope he resolves to share his secret with Bruno and Buffo, 'of whom he was particularly fond'. He points out to them that, once they have found the stone of invisibility, they need only go to the money-changers' tables and take as much as they like. Here Calandrino admittedly shows greed and dishonesty, but he also shows a better side in his wish to give his friends a share of the spoils. Yet these are the very friends who are plotting to deceive and humiliate him.

Calandrino goes with Bruno and Buffo to the desert place where heliotrope supposedly lies, and searches as directed. He has been told that the magic stone will be black, but that most black stones will lack the magic touch. Having made a large collection, he hears Bruno say to Buffalmacco, 'Where's Calandrino?' Since the others evidently cannot see him, Calandrino deduces that he has found the magic stone and has become invisible. But, since he cannot be sure which stone in his collection is the precious one, he must keep carrying the whole load. Meanwhile, Bruno and Buffalmacco pretend to get angry. They tell each other that since Calandrino is nowhere to be seen he must have sneaked off home, leaving them to search for a non-existent magic stone in a desert place. 'Who else apart from us', they ask one another, 'could have been so stupid as to believe that such stones were to be found here?' Once again we encounter the confidence-trickster's principle: a victim may fail to grasp the truth if you place it under his nose. Who indeed would believe that a stone of invisibility could lie close at hand without anyone taking advantage of its properties? Why, if such a stone has been discovered, should the person who discovered it blab, instead of keeping quiet about it and exploiting it himself? What induces Calandrino to swallow such a tall story is his willingness to think that he could be given an opportunity denied to everyone else. It is on the fool's vain conviction of his own privilege and importance that the rogue or trickster plays.

As Calandrino staggers away with his load of stones, the other two, still pretending not to be able to see him, discuss the punishment Calandrino deserves for stealing off and leaving them in a stony gully far from home. 'How I'd like to hit Calandrino in the kidneys with this pebble,' sighs Buffalmacco, and he suits the action to the word. By the time Calandrino gets home he has been pounded with stones: he is also exhausted from carrying his large collection of pebbles. But he still thinks he is invisible because the friends whom he meets on the way, and who usually stop to chat with him or invite him in for a drink, pretend not to see him: they have all been primed by the tricksters in advance. The climax, or anticlimax, is when Calandrino gets home and is greeted by his wife, who has no idea that he is supposed to be invisible and berates him for arriving late for his meal. In his rage and disappointment, Calandrino beats his wife ('a beautiful and accomplished woman' as the narrator calls her), pulling her hair, punching her and kicking her in spite of her cries for mercy. If this is still comedy (and the *facezie* are certainly intended primarily to arouse laughter), it is close to what Northrop Frye calls 'the condition of savagery, in which comedy consists of inflicting pain on a helpless victim, and tragedy in enduring it'.

Behind the Calandrino stories, as so often in comedy, lie several rather contradictory principles. One is the principle of inflicting suffering. All the tales bring injury or loss to the victim, in such forms as theft, beatings, stonings, and the administration of foul medicines. Another is the principle of comic justice, which tries to establish some sort of pretext for the deceits apart from the sheer pleasure of laughter at another's expense. It is noticeable that, in the *Decameron*, several different narrators tell stories about the same quartet of characters (Calandrino, Bruno, Buffalmacco, and the former's wife Monna Tessa) and that the later ones elaborate on the original hint about Calandrino's selfishness and avarice as a justification of the tricks played upon him. They also focus increasingly on the idea of Calandrino as an enemy of festivity. When he receives some small windfall, his friends feel he should hold a party on the proceeds. When, instead, he keeps the money or food for himself, they resolve to trick him into paying for a party in any case, and inflict other indignities on him along the way. One of the best tricks is to persuade Calandrino that he is pregnant. He is then made to pay handsomely for a medicine (really a harmless and worthless placebo) to procure an abortion.

Calandrino is close to the kind of comic character whom Aristotle calls the *agrikos* or boor. He is not only stupid but graceless and lacking in generosity. He has a better wife, and more money, than he deserves. Much of the resentment against him seems due to his undeserved good luck: fortune should favour the witty and bold, not the cowardly and dull. Luckily a fool and his money are soon parted, and the false friends Bruno and Buffalmacco enter zestfully on the task of parting them. But while most readers enjoy the Calandrino stories, many feel guilty about doing so. The Renaissance critic Castelvetro hints that the first to feel guilty may have been Boccaccio, who comments at one point: 'The ladies had laughed long and loud at Calandrino, and would have laughed even more had it not annoyed them to see him robbed of his capons by those who had stolen his pig.' Castelvetro observes on his own account that the stupidity of Calandrino provokes laughter, but only because in the end he suffers no great harm. Clearly there is a type of tale which invites us to laugh at stupidity for its own sake and abandon other criteria of justice. But stupidity alone is never quite enough: other vices, such as niggardliness, have to be produced to help justify the dupe's humiliation, and even then readers will worry as to whether the punishment is too harsh.

The quality of cumulative, almost unrelenting, gulling and deception found in the Calandrino stories also marks Molière's *Monsieur de Pourceaugnac*. The trickster Sbrigani helps two young people to foil a plan to marry the girl to a rich booby. But it is the gulling of the victim, not the devotion of the lovers, which is the focus of the play. Pourceaugnac is a business-correspondent of Julie's father: he lives in a provincial city and has hitherto met neither father nor daughter. The marriage is meant to cement a commercial alliance. However, though the two rich men breach the laws of comedy by treating Julie as a commodity, their avarice is not much stressed. More important pretexts for tormenting Pourceaugnac are that he is a booby, that he comes from the provinces, and that he is not the man Julie wants.

The strategy for preventing the marriage will be two-pronged. Oronte must be persuaded that Pourceaugnac is not a desirable son-in-law; Pourceaugnac must be convinced that Julie is not a desirable bride. A man posing as a foreign merchant tells Oronte that the prospective bridegroom has debts and plans to use Julie's fortune to pay them. Meanwhile Pourceaugnac is told that Julie, if not actually unchaste, is a 'coquette achevée', an accomplished flirt. So by the time Oronte and Pourceaugnac actually meet, neither of them wants the marriage to proceed; each, however, assumes that the other desires it from the worst of motives. The only person who still seems enthusiastic about the wedding is

Julie: she drools shamelessly over Pourceaugnac, interrupting the men's conversation with cries of admiration and impatience. This is comedy of situation, with everyone's role hilariously reversed through contrived misunderstanding: there is no subtlety of 'psychology' or feeling, merely a confrontation full of mutual suspicion and hurt pride. Molière's aim will be to top this, and to keep topping it, by adding more and more misunderstandings and deceits. Pourceaugnac will be accused of bigamy, a capital offence, then made to believe that the gallows has been prepared for his execution. He will be advised to don female disguise to escape capture. Once disguised, he will be pestered by men who stop to flirt with him and to invite him to come with them to the execution. Next he will be forced to bribe a policeman, who sees through his disguise as unhesitatingly as the other men seemed to accept it, to let him go. All these are, needless to say, contrived impostures and deceits. There is a moment of pathos when the victim, at last free to escape, turns to thank Sbrigani as 'the only honest, decent man I've found in this town': it is in fact Sbrigani who has contrived all the deceits and humiliations. But the audience's feeling of pity is fleeting. It is overpowered by wild laughter, not only at the nerve and skill of the tricksters but at the folly and discomfiture of the victim.

We have seen that trickster-comedy usually provides its audience with some pretext for its derision. The dupe is mean; he is dishonest; he is richer than he deserves; he is exploiting his money or social status to force a marriage on a woman who doesn't want him. Sometimes, of course, this quasi-moral justification for trickery seems overdone; certainly it is, as we have suggested, a pretext, not the real point of the play. Nevertheless it is doubtful whether this element in trickster-comedy can ever be abandoned completely. Northrop Frye suggests that it is the element of play which separates art from savagery, and that 'playing at human sacrifice seems to be an important theme of ironic comedy'. Play, in some of our examples, consists in the proliferation of trickery and mystification for their own sake, with a climax at the moment when the victim is brought (or apparently brought) close to death. 'Playing at human sacrifice' seems an apt phrase here. Part of the excitement is in the terror: we are never quite sure that the barrier will not crumble, that the condition of savagery will not be restored, that the play will not become earnest. But the norms of responsible behaviour never quite lose their hold. Some whiff of evaluative judgement on the victim seems indispensable: 'play' and inventiveness for their own sakes are not quite enough to keep the 'condition of savagery' at bay.

The appeal of grotesque deceit and trickery did not die with the seventeenth century, nor is it confined to what we may call ruthless comedy. Consider, for example, the extended episode of trickery for its own sake that occurs towards the end of *Huckleberry Finn*. By the time it begins, Huck's journey down the river is over; he is back with Tom Sawyer on an extended vacation at the Phelps farm. Old Phelps is keeping Jim, whom he thinks of as a 'runaway nigger', shut up in a shed while he tries to find out who owns him. Huck and Tom, not letting on that they know who Jim is and where he comes from, set about helping their friend escape. The episode, which is spun out over several chapters, has annoyed and disturbed critics. In the course of the main story, Huck has endured and learned much: he has encountered the adult world. The episode with Jim seems like a regression to childishness: Huck, who has been through so much more than Tom has, tamely submits to the will and fantasy of his friend. When he suggests direct and practical ways of releasing Jim, Tom pours scorn on them: he wants something 'real mysterious and troublesome and good', 'a way that's twice as long'. And Huck agrees because Tom's schemes always have so much 'style'. To the reader, preoccupied with the question of whether and how the boys will win Jim his freedom, Tom's insistence on style, and Huck's complicity in it, are irritating. Even more frustrating, if anything, is the later revelation that Jim has been legally free all the time, since his owner has died and bequeathed him his freedom, and that Tom knew this all along. 'To keep [Jim] in unnecessary suspense for days', writes George P. Elliott, 'is shockingly cruel of Tom.'

In the web of intrigue that surrounds Jim's release Mr and Mrs Phelps function as dupes. But there is no temptation on the reader's part to conclude that the old couple deserve to be fooled. Not only are they, as Tom remarks, 'so confiding and mullet-headed' that deceiving them is almost too easy: they are also unfailingly kindly and concerned. Admiration for these virtues is not, however, allowed to interfere with the boys' plans. In pursuit of their schemes of romantic escape the two purloin a shirt, a sheet, three knives, a saw, six tallow candles, three tin plates, and other items. Huck, adopting his father's terminology, calls this borrowing, but Tom rules that it is stealing and would not be justified but for the need to release a prisoner. When Huck steals a water-melon from the slaves' vegetable patch, Tom insists that he must find a way to pay the owners back. Huck laments: 'I couldn't see no advantage in my representing a prisoner if I got to set down and chaw over a lot of gold-leaf distinctions like that every time I see a chance to hog a watermelon.' But he keeps his grumble to himself. The joke here is the clash between two sets of rules, each of which conflicts rather sharply with the rules prevailing in adult society. Different people acknowledge different rules: my qualm of conscience is your gold-leaf distinction.

Another joke, a deliberately painful one, is the effect of Tom's and Huck's trickery on the victims. When items keep disappearing and reappearing, as also when rat-holes keep getting stopped up and then unstopped by some mysterious agency, the old couple begin to feel that they are no longer in command of their senses. Witchcraft, haunting, and madness are all evoked: the everyday laws of cause and effect seem to have been temporarily suspended.

How are we likely to feel about the effects of the boys' deceits on the innocent Mr and Mrs Phelps? Hazlitt, contemplating similar trickeries in *The Thousand and One Nights*, appeals to what he calls 'the principle of callous indifference', and while that description is too simple it does explain a lot. Indifference, in this context, extends not only to the feelings of others but also to one's own physical safety. On the night of Jim's rescue the Phelps property is guarded by a posse of armed farmers, since Tom has decided that the escape will not be stylish unless the prisoner's guards are warned (anonymously) in advance. The release of Jim goes as planned, but as the prisoner and rescuers run off the farmers' bullets whizz about their ears. When everyone is safe, Huck records, 'We was all glad as we could be; but Tom was the gladdest of all because he had a bullet in the calf of his leg.'

It is noticeable here that the feelings of the characters are dominated by romantic exaltation rather than amusement or laughter. It is the reader who laughs, and the laughter has a touch of hysteria about it. The plot hatched for Jim's escape has involved terror, confusion, gunfire, and a wound, and could, as the text invites us to infer, easily have involved a death. The feelings of two nice old people, warned to expect an armed attack on their home, have been sacrificed to the needs of the exhilarating but unnecessary scheme. Not only are the Phelps's ordered lives disoriented before and during the escape: the two are subjected to needless anxiety afterwards, since Tom fails to come home and Huck conceals the fact that his friend, though wounded, is safe. Blood, terror, and mystery are the essence of the comedy: at one point before the rescue Tom wondered whether the artistic integrity of the plot might not require the amputation of Jim's leg. We are reminded of the comic-horrific incidents cited by Hazlitt from the *Thousand and One Nights*. One man's hand is cut off in an affray and 'this is felt as an awkward accident'. Another is in danger of 'losing his head for want of saying who he was, because he would not forfeit his character of being "justly called the Silent" '. This last, Hazlitt observes, 'is a consummation of the jest, though, if it had really taken place, it would have been carrying the joke too far. There are a thousand instances of the same sort in the *Thousand and One Nights*, which are an inexhaustible source of humour and invention.' Examples from this and other sources suggest that the most hilarious laughter is that which comes closest to the point where the joke is indeed taken too far. The prospect, at least momentary, of mutilation or death (Pourceaugnac supposedly wanted on a capital charge, Jim bitten by a rattlesnake or threatened with amputation, Monna Tessa beaten and pulled by the hair) arouses the wildest hilarity.

The 'principle of callous indifference' is indeed a powerful one. Twain's novels, where the main characters are children, afford an important clue to its workings. It belongs to the period when the child is still able to contemplate possible disasters without fully taking in their likely consequences, and without fully distinguishing fantasy from reality. What sets Twain's trickster-comedy apart is its self-consciousness. Here the principle of indifference is not taken for granted: it is questioned, its nature explored and revealed.

8

The Fool

The gull or dupe thinks of himself, most of the time, as a person of normal intelligence. He is ridiculous because his self-image is awry. His capacity for dealing with the world on its own terms is less than he thinks; he is not wary or astute enough to perceive, until too late, the deceits, frauds, and hypocrisies of other people. In everyday usage such gulls and dupes would be described as fools. But we shall reserve that term for the possessors of another, more esteemed, kind of folly. These fools are, and know themselves to be, set apart from the everyday world. As Kolakowski writes,

Although an habitué of good society, [the jester] does not belong to it and makes it the object of his inquisitive impertinence; he . . . questions what appears to be self-evident. The jester could not do this if he himself were part of the good society . . . A jester must remain an outsider.

The fool, unlike the gull, acknowledges his apartness and is, up to a point, respected for it. A character in Chapman's Renaissance comedy *The Gentleman Usher* who confesses, 'I am the veriest fool of you all' earns the reassuring response: 'Therein thou art worth us all, for thou knowest thyself.' In Rostand's *Cyrano de Bergerac*, three centuries later, the heroine's handsome but stupid lover laments, 'Alas! I'm such a fool that I could kill myself for shame!' Cyrano generously reassures him: 'No, you are no fool if you are able to see yourself as one.' With the fool's recognition of his own limitations goes another special characteristic: integrity, single-mindedness, innocence, even holiness. This explains why, though he may be cheated or exploited, this type of fool is not despised as the gull or booby is. His folly (often thought of as bordering on madness) carries with it a wisdom that is not the wisdom of this world.

One embodiment of wise folly is the peasant. Though neither mad nor, necessarily, mentally defective, he is doomed by his narrow upbringing and restricted experience to appear 'simple' in the eyes of his betters. Don Quixote's Sancho Panza, a rural labourer led on by delusive hopes of winning an island kingdom, is constantly being duped or deluded, but proves unexpectedly competent when sitting as a magistrate in a country village. Like Azdak in Brecht's *Caucasian Chalk Circle* Sancho gives wise-foolish, corrupt-honest judgements which show intuitive understanding of the realities of village life. The fool in his quality of country bumpkin will often make remarks that confound the wisdom of rulers and philosophers. Antonio, the gardener in *The Marriage of Figaro*, is reproved for drunkenness. 'Drinking when they aren't thirsty, and mating in and out of season', he retorts, 'are the only things that distinguish human beings from beasts.' Among innumerable attempts to find a defining difference between humans and animals, Antonio's stands up as well as most.

Oddly enough, those who assume the mantle of folly self-consciously, as a kind of disguise, like Socrates in the accounts that have come down to us, qualify for this special status just as the 'natural' fool or rustic simpleton does: they are not considered affected or hypocritical. Lane Cooper detects 'a kind of generalized Socrates, often comic' in Plato's dialogues: this figure, like later 'fools', affects innocence and simplicity. Erasmus in the *Praise of Folly* explains: 'Socrates . . . would not take upon him the name of a wise man, but rather ascribed it to God alone.' However, Socrates led on supposedly wiser men by harmless-sounding questions until their later answers contradicted their earlier ones: he made those who claimed to be wise look foolish. The same strategy is used by the Shakespearian fool. The Fool in *King Lear* regularly traps the King into confessing, and thus perceiving, his own folly. Touchstone in *As You Like It* makes 'very swift and sententious' repartees: other characters see that 'He uses his folly like a stalking-horse, and under the presentation of that he shoots his wit.' Feste in *Twelfth Night* tricks Olivia into proving herself a fool. Don Quixote, himself a kind of wise fool, knows that 'The cunningest part in a play is the fool's, for a man who wants to be taken for a simpleton must never be one.'

Predictably, the wise fool sometimes chafes at his confinement within the role. 'I wear not motley in my brain', insists Feste, anxious to set himself apart from the 'ordinary fool, that has no more wit than a stone' mentioned elsewhere by Malvolio. This is reminiscent of Sartre's essay on the comic actor, who loses authenticity by living through roles. Though aware of the part they are playing, fools seldom seem to be playing it by free choice; their ability to make contact with other worlds arises from their awareness that they do not fit comfortably into this one. In some societies this apartness is recognized and privileged: fools are allowed, even encouraged, to make jokes not permitted to other people. But the privilege is precarious. The Fool in *King Lear* complains that he is sometimes whipped for telling the truth, sometimes for lying, and sometimes for keeping silent: he would 'rather be any kind of thing than a fool'.

So far we have mostly seen the fool as offering a contrast to the rogue or trickster, but sometimes the contrasting roles meet and blend. In *Twelfth Night* Feste is proud to assist with the gulling of Malvolio: elsewhere in Shakespeare the words 'knave and fool' often occur in the same sentence in ways that suggest a simultaneous contrast and comparison. The fool's sexual potency, too, was proverbial, and the bauble he carried was phallic. In Cleland's pornographic novel *Fanny Hill* the girls decide to put the fool's proverbial virility to a practical test: the results are positive. Fools, then, may be associated with knavery, deceit, swindling, thieving, and tireless sexual activity. Susanne Langer sees the fool as 'a red-blooded fellow, . . . close to the animal world; . . . all motion, whim, and impulse—the "libido" itself'. The fool's spontaneity entails a certain emancipation from the restraints that beset 'normal' people: in Marguerite of Navarre's *Heptameron* it is asserted that fools live longer than wise folk because they do not bottle up their emotions. This rejection of restraint can lead to an association of the fool with temptation: David Willbern suggests that a remark of Shakespeare's Feste 'echoes the voice of the arch-deceiver, perched on his victim's left shoulder'. But another critic, R. H. Goldsmith, finds Feste a 'moral being', the 'moral touchstone of the play', and Willbern too finds a weighty and even sermonizing quality about some of his speeches.

The fool shows, indeed, an unexpected affinity with the preacher: this affinity is at least as close as his kinship with the devil, the trickster, or the rogue. To some extent, admittedly, the relation between fool and priest is parodic. In the medieval Feast of Fools the fool mocked clerics, sermons, and the liturgy: there seems to have been a visual resemblance between the fool's cap and the monk's cowl. However, the function of the fool as preacher was not confined to mockery of religion: at times he seems to be the repository of grace, rather than an emissary of Satan counselling people to put their grace in their pockets. Erasmus' Dame Folly, who makes an exuberant speech in her own praise, quotes St Paul to show that foolishness is an attribute of the saintly, and even of the divine, nature: 'We are become fools for Christ's sake. . . . Whoso seemeth to be wise amongst you, let him become a fool, to the end he be wise indeed.' Not satisfied with this, Folly ventures the even more audacious argument that the great exemplar of Folly is Christ himself, who 'minding the relief and redemption of mankind's folly, although he was the ineffable wisdom of the Father, became yet a manner fool.' In worldly terms Christ was foolish because he sacrificed himself for a humanity which only dubiously deserved such a sacrifice; because he voluntarily exposed himself to suffering; because he did not put his own interests first. This is presumably what Enid Welsford has in mind when she writes of the 'essentially "Christian" nature' of fool literature. Writers on Renaissance comedy such as M. A. Screech have shown in detail how Rabelais and Erasmus drew on St Paul's epistles for their concept of divine or sanctified folly, holding that comedy and folly are closer to the spirit of Christianity than tragedy and seriousness. William Willeford has noted that, in societies in which magic is important, the clowns sometimes perform it: their magic contrasts with (but also, presumably, complements) 'the more "rational" magic of priests and magicians who are not clowns.'

This eerie linkage between fool and priest seems endemic to comedy. In eighteenth-century England it marks Fielding's Parson Adams, Sterne's Parson Yorick, and Goldsmith's Vicar of Wakefield, who are not merely holy fools but actually in holy orders. Each is able to fill the fool's role because he never becomes a plausible authority-figure, however much he may like to think of himself as one. None of the three is rich, none stands well with the Church hierarchy. Each has a sense of humour, yet each unwittingly becomes an object of ridicule. In *Tristram Shandy* Sterne laments the passing of the court fool and explicitly identifies Yorick as his descendant. Yorick, like other fools from Lear's onwards, comments shrewdly on the ways of the world but cannot apply the lessons he has learned. Other men, while pretending to enjoy his satirical gift, smart from it and yearn for revenge: Yorick remains blithely ignorant of their malice. His innocence and vulnerability are typified in the incident where a sizzling chestnut rolls off the dinner table into 'that particular aperture' of a fellow-clergyman's breeches 'for which, to the shame and indelicacy of our language be it spoke, there is no chaste word throughout all Johnson's dictionary'. Since Yorick has a reputation for jokes, and is known to disapprove of the scorched pastor's book on concubines (believed to have inflamed many men in that part of the body where the burning chestnut fell), the victim assumes that Yorick caused the nut to fall where it did. The grudge which he conceives blights Yorick's prospects of advancement; Yorick, neglected and a failure, pines and dies. In a world where many people see wit as incompatible with innocence and goodness, his best actions are misconstrued and his sermons have gone largely unheeded.

The fool's attachment to Christianity, though often strong, is always problematical. Nietzsche writes in *The Birth of Tragedy* of 'the fantastic and seemingly so offensive figure of the wise and rapturous satyr who is at the same time "the simple man" as opposed to the god—the image of nature and its strongest urges, even their symbol, and at the same time the proclaimer of her wisdom and art—musician, poet, dancer, and seer of spirits in one person.' His description perfectly fits the fool, simultaneously a sacred figure and a potentially offensive one. The fool is associated both with heaven and with nature, with the spirit and the body, with the god and with the simple man, with holiness and with irreverence. Sterne's Yorick, like Don Quixote, can preach a fine sermon, but his dignity is repeatedly compromised by involvement with such worldly and bodily concerns as feasting, childbirth, midwifery, horse-flesh, and hot chestnuts.

This pattern of contrary associations is not confined to European literature: the ambivalent figure of the fool seems to serve a widespread cultural need for a bridging of the gap between what is wise and what is foolish, between what is earthy and what is heavenly, between what is dignified and what is ridiculous. In Kalidasa's *Sakoontala* (India, fifth century AD), a romance with some comic elements, the jester Mathavya is a privileged person who gives cheek, in the manner of Lear's fool, to the king and his general. Like Shakespeare's Touchstone, he grumbles about being buried in the country at the whim of his social superior. He is associated with food and bodily urges; a long, rhapsodic speech of the king's annoys him because it keeps the two of them from dinner. He is afraid of demons (which the King has power to banish) and seems at times to have little understanding of sacred things. When he hears that one of the king's wives is in a jealous rage he fears to go near her in case she seizes him by the hair and beats him to a jelly. (Evidently the privileges of the Indian jester, like those of his Elizabethan counterpart, were sometimes infringed.) Thus far Mathavya seems not merely earthy but cowardly and self-centred. But this represents only the less dignified aspect of his role. Mathavya is intelligent: he knows more about the king's affairs than the king himself realizes. He is highly esteemed: the king calls him 'dear friend' and 'Holy Brahman', and when his royal master is unhappy Mathavya is sent for to comfort him. When the Queen Mother calls her son home to the city for an important ceremony, at a time when the hermits need him in the country, the king sends the jester home to take his place: this will be acceptable to the Queen Mother, who has already adopted Mathavya as her second son. Elsewhere, when a cry of distress is heard from the jester, the king calls out in anger, 'Who dares insult the worthy Mathavya?' In fact Mathavya has been kidnapped by a god, who explains that the broken-spirited king could not have been aroused except by an act of extreme provocation. An attack on Mathavya was serious enough to rouse him. The example of *Sakoontala* encourages us, then, to accept the wise or holy fool as somehow necessary to the imaginative literature of advanced cultures. His leading characteristic is the combination of contrasting qualities: dignity and indignity, earthiness and sacredness, wisdom and folly.

The strain involved in maintaining the paradoxical character of the fool often results in a splitting of the archetypal figure. The classic instance is that of Don Quixote and Sancho, spirit and body, one standing closer to God while the other allies himself to nature. But this, as E.C. Riley sees, is only one example of many similar pairings: 'Joseph Andrews and Parson Adams, Mr. Pickwick and Sam Weller, . . . the robots C3P0 and R2D2 of *Star Wars*'. The last two examples call attention to a recurring characteristic of the fool: his indestructibility, the care apparently taken of him by providence. Mr Pickwick, staying at a rambling hotel in Ipswich, takes a wrong turning during the night and stumbles into a strange lady's bedroom; he has to be rescued by his servant Sam, who observes: 'You rayther want somebody to look arter you, sir, wen your judgement goes out a wisiting.' When Pickwick goes to prison his protectors fear that his innocence will make him vulnerable: the other prisoners will 'eat him alive'. But somehow Pickwick always pulls through. Sam, for his part, is shrewd in some situations but ridiculous in others, as when he pens his ill-spelled and weirdly expressed Valentine, or allows himself to be taken in by the hypocritical Job Trotter. But Sam, like his master, is both lucky and resilient: he wins the woman he loves and turns the tables on his adversary. Like Sancho, Sam is a lovable mixture of trickster and earthy fool.

Riley's other example, the pair of comical robots in *Star Wars*, is equally instructive. R2D2, carrier of secrets and repository of truth, needs help and protection as the holy fool so often does: the role of C3P0 is to escort and shield his fellow and to take the knocks. C3P0's share of the fool's role is to be gossipy, vain of his knowledge, self-important, unwary at some moments (as when he risks demolition by beating the Wookie at chess) and excessively cautious and cowardly at others. But he has the indestructibility of his kind: though regularly dismantled he is invariably put together again.

Indestructibility, or something like it, is an especially strong characteristic of the modern fool, who often emerges as the miraculous survivor in an indiscriminately murderous universe.

The army chaplain in Joseph Heller's war-novel *Catch-22* is a holy fool who survives almost in spite of himself. His innocence, sincerity, and helplessness make Yossarian, the central figure, love him at first sight. This does not prevent Yossarian mischievously signing the chaplain's name to an erotic invitation on a letter he is censoring: later this causes the chaplain to be brought before brutal intelligence officers armed with the latest interrogation techniques. But the victim somehow escapes actual torture or imprisonment and is allowed to go free. In the course of the book he has to bear many crosses, including loss of religious faith, a demand for church services which don't mention God, and an unjust accusation of stealing a black-market tomato. But by the end he has recovered his faith and is still alive and free. Another feature that links Heller's chaplain with earlier holy fools is a counterpointing with an earthy, wise fool who has associations with nature and who survives by his own efforts, not by luck.

The recovery of faith in providence by the holy fool, the chaplain, is boosted by the good news he receives about the wise fool, Orr. Orr goes through life with his cheeks full of pebbles and a ridiculous grin on his face. On bombing missions he always ditches his aircraft. When he invites Yossarian to join his crew the latter refuses because of Orr's incompetence as a pilot. But on the ground Orr proves oddly adept at building luxurious accommodation for Yossarian and himself, and he spends hours dismantling and reassembling intricate pieces of machinery. When Orr ditches his plane for the last time and disappears, Yossarian assumes that yet another friend has been killed in action. Only when he hears, towards the end of the book, that Orr has turned up in neutral Sweden does Yossarian see the truth. Orr stuffed his face with pebbles to make himself look stupid: his ditchings of aircraft, like his tinkering with machinery, were part of an elaborate rehearsal for escape. One of the last and most striking images in the book is that of the grotesque-looking Orr paddling manically towards Sweden in a rubber dinghy. Once again it is the fool who rises above the craziness of the world.

The fool's blend of wisdom and folly is disarming, but can be confusing. Shakespeare sometimes uses pointers such as 'This is not altogether fool, my lord' to warn audiences not to ignore the fool's wisdom. Cervantes keeps reminding readers that the Don speaks sense on any subject not connected with knight errantry. Jaroslav Hašek in *The Good Soldier Švejk*, a novel which anticipates Heller's device of contrasting the wisdom of the fool with the lunacy of warfare, makes several characters wonder whether Švejk is a real or pretended idiot. Actually the writer's own attitude to the fool often changes in the course of the work. In the early chapters of *Quixote* and *Pickwick* the protagonists are, respectively, very mad and very gullible; positive qualities such as goodness, kindly innocence, and unworldly wisdom develop gradually as the tale goes on. The case of Švejk is slightly different. Early in the book, when war has just been declared, Švejk has himself pushed down the street in a wheel-chair, shouting patriotic slogans as he goes: in this instance even the military can see that he is not a real idiot or fanatic, and that his show of enthusiasm for the war is in fact a satire on war. But Švejk is not at this time, and never becomes, an altogether wise fool: some of his actions can only arise from real, unaffected stupidity. He seems genuinely fond, for example, of Lieutenant Lukáš, one of the few officers in the book who is neither brutal nor incompetent: at times Švejk makes heroic sacrifices to avoid getting Lukáš into trouble. But most of them are in vain: for example, there is a hilarious incident where Lukáš's love-life is exposed in the newspapers as a result of an indiscretion of Švejk's, despite the latter's belated act of devotion in swallowing an incriminating letter.

That Švejk should at times seem genuinely foolish is as it should be. There is something unsettling about fools such as Shakespeare's Feste, who have become so refined that they retain few traces of 'natural' folly. The fool should remain a fool in at least part of his being. Švejk, in one of his most lucid intervals, explains the fool's function in life and art: 'Stupid people have to exist too, because if everyone were wise there would be so much good sense in the world that everyone would be driven crazy by it.' Many twentieth-century writers would go further, hinting that in a crazy world none but the fools are really sane. In Tom Stoppard's *Every Good Boy Deserves Favour* the Doctor says contemptuously, 'The idea that all the people locked up in mental hospitals are sane while the people walking about outside are all mad is merely a literary conceit, put about by people who should be locked up.' But this doctor is working in a Russian psychiatric hospital used for the confinement of political dissidents, who are diagnosed as insane for no other reason than that their views conflict with those of the government. For the audience, the Doctor's comment only reinforces the view he is trying to refute, and indeed the 'literary conceit' that he mentions is one of the most pervasive of modern times. Kikuchi Kan's Japanese play *The Madman on the Roof* (c.1916) is informed by it. It can appear in commercial comedies as well as in those with higher intellectual pretensions: in the 1950 film *Harvey* the protagonist, who believes he is being protected by a guardian spirit in the shape of an enormous rabbit, proves saner than the other family members who are seeking to have him locked away.

Critics and philosophers have always been aware of the importance in humour and comedy of the rogue, the trickster, and the fool. In a sense these figures are marginal to the classic comedy-intrigue of two young people who overcome obstacles to their marriage; but this in its turn reminds us how uninteresting those two figures can sometimes be. What the rogue, fool, and trickster have in common is their capacity for escape from the normal, rational world. The fool is aware of the existence of more than one level of reality. The trickster loves to impose a whole perceptual world on the victim. Comedy itself is often thought of as a world of mistakes and illusions (some contrived, some accidental) where, as Shakespeare's Feste puts it, 'Nothing that is so is so.' Had we to deal only with the fool and the trickster, who take a childish delight in illusion for its own sake, we might conclude that the spirit of comedy was that of childishness or adolescence, with the fool as the lovable lunatic who has never grown up and the trickster as the mischievous older child or teenager who enjoys sowing confusion in the orderly adult world. And there is, indeed, much truth in that view. But we cannot ignore the relation of these less harmful figures to the more disturbing figure of the rogue, whose illusions and trickery are goal-orientated and whose attitude to his victims is ruthless. Nor can we ignore the closeness of many comic punishments and put-downs to 'sheer barbarity', 'callous indifference', and 'the condition of savagery'. In the course of the last few chapters we have examined some of the strategies comic writers use to keep these connotations under control. But there is no denying that control becomes precarious at times, or that comic trickery and deception often threaten to leave the realm of the mischievous for that of the demonic.

In this situation the role of the fool emerges as curative and redemptive. It helps us to avoid treating as categorical the rule cited by Todorov: namely, that stupidity is a crime in itself. There is much to tempt us to sympathy with the rogue and harsh trickster, and with the demonic element in comedy: they represent energy which, as Blake said, is eternal delight. But to identify too closely with the rogue is to be tainted with his hubris, his arrogant contempt for his victims and for the law-abiding world in general. The fool—as distinct from the merely ridiculous gull—helps us to avoid this error because he (or she) demands a share of identification too. We can pity a gross dupe like Calandrino, but we cannot identify with him. In the wise or holy fool, on the other hand, there are many characteristics which we would like to appropriate. If the wise or holy fool never feels quite at home in the world, his *Angst* is one which we all experience from time to time. We enjoy the idea of tricking others, but we are never quite immune from the fear of being tricked ourselves: we enjoy laughing at others, but we know what it is to be laughed at. Above all, we find it disturbingly easy to imagine being written off as mad in a world which is only dubiously sane.

9

The Language of Comedy

One of the richest sources of comedy is language. While not all jokes depend on turns of language, the majority do; some uses of language in comedy and humour will, then, be the subject of this chapter. Perhaps the first characteristic that we learn to expect from comic dialogue and narrative is that they will approximate to what students of language call naturally occurring speech. While tragedy is expected to aspire to sublimity or elevation of diction, comedy is generally supposed to be written in what Ben Jonson, in his preface to *Every Man in His Humour*, approvingly called 'language such as men do use'. Other writers seem equally anxious to stress that the language they use is close to everyday speech. J. M. Synge wrote of *The Playboy of The Western World* (which, while not a pure comedy, is full of comic scenes and effects) that he had used in it 'one or two words only that [he had] not heard among the country people of Ireland, or spoken in [his] own nursery before [he] could read the newspapers'. However, Deirdre Burton, in her book *Dialogue and Discourse*, points to a general agreement among linguists that 'nobody speaks at all like the characters in a novel, play, or film'. And if we test the statements of comic playwrights against their practice we shall find that it is not they but the students of linguistics who are right. The slanging match at the beginning of Ben Jonson's *The Alchemist*, the dream of power and riches given to Sir Epicure Mammon in the same play, and much else in Jonson's comic drama, go far beyond 'language such as men do use'. Even Synge may be suspected of exaggerating the lyrical and imaginative riches of provincial Irish speech.

The most obvious and distinctive feature of comic dialogue and narrative is, of course, the joke. Jokes, though encountered fairly frequently in everyday conversation, represent tightening or heightening of language of a kind that is unnecessary to, and sometimes actively disruptive of, the normal pragmatic and informational functions of language. Many, perhaps most, jokes will be found to arise from a phenomenon which is in pragmatic terms a potential source of confusion: from what Bergson, in his essay on laughter, calls 'the reciprocal interference of series'. One type of interference of series occurs when two contrasting modes of speech (serious and comic, heroic and unheroic, learned and unlearned, native and acquired, upper-class and lower-class) are placed in ludicrous juxtaposition with one another. In another type, the same word or sentence carries two divergent meanings. In a third, two semantically remote words or phrases cause enjoyable confusion because of the ease with which they can, graphically or phonetically, be mistaken for one another.

The most obvious explanation for the comic effects generated by these convergences is incongruity. The common printing error 'immoral' for 'immortal' is amusing because it substitutes an undignified word for a dignified one. When a theatre audience is suddenly made aware that 'our souls', in many dialects of British English, is homophonous with 'arse-'oles' (this last example is taken from Brendan Behan's play *The Hostage*), the effect is that of a *discordia concors*, a bringing together at one level of elements which do not meet on any other level.

In addition to incongruity, humour based on language may also arise from a sense of psychic release. When we laugh at a low-life word which underlines a dignified word, or at an insult which lurks behind a compliment, or at a threat veiled in polite language, the child in us is defying the adult censor who normally forbids us to use threats, insults, or low words. The most obvious and most time-honoured example of verbal humour arising from psychic release is the sexual joke. In a well-known twentieth-century tavern anecdote a society woman asks to see a prospective employee's testimonials (or credentials), with ludicrous results. A similar play on words can be found in Charles Johnson's eighteenth-century comedy *The Country Lasses*, where a hero says to a villain, 'But that I have a decent regard to posterity, I would have cut away the only credentials you have of humanity, and made a walking sign of you.' As far back in the history of comedy as Plautus' *Braggart Soldier* we find the braggart being frightened by an enemy who brandishes a knife, telling him that he will be lucky if he gets away with 'his bearers of testimony intact' (*salvis testibus*). In the example from Plautus the pun is unmistakable, for it is repeated several times within the scene by means of cognate words such as *intestatus* and *intestabilis*. So in the course of two thousand years we can see a series of remarkably similar puns being used as a means of psychic release. However, the type of psychic release obtained is not the same in all three instances. In the modern example the language of the tavern is imagined as intruding, uninvited, on the language of the drawing-room. In the earlier instances threats and insults, of a kind which few members of the audience would venture in similar circumstances, are offered with impunity to a swaggerer or braggart. In all three cases the joke generates an enjoyable feeling of transgression.

Verbal humour generally depends on ambiguity: on the use of a word, phrase, sentence, or longer unit which can be understood in two different, usually conflicting, ways. This in turn relates to the tendency, inherent in language, for different phonetic and semantic chains to cross one another. We have all encountered the type of utterance which, made in all innocence, is suddenly seen to carry a second possible meaning which clashes with the first. Usually the sender fails to realize that the receiver might take the message in the wrong way. Victor Raskin quotes a story about a clergyman who cabled his bishop to announce the sudden death of his wife, and to request a substitute for the following Sunday. To the sender of the cable, it would be clear that what he wanted was a substitute preacher: the possibility that he might seem to be asking for a substitute bedfellow would not cross his mind. This kind of joke is complicated, and enriched, by suspicions of unconscious motivation. We may think of the clergyman (real or fictional) as having made a Freudian slip: perhaps he unconsciously chose a form of words expressive of his hidden desire.

Raskin uses the story of the clergyman to illustrate his theory that most, perhaps all, jokes arise from a clash between two rival 'scripts' or realms of meaning. In the case of the clergyman's cable the two 'scripts' involved are that of sex and that of religion. As this example shows, it is necessary for the two scripts to appear, on the surface, to be divergent, even antithetical: the double meaning reveals an unexpected connection between two realms of meaning which seemed far apart. Raskin's theory may not, then, be very new: it is perhaps best viewed as an elaborated version of Bergson's 'convergence of series' or the even older notion of the *discordia concors*.

It will be seen that verbal humour often manifests itself on a relatively small scale, at the level of the word or phrase. The most obvious type of small-scale linguistic joke is the pun, some examples of which we have already considered. Puns, as Jonathan Culler reminds us, were once considered among the lowest form of wit: Samuel Johnson, in the eighteenth century, deplored Shakespeare's fondness for them, and Swift expressed his irritation with puns by fancifully deriving the word from 'the French word *punaise*, which signifies a little stinking insect that gets into the skin, provokes continual itching, and is with great difficulty removed'. Twentieth-century commentators have laboured to reinstate puns in the more prestigious position they enjoyed in the time of Donne and Shakespeare. One frequently encountered, and perfectly valid, argument is that some puns, far from being tasteless intrusions of humour into serious discourse, are intended seriously. Donne's 'A Hymn to God the Father' contains the line, 'When thou hast done, thou hast not done': this puns on the poet's name, which was identical in sound with the word 'done'. It is unlikely that any humour was intended in this instance.

However, there is no reason why this overtly serious type of word-play should be the only kind to attract serious attention. Jonathan Culler notes that 'in Freud's dream analyses, the link between a dream image and the day's residue [repeatedly] turns out to be a word functioning as a pun'. Elsewhere the same writer cites with approval 'a kind of wordplay which, by its subliminal fluidity, resembles Freud's theory that the truth of the unconscious can be revealed through word association'. Thus the neo-Freudian Jacques Lacan 'takes paranomasia as central rather than marginal' to the understanding of the relationships between language and mind. If Freud and his commentators are right, then all punning, comical or serious, deserves attention. In modern literary criticism there is a growing tendency to distinguish between the type of writer in whose work, as Anthony Burgess puts it, 'language is . . . transparent, unseductive, totally damped', and the type to whom 'it is important that the opacity of language be exploited, so that ambiguities, puns and centrifugal connotations are to be enjoyed rather than regretted'. Burgess concedes that writing of the first class, 'transparent' writing, can 'be elevated to a high level of aesthetic interest through wit, balance, euphony, and other devices of elegance'. But he contends that 'elegance . . . is the most that Class 1 prose can achieve; for dandyism one must go to Class 2 writers.' 'Dandyism', which Burgess uses here as a term of approval, points to the element of what is playful, exuberant, ludic, comic in 'Class 2' writing. This latter class is clearly the one that Burgess, and many other recent commentators, esteem most highly.

Culler prefers to 'take pun as paradigm for the play of language' rather than seek to 'circumscribe it or discriminate it from other forms of wordplay', and there is something to be said for broadening the definition in this way. However, our discussion of word-play will move next to a consideration of phonetic confusions and coincidences, which are closest to what is normally understood by the word 'pun'. Baldesar Castiglione, who devoted a whole section of *The Book of The Courtier* to jokes, records that witticisms which depend on 'changing a word by adding or taking away a letter or syllable' have a special name, *bischizzi*: the example he gives turns on a confusion between *latina lingua*, 'the Latin language', and *latrina lingua*, 'lavatory language'. Though not all languages can boast a technical term for this type of humour it is, of course, widespread. An enjoyable modern instance occurs in the film *Bedazzled*, a comic version of the Faust legend, where the devil-figure changes the newspaper headline 'POP STARS IN SEX AND DRUGS SCANDAL' to read 'POPE STARS IN SEX AND DRUGS SCANDAL'. Humour of this type can, of course, be generated either intentionally or unintentionally. Consider the story of a Finnish woman who, when asked her age by some official, replied, 'I am dirty, and my husband is dirty too.' Here, apparently, a particular English sound proved difficult for the foreigner, so she regularly substituted another. The result was the simultaneous production of two different meanings. It will be noticed that such naturally occurring mistakes often need artificial heightening in order to become acceptable as jokes. In the example cited, the comic effect depends on accumulation. 'Dirty' for 'thirty' isn't especially amusing by itself, but the addition of 'dirty too' for 'thirty-two' (which fits into both the relevant 'scripts', that of age and that of uncleanliness) improves the joke. The story may indeed be based on a real exchange, but we may suspect that the original version has undergone some polishing.

Jokes based on the speech of foreigners, provincials, or minority groups are common in stage comedy: their success depends to a great extent on the audience's feeling of superiority. The ability to see a double meaning depends on the hearer's fluency in a particular tongue: the less fluent speaker becomes, by contrast, an object of ridicule. Pleasure in superiority is also present in our response to characters who mistake words for one another, such as Shakespeare's Dogberry and Elbow and Sheridan's Mrs Malaprop. When Mrs Malaprop says 'atmospherics' but means 'hysterics', the audience not only needs to realize that the speaker has hit on the wrong word but must also be able to infer which word she intended to use. This will confer a feeling of superiority to the fictional character.

However, part of the humour in these instances derives from sheer pleasure in the perfidy of language, the ease with which a minute alteration can bring about a transformation of meaning. This same perfidy is evident not only in malapropisms, where a word which does not belong in a sentence is substituted accidentally for one which does, but also in cases where two words of the intended or expected utterance are deftly reversed to create ludicrous effects. Sancho Panza in *Don Quixote* praises his master for giving drink to those who are hungry and food to those who thirst; Oscar Wilde describes work as the curse of the drinking classes; the cartoon character Roger Ramjet temporarily deserts crime-fighting for show business, becoming intoxicated with the roar of the footlights and the smell of the audience.

We have now moved to sources of linguistic humour and comedy which lie beyond what are usually recognized as puns, but which still depend on the agreeable duplicity or perfidy of words. Further instances of these are palinlogues and acrostics, apparently trivial devices for arousing laughter which have attracted the attention of some unexpectedly eminent writers. The comic palinlogue is exemplified in Llareggub, the fictional township in Dylan Thomas's *Under Milk Wood*; at first glance the name looks appropriately Welsh and folksy, but it becomes less so when reversed. The palinlogue also appealed to Jaroslav Hašek, who took a room in a shady hotel and registered as a Russian at a time when Russians were regarded with suspicion in the Austro-Hungarian territories. Hašek's register entry looked like a genuine Russian name, but when read backwards it spelt out a coarse phrase in Czech. In both these instances the palinlogue gratifies the wish of the author or informed reader to feel superior to those who fail to see the joke. Acrostics work in much the same way. The Australian poet Gwen Harwood, after a quarrel with the editor of a journal which had published some of her work, submitted two apparently high-minded poems under an assumed name. Issues of the journal had to be recalled after it was discovered that the initial letters of each line spelt out a farewell to the journal and a caustic suggestion as to the proper fate of editors. The poet, and those readers who spotted the concealed message, could feel superior to the editor and staff of the journal, who had missed it. However, these types of humour depend at a more fundamental level on incongruity: on the ease with which language, often by very slight adjustments, can be diverted from its day-to-day informational and pragmatic functions and made to subvert these functions.

A favourite game among comic writers of most countries and periods has been the use of meaningful fictional names. This appears at its simplest in such characters as Lady Haughty and Sir Amorous La Foole in Ben Jonson's *Epicoene*, whose names allude directly to their natures. But some comic writers play the game of giving their characters conspicuously inappropriate names, or names containing internal contradictions. In Pynchon's *The Crying of Lot 49* Dr Hilarius, an ex-Nazi psychoanalyst, is neither cheerful nor amusing, while Genghis Cohen is not a ruler obsessed with conquest but a gentle Jewish stamp-collector. The protagonist's husband Mucho Maas, whose name is close to a Spanish phrase meaning 'a whole lot more', has less to offer to women than other people: Mucho is not macho. In like manner the first name of the theatre-director Randolph Driblette is sometimes shortened to Randy, with the result that his two names stand in ludicrous contradiction to one another. The name of the book's central figure, Oedipa Maas, seems to suggest some kind of Freudian meaning. But some commentators have noted that it can be read 'Oedipa my arsc', a possibility which ought perhaps to deter readers from more straight-faced interpretations. To add to the confusion some names, such as that of 'the beautiful Spanish exile Remedios Varo', are those of real people, of whom a given reader may or may not have heard: if I find myself seeking a recondite meaning behind such a name, the joke will be on me. Pynchon, it seems, is playing a game with his readers, a game whose rules he feels entitled to change without warning in the course of the book. Here, as is so often the case, the key to the humour lies in incongruity. For the reader (though perhaps not for the author) the additional satisfaction of superiority is only fitfully present: the fear that at any moment we may be missing something keeps the feeling of superiority at bay.

One of the sustained jokes behind *The Crying of Lot 49* is that, while both protagonist and reader are constantly invited to look for hidden signs, there is seldom any certainty as to whether a particular sign has been interpreted correctly, or even (in some instances) whether it is justifiable to assign it a meaning at all. Messages are constantly being intercepted, distorted, or given dubious interpretations. 'Communication is the key,' Oedipa is assured by one of the more sinister characters, but there are few occasions in the book when the key perfectly fits the lock. A notable exception is a dance in which Oedipa finds herself involved, at which all the other dancers are deaf-mutes. Nobody but Oedipa (who, since she is a woman, must follow her partner's lead) can hear the band; each couple dances 'whatever [is] in the fellow's head'. Oedipa waits for the collisions, but they do not come: at last she has to conclude that 'some unthinkable order of music' is at work, something 'they all heard with an extra sense atrophied in herself'. In any case the deaf-mutes, deprived both of music and words, communicate, in this instance, more efficiently than any other group or pair of human beings encountered in the novel.

It is an incongruity which points us beyond the language of comedy to its semiotics. For comedy thrives not only on games played with verbal language but also on body-language and on other types of non-verbal communication. In the 1986 film *Ruthless People* the shoulders of a man with his back to the camera begin to shake when he hears of his wife's death. To some of the onlookers he appears to be sobbing, but in reality he is shaking with triumphant laughter: he has been trying to get rid of his wife since the beginning of the film. Earlier the wordless cries of a woman in an (admittedly simulated) orgasm are taken for the agonized shrieks of a murder-victim: this initial misunderstanding generates many more as the plot unfolds. At yet another point in the film two policemen go to interview a suspect: to elude them he pleads stomach flu, and shuts himself into the men's lavatory. The policemen, listening at the door, hear grunts, which they innocently interpret as symptoms of an upset stomach. In fact the suspect has tried to escape through the lavatory window, which is on the first floor. Then, hearing a third policeman tell the first two that another man has been taken in for questioning, the climber abandons his plan of escape and tries to get back inside. The grunts heard by the detectives are caused not by stomach pains but by the effort of scrambling back through the window. Each of these instances involves the non-verbal equivalent of a pun or double-meaning: the same sign or group of signs can be interpreted in contrasting ways.

We need not labour the point that laughter and comedy can exist independently of spoken or written language. The art of the mime and of the silent-film comedian depends on non-verbal jokes. (It is notable that most mime is comic rather than serious: there is an in-built incongruity in the idea of human beings, those uniquely articulate creatures, attempting to communicate without the aid of words.) A comic or satiric print by Hogarth or Rowlandson may likewise act on us with minimal assistance from language, while some of the better modern newspaper cartoons achieve their effect without words of any kind.

Some of the types of wit and humour already discussed in this chapter look at first sight as if they belong to the discussion of laughter rather than to that of comedy. A pun, a palinlogue, a comic name, or a sight-gag may seem like an incidental device, here one moment and gone the next. In fact such devices often go far beyond merely incidental sources of humour: when used repeatedly they can permeate a play or novel, helping to determine its tone and communicate its ethos. Such are the use of comic names in Pynchon or of puns in Joyce. Moreover, language itself often becomes a theme of comedy: several comic works undertake an explicit critique of language, evaluating the uses of different systems of communication in life or literature. In Ben Jonson's satirical comedy *The Poetaster* a writer accused of using obscure and pretentious words ('wild outlandish terms') is given an emetic. Shortly afterwards he begins to vomit up the offending words into a basin: among the more outrageous are 'glibbery', 'lubrical', 'snotteries', 'furibund', and 'obstupefact'. A rather similar exercise is undertaken in Molière's *Précieuses Ridicules* and *Femmes Savantes*, where the use of affected or over-refined language is treated as a grave personal failing, a sign of hypocrisy and even sexual frigidity in the speaker. The no-nonsense language of householders and the pleasing country dialects of maids and lackeys are deliberately used to make the linguistic fastidiousness of the society women sound ridiculous by comparison.

A rather different case is Shaw's *Pygmalion*, which dwells on the disadvantages suffered in English society by those who do not speak in the accepted upper-class register. One of the jokes here concerns the number of different levels on which language works. The scene in which Professor Higgins introduces the former flower girl Eliza Doolittle into his mother's drawing-room demonstrates that carefully modulated vowel sounds are not in themselves enough to guarantee social acceptance; the subject's grammar, choice of words, and choice of topics need equally careful attention:

MRS EYNSFORD HILL. But it cant have been right for your father to pour spirits down [your mother's] throat like that. It might have killed her.

LIZA. Not her. Gin was mother's milk to her. Besides, he'd poured so much down his own throat that he knew the good of it.

MRS EYNSFORD HILL. Do you mean that he drank?

LIZA. . . . It never did him no harm that I could see. But then he did not
  keep it up regular. [*Cheerfully*] On the burst, as you might say, from
  time to time. And always more agreeable when he had a drop in.

Shaw's concern in *Pygmalion* was mainly with the social aspect
of language. Often, however, a comic treatment of language will
point to philosophical paradoxes about the nature of language as
such. In the British television series *Fawlty Towers* the hotel
proprietor uses the word 'burro' in a conversation with his Spanish waiter: he wants it to mean 'butter' (which it does mean in
Italian), but the waiter fails to understand because in Spanish the
word means 'donkey'. The fact that a word can mean 'butter' in
one language and 'donkey' in another points towards the inherently arbitrary character of the relation between words and their
meanings.

  When we learn a language, we have to struggle to attach the
right words to the right meanings. We do so by means of inference, observation, and practice: we try to correlate people's
actions and facial expressions with their words. But there is
always room for confusion. As Wittgenstein notes, if I point to
two apples I may be drawing attention to the fact that they are
apples as opposed to pears, or to the fact that there are two rather
than one or three: my gesture may be misinterpreted because it
may apply to either of two possible classes, the class of numbers
or the class of objects. Likewise, a person may try to learn a
language by watching and listening to builders on a site. Hearing
a man shout a particular word and seeing another pass him a
plank, the observer may conclude that the word means 'plank'.
But the inference may be false. The word called out by the first
labourer may have meant 'Ready'; the second man, knowing in
advance which object would be required, may have passed him
what he wanted without having it named.

  The comic consequences of this are played out in Tom
Stoppard's *Dogg's Hamlet*. The majority of the characters in the
play speak a lingo called Dogg. All the words in Dogg also occur
in English, but most have different meanings: a polite sentence in
Dogg is offensive in normal speech. For instance, 'Cretinous
pig-faced, git?' means 'Have you got the time please, sir?' The

audience is invited to infer the Dogg meaning of the sentence from the context. A schoolboy uses it in talking to his head-master; his tone is deferential; the headmaster shows no signs of anger, but instead looks at his watch and gives an apparently polite reply. We infer that the phrase cannot mean what we nor-mally take it to mean; the context enables us to feel fairly confident as to what it means in Dogg. The game of inference continues throughout the play.

The framing action of *Dogg's Hamlet* is a school speech day with the presentation of a play (a fifteen-minute version of Shakespeare's *Hamlet*). Just as the audience is beginning to make sense of the situation, and of Dogg, a new character appears. He is a construction worker called Easy, with a van full of planks and blocks to build the temporary stage. Easy speaks English and knows no Dogg. When hailed in blank verse by a boy who claims to be William Shakespeare, and later addressed by another boy as a useless git, Easy concludes that the pupils and teachers are mad or inexplicably hostile. Gradually, however, the need to co-operate with them on the job of unloading the equipment and setting up the stage forces him to start picking up Dogg, though not without several more misunderstandings. The audience can enjoy these since its own knowledge of Dogg is several steps ahead of Easy's: he arrives only after several revealing exchanges have taken place. Here, as in *Pygmalion*, the feeling of superiority joins with the feeling of incongruity to produce comedy: a character struggles to master a language or dialect which the audience already has at its command.

Dogg's Hamlet takes its inspiration from a passage in Wittgenstein's *Philosophical Investigations* (I. ii–x). But it can be understood by an alert audience with no knowledge of Witt-genstein, for it appeals to a fundamental source of linguistic humour: the phenomenon by which the same utterance can carry two different, and often ludicrously contrasting, meanings.

The extreme example of linguistic humour, the kind which stands furthest from pragmatic and informational uses of lan-guage, is nonsense-humour, best known to English-speaking readers in the works of Lewis Carroll and Edward Lear. Freud saw nonsense as an enjoyable rest for the mind from the pressure of meaning, one of the diverse forms of human play. Part of the fun of nonsense is that it apes sense, playfully pretending to a rational meaning. Chomsky's famous sentence 'colourless green ideas sleep furiously' uses normal sentence structure, and thereby challenges us to tease out a coherent message. Though formulated to illustrate a serious linguistic theory, it is incidentally amusing by virtue of the incongruity, in semantic terms, of its different parts.

Nonsensical sentences whose unimpeachable structure challenges readers to find a meaning are also found in Carroll's Jabberwocky, the language which puzzles Alice in *Through the Looking Glass*:

> 'Twas brillig, and the slithy toves
>   Did gyre and gimble in the wabe,
> All mimsy were the borogoves
>   And the mome raths outgrabe.

When Alice first hears this poem she says to herself, 'It seems very pretty . . . Somehow it seems to fill my head with ideas—only I don't exactly know what they are!' Evidently Alice feels she should be able to discern a meaning in the words, but she doesn't find it easy. Later, when she meets Humpty Dumpty, she asks him to help, since he seems so clever at explaining words. Humpty Dumpty is confident that he can 'explain all the poems that ever were invented—and a good many that haven't been invented just yet', so Alice repeats the first verse for him. But Humpty Dumpty's way with words is overbearing: he insists on mastering them, evidently afraid that they might otherwise master him. *Outgribing*, he explains, is 'something between bellowing and whistling, with a kind of sneeze in the middle'. *Toves* 'are something like badgers—they're something like lizards—and they're something like corkscrews'. Humpty's allocation of meanings is creative, but a little high-handed. It does not occur to him to enjoy nonsense by letting it play unhindered upon the mind. Though Alice's attitude to this donnish figure is deferential, the reader is liable to feel superior, setting down Humpty Dumpty as an object of ridicule. (Even Alice, when Humpty Dumpty offers to recite some poetry, quickly forestalls him with the assurance that 'it needn't come to that'.) We feel superior to Humpty Dumpty because he has missed the point of Jabberwocky. It is spoiled by any attempt to tie it down to a set meaning. It is a code which we should not try to crack.

In Jabberwocky, Carroll created a language which was largely new, in vocabulary if not in grammar. This feat is not as rare as we might suppose. Something like it is to be found not only in *Dogg's Hamlet* but in Anthony Burgess's *A Clockwork Orange*, where the young vandals create an argot of their own based largely on Russian; in John Barth's *Giles Goat-Boy*, where the world is described in terms of the structure of a university (the Messiah being the Grand Tutor, to be damned being to be flunked, etc.); and in Malcolm Bradbury's *Rates of Exchange*, where the imaginary Balkan country is assigned an artificial, but remarkably plausible, language. These fictional tongues differ somewhat from nonsense-language. If the advantage of nonsense is its offer of a rest from the pressure of meaning, the invented languages of Stoppard, Burgess, Bradbury, and Barth offer us the alternative pleasures of decipherment. A likely meaning can usually be inferred; this time the reader is allowed to feel superior at having found a plausible solution.

The primary function of language is that of making sense: comedy recognizes this function but often shows it being supplemented or subverted. Nonsense, the most subversive variety of comic language, seems antithetical to sense and reason. Yet Elizabeth Sewell shows that it exploits, though in parodic fashion, the forms of syntax, reason, and logic. Modern commentators, though unwilling to hand over comedy and nonsense-humour to the undisputed control of reason, mostly see it as having closer kinship with play, which is always rule-governed and thus in a sense logical, than with dreams, which defy logic. Yet comic language does seem to have a foot in two realms: it is both a self-referential world of words and an outwardly directed commentary on reality. Sewell notes that even nonsense, quint-essentially a world of words, keeps ostentatiously in touch with objects: with 'shoes—and ships—and sealing-wax', with 'cabbages—and kings'. Uses of language, and thinking about language, can easily become dominated by its pragmatic functions: comedy arouses our sense of the incongruous by setting direct, pragmatic uses of language in ludicrous juxtaposition with circumlocutory, fantastic, oneiric, ambiguous, or frankly ludic uses. Writers of comedy, and their characters, often declare their allegiance to practical, unpretentious, down-to-earth speech and writing. ('I live on good hot-pot, not on fancy language' observes a character in Molière's *Les Femmes Savantes*.) However, a comedy which restricted itself to pragmatic uses of language would be a contradiction in terms, since the composition of a comedy is one of the least pragmatic uses of language that could be imagined. Comedy is by its very nature festive, ludic, and creative. Preciosity is mocked, but at the same time enjoyed and exploited. The forms of everyday speech are praised but transcended: copiousness of insult, fluency of repartee, and inventiveness of word-play go far beyond anything encountered in the everyday world.

10

Reality and Fantasy

In the first century BC Cicero described comedy as a mirror of
manners. Many later writers have agreed. During the Italian
Renaissance Baldesar Castiglione saw comic writing as the mode
which could 'express better than the rest, the trade of man's life'.
In Elizabethan England Ben Jonson, in *Every Man out of his
Humour*, quoted the Ciceronian definition with approval and
rejected romantic comedy in favour of what was 'familiarly allied
to the time'. In the eighteenth century the critic John Dennis
declared, 'Comedy is nothing but a picture of common life, and a
representation of humours and manners.' Early in our own century Jaroslav Hašek, in the epilogue to the first part of *The
Good Soldier Švejk*, claimed that the language and characters
of his exuberant comic novel were drawn from experience. The
literary critic Stuart Baker, in a book first published in 1976, still
felt able to assert: 'Comedy can be judged by how well, how pro-
foundly, or how cleverly it portrays the real world.' (Baker did,
however, think it normal for comedy to contain some unrealistic
elements.)

Other writers on comedy during the last thirty years have been
more inclined to emphasize the disparity between comedy and
everyday life. Ian Donaldson, for example, in his book *The
World Upside Down*, shows how apt comedy is to portray a
topsy-turvy world, in which patterns of authority found in the
real world are reversed: greybeards go to school; justices are put
in the stocks. And it is a commonplace of criticism that comedy
thrives on disguisings, deceptions, and mistakings: that is to say,
on the provisional nature of our perceptions and interpretations
of reality. There are many moments when comedy portrays the
confusion or disruption of these perceptions, tempting us to say,
with Shakespeare's Feste, 'Nothing that is so, is so.' In Renaissance comedy, for instance, it is common for a male character to
be saddled with such delusions as that he is mad, dead, haunted,
pregnant, or flying through the air on a winged horse; characters

are regularly tricked into accepting a man as a woman or a woman as a man; lowly peasants and labourers are made to believe that they have been transformed into kings or noblemen.

Since the topic of the relationship with reality arises so persistently in discussions of comedy, this chapter will be devoted to a consideration of that relationship. We shall examine the closeness or remoteness of the world of comedy, on the one hand to the everyday world, and on the other hand to the alternative world of fantasy. In the course of the investigation we shall need to keep in mind the wide range of meanings that can attach to the word 'reality', especially in relation to comedy. Our conclusion, on the whole, will be cautious. We shall accept the view of the psychoanalyst Charles Mauron that comedy moves away from the hauntings of dreams towards everyday experience. But we shall remember, as Mauron does, that comedy, though its world is not the same as the dream world, does border on it: everyday reality is not all that comedy brings into play.

The quotations from Cicero, Castiglione, and Jonson which began this chapter all pointed to a particular feature of the relation between comedy and reality: the topicality of comedy, its relation to the 'manners' (customs) of ordinary people at a particular place and time. Let us, then, test the notion that comedy should remain faithful to reality against a type of comedy which seems to promise this topicality and particularity: the regional comedy of colourful, but unsophisticated, village life. A lively specimen is Heinrich von Kleist's *The Broken Jug*, written in German in 1805 and set in a small village in the Netherlands. John Allen writes that Kleist 'tried to depict peasant life with new truthfulness', but he also detects 'a certain generality about the theme of the play' which should enable it to transpose readily into 'any authentic dialect'. This may suggest to us that, while local and topical details are used to good effect, they are not of overriding importance.

The main character in Kleist's play, a village magistrate called Adam, is first seen in his bedroom in the early morning. His clerk enters to tell him that an inspector from the city will be in court during the day. The last magistrate to be inspected, the clerk adds, received his dismissal in his own courtroom, and hanged himself from a rafter the following night. The Judge's whole world is at once threatened: he knows that when he enters the court on this day it will be he who is on trial. To make matters worse, the Judge is on this occasion in no condition to preside in court. He has lost his wig, one of his emblems of office; his bald head is covered in bruises, which he says he got in a fall. The audience infers that the magistrate has been involved in some disreputable activity on the previous evening. It foresees that he will abuse his office in an effort to blame his own misdemeanours on someone else.

The facts of the case which the Judge is asked to try are that Eve, the prettiest girl in the village, has been caught with a man in her room. In the excitement a valuable jug, decorated with scenes from Dutch history, has been broken. Eve's mother says the rumpus began when she found Ruprecht, Eve's fiancé, in her daughter's bedroom. Ruprecht says that he burst in because he heard Eve in the bedroom talking to another man. There was a struggle; the jug was broken. The intruder escaped out of the window, but Ruprecht hit him on the head with the doorknob. The audience, hearing this detail, guesses how Judge Adam got his bruises. The Judge tries to divert suspicion on to others, but evidence that it was he, not Ruprecht, who tried to seduce Eve accumulates. Tracks in the snow show that the intruder had one normal foot and one shaped like a hoof, prompting the local witch to conclude that he was really the devil. But the Inspector notices that one of Adam's boots is oddly shaped. It emerges that Adam has one leg shorter than the other: the special boot made to fit the shorter leg has a hoof-shape. Finally the witch produces a wig, which was found caught in the vines on Eve's balcony. It is Adam's.

On one level, then, the play poses as a representation of reality. Realistic details of the kind later to be found in detective stories accumulate until the audience is in possession of a rational explanation of events. Yet on this rational level the play does not quite stand up to scrutiny. Would villagers, who proverbially notice everything about their neighbours, ignore for years the secret of Adam's deformed foot and oddly shaped boot, which the visiting Inspector notices at once? Equally revealing is the fact that the witch's hints of supernatural intervention, ridiculous on the realistic level, nevertheless influence the audience's reception of the play. The Judge, presented in the early scenes as a mere fallible human being, takes on a steadily more sinister cast. We hear that as he fled from Eve's bedroom his bald head seemed to glow in the dark, and his lame leg left the prints of a beast. And at the end of the play, when he flees from the courthouse after his exposure, Adam's aspect is less bestial than diabolical: 'Look, there he goes! Straight up the hill—as if, this time, the Devil really were abroad!' This is a blatant and enjoyable escape from reality: Adam is no longer a human figure but a carnival demon, a representative of discord who is to be cast out with joyous laughter. Yet at the same time there is, as is usually the case with comic demons, something attractive about him. He epitomizes the anarchic force which is always present beneath the calm surface of provincial life.

There are passages in *The Broken Jug* which evoke Netherlands village life in all its specificity. But they are only one source of the play's appeal. A more important aspect is the element of what Robert Scholes calls 'fabulation' or ethically directed fantasy. And the 'ethics' involved are not exclusively those of good and evil, of satire on the corrupt judge and praise for the impartial Inspector. Adam's failings, and Adam himself, are essentially comic: this carnival figure of anarchy and evil will be allowed back into the village, for the good reason that he is always there in any case and we cannot forgo the fun of expelling him again next year. At the opening of the play, as we have seen, hints are dropped that if Adam's corruption is exposed he may commit suicide, as another discredited local magistrate has done. But by the end this is seen to have been no more than a piece of artful deception designed to lure the audience into judging Adam's behaviour by the canons of everyday human motivation. By the final curtain the notion that Adam might commit suicide no longer looks plausible, because we are no longer thinking of him as a man but as a spirit of disorder. 'Reality' in its everyday sense seems to have been left behind.

In basing itself in reality while leaving an escape-route open to fantasy or carnival, Kleist's *Broken Jug* is in no way a special case. To demonstrate this we shall turn to another play about provincial life, J. M. Synge's *The Playboy of the Western World*, set on the west coast of Ireland. Synge was emphatic about the closeness of the relationship of his characters to observed reality. 'I wrote the *Playboy* directly, as a piece of life, without thinking, or caring to think, whether it was a comedy, tragedy, or extravaganza,' he told an admirer. Though perhaps a tragedy for Pegeen, the publican's daughter who finds and then loses 'the only Playboy of the Western World', it is otherwise for Christy, the weak-kneed youth who hardly dares speak to a woman at the beginning of the play, is lauded as a hero, tearaway, and swaggerer throughout the middle section, and becomes a genuine 'playboy' by the end. Christy's release from his father's domination through a rash blow with a shovel, his adoption as a romantic hero by a group of villagers who believe he has 'destroyed his da', and his final determination to live the roistering legend which his hosts have foisted on him, are comic triumphs. In particular, the play's handling of the rebellion of child against parent affords a neat illustration of Ludwig Jekels's theory that in comedy the Oedipal pattern is reversed with guilt displaced from the son on to the father. But to what extent is the play, as Synge thought, 'a piece of life'?

It opens in an atmosphere of turbulence and fear. Many people are said to be on the run from the police as a result of disturbances created by 'the broken harvest and the ended wars'. Pegeen resents being left alone in the house by her father; she fears 'the harvest boys with their tongues red for drink, and the ten tinkers is camped in the east glen, and the thousand militia—bad cess to them!—walking idle through the land'. These details seem calculated to anchor the play in Ireland at a particular time and place, and so they do; but an alert reader or auditor may notice that allusions to the troubled times decrease sharply after the first few exchanges. The movement away from historical precision is accompanied by a move away from seriousness and towards comedy. The initial impression of turbulence is swiftly replaced by one of timeless village calm in which drinking and yarning, rather than fighting, are the main activities. Some of Pegeen's speeches suggest that there is too little larrikinism rather than too much: 'Where now will you meet the like of Daneen Sullivan knocked the eye from a peeler; or Marcus Quin, God rest him, got six months for maiming ewes . . .?'

If the careful siting of the *Playboy* in time and place begins to look spurious, those aspects of Irish life which are less subject to change seem to be evoked more convincingly and more specifically than the details of Dutch life in *The Broken Jug*. The villagers can get drinks outside normal hours because they count as travellers: the shebeen is several miles away from the village by road, but only a step if you take the footpath across the stream. The goats leap off the hillsides on to the roofs of the crofts and crop the grass growing among the thatch. The widow Quin, if she cannot get Christy for a husband, will content herself with 'a mountainy ram, and a load of dung at Michaelmas' when he marries Pegeen. The quarrel between Christy and his father took place when they were 'digging spuds in his cold, sloping, stony, divil's patch of a field'.

Yet documentary realism quickly modulates into lyricism and myth. The widow Casey, to whom Old Mahon threatened to marry his son Christy, is 'a walking terror from beyond the hills, and she two score and five years, and two hundred-weights and five pounds in the weighing scales, with a limping leg on her, and a blinded eye, and she a woman of noted misbehaviour with the old and young'. This is a comic archetype, not a description of a real woman. The goats, the donkeys, the dung; the cowards, rouseabouts, priests, and witches; the hard-drinking publicans, wild barmaids, and formidable widows: all these, though no doubt they have their counterparts in the real world, take on mythic and symbolic overtones within the world of the play.

One of the play's most beguiling implications is, indeed, that the things of everyday can be taken up and refashioned, by whoever has the gift of narrative, into mythic or fantastic transformations of reality. The supreme example is Christy's description of the slaying of his father: even the first telling was an exaggeration (since the old man was never dead in the first place), but each repetition brings it further from reality and closer to the realm of art. Christy himself rises, as we watch, from a timid skulker behind hedgerows to a swaggerer and roisterer who means to 'go romancing through a romping lifetime from this hour to the dawning of the judgement day'. Our consciousness of Christy as a teller of tall stories may prevent us noticing that Synge is exercising the same art. The play itself, far from being realistic, is a tall story to end all others, an inverted Oedipus-legend whose hero enjoys, simultaneously, the benefits of killing his father and those of failing to do so, the sympathy accorded to the weak and the admiration reserved for the strong.

No doubt Synge was telling the truth when he wrote:

Anyone who has lived in real intimacy with the Irish peasantry will know that the wildest sayings and ideas in this play are tame indeed, compared with the fancies one may hear in any little hillside cabin in Geesala, or Carraroe, or Dingle Bay. . . .

But the word 'fancy', used here to denote something creative and imaginative, almost in the sense of 'fantasy', is revealing. Despite Synge's emphasis on the element of reality in *The Playboy of the Western World*, it should be obvious that the play depends just as heavily on imaginative transformations of reality. When Old Mahon declares: 'I'm after walking hundreds and long scores of miles, winning clean beds and the fill of my belly four times in the day, and I doing nothing but telling stories of that naked truth', we know that the truth was not naked but richly adorned. It is this kind of truth that wins the story-teller a bed for the night, and it is this kind of truth that pervades Synge's play.

Fantasy is sometimes considered as the antithesis of realism. Kathryn Hume, for example, describes fantasy in her book *Fantasy and Mimesis* as 'the deliberate departure from the limits of what is real and normal'. However, Hume sensibly adds: 'Departure from reality does not preclude comment upon it: indeed, this is one of fantasy's primary functions.' How, then, does Hume visualize the relationship between fantasy and comedy? There are times when, in contrast to the neo-classical critics quoted earlier, she seems to see a strong element of fantasy as characteristic of comic and humorous literature. 'Most humorous narratives', she suggests, 'build a world noticeably better than ours because funnier, but these worlds are not offered as if they might be real.' Hume is certainly right in suggesting that comic fantasy may comment on reality without necessarily reflecting it. And we have seen, from the examples so far considered, that fantasy is inclined to infiltrate even those comedies whose worlds are, in some respects, presented as if they might be real. What, though, of those more radical fantasies which deliberately emphasize their own remoteness from reality? How close is the connection of this kind of writing with comedy?

The fantasy of fantasies is, or was until recently, flight to other plancts. And it so happens that most of the earliest examples of fictions involving space travel are recognizably comic or satiric. Aristophanes in the fifth century BC, and Lucian in the second century AD, sent comical characters to Cloud-cuckoo-land, to the moon, and to the abodes of the gods. As late as the Renaissance period a comic-chivalric epic, Ariosto's *Orlando Furioso*, has the English knight Astolfo mounting a Hippogriff and flying to the moon, where the wits of those who have lost their senses are stored. Astolfo's aim is to recover the lost wits of his friend Orlando, but he also finds a remnant of his own wit which deserted him when he fell in love. Fantasies such as these took comedy, from a relatively early stage in its development, beyond the realm of the mundane and everyday in which Aristotle and Cicero sought to confine it. Yet they also commented, obliquely but unmistakably, on the everyday world.

More recently Italo Calvino, an admirer of Ariosto, has given us *Cosmicomics*, in which each chapter germinates from a scientific hypothesis about some stage in the creation or development of the universe. The first tale, for example, exploits the hypothesis that the moon was once much closer to the earth. The story is set in a time when human beings can row boats out to a position underneath the moon, put a ladder against it, and climb up. Inch by inch, however, the shining satellite drifts away, until the characters realize that they will have only one more chance to make the ascent. The narrator's deaf cousin, the best moon-walker of all, has always intuitively understood that the moon will one day cease to be accessible, and has not seemed to mind. But the wife of the Captain of the vessel on which the narrator travels, frustrated in her love for this magus, elects to stay on the moon as it floats away from the earth. (Perhaps she longs, as

Lacan would say, to become 'the scene of desire'.) There is nostalgia in this tale, a longing for a time of lost innocence, but there is also an undeniable element of comedy: Calvino attributes to early human beings the same self-delusions and unfulfillable longings that we experience today.

In an interview printed in his critical miscellany *The Literature Machine*, Calvino defended his practice of 'inventing human figures and language in the primeval void'. He sees this procedure as 'linked to one of primitive man's earliest explanations of the world: animism'. He also postulates a continuity between literary fantasy and scientific theory: for him it is 'no coincidence' that Ariosto, 'cosmic and lunary poet that he was', was admired by the scientist Galileo. The theories about the universe on which *Cosmicomics* is based consist of informed speculation, which is a type of fantasy: they look, in fact, rather like updated creation-myths. What is intriguing for our purposes is that Calvino's imaginative treatment of these theories, his recasting of them in fantastic, quasi-mythical form, should take on such a decisively comic colouring. Most of the comedy comes from the incongruity of imagining ordinary human beings trying to cope with great cosmic changes. The narrator, Qfwfq (who is more or less human most of the time, and is certainly always 'our' representative), is usually caught napping by them. In some stories he is confident that life will go on as before; in others he is aware that changes may take place, but his prediction of future developments is spectacularly wrong. He is, in fact, a normal thinking creature, as opposed to a genius: this makes him, in turn, an essentially comic, rather than tragic, figure.

The manner in which Calvino uses this fantastic creature to comment on real human concerns and affairs may be conveniently illustrated from the seventh story of *Cosmicomics*, set in a prehistoric period when some creatures have recently left the water to live on land. Qfwfq and most of his kinsfolk stand at this time near the middle of the evolutionary scale; they are much distressed that one eccentric uncle is lagging behind the rest of the family, having refused to leave the water. Qfwfq is especially troubled at having a relative who is still a fish: he has a girl-friend whose family has evolved even further than his own, and who can be expected to disapprove of the aquatic uncle's regressive tendencies. At last Qfwfq admits to his sweetheart that he has a relative who lives in the water, and introduces the two to one another. The result is the opposite of what he expected: his girl-friend decides to marry the uncle instead of the nephew, and goes back with him into the water.

Here we are clearly in the presence of 'significative' comedy. The tale ridicules those simplistic accounts of evolution which make it sound like a process of continuous forward movement. Calvino's story brings into play more recent and more flexible theories, according to which certain creatures, having at one stage emerged from the sea, went back to it several millennia later. Evidently one stage of evolution may be only relatively, not absolutely, preferable to others: change should perhaps be thought of in terms of a cycle or spiral, not a straight line. But if the story of the aquatic uncle satirizes certain versions of evolu-tionary theory, it also alludes impishly to everyday realities like snobbery and social climbing. The incongruity between two lev-els of interpretation, the cosmic and the parochial, is responsible for much of the humour. We owe these enjoyable comic effects to Calvino's recognition of what he calls, in *The Literature Machine*, 'the impossibility of thinking about the world except in terms of human figures or . . . human grimaces and human bab-blings'. Fantasy provides us with a more accessible, and more playful, means of speculating on the relations between ourselves and the rest of the universe than conventional scientific discourse can offer.

Comic fantasy, then, seldom consists of pure imaginative play: it offers a creative critique of our modes of thought, especially those (such as traditional objective science, utilitarian and positivistic philosophy, Cartesian logic, the analytic mind, behaviourist psychology) which seek to impose a rigid or unimaginative conception of reality upon humankind. Indeed it is no exaggeration to say that, when science fiction turns to satire and comedy, conventional science is its usual target. Thus in Woody Allen's film *The Sleeper*, where a man deep-frozen in the mid-twentieth century wakes up some centuries later, the hero announces scornfully, 'I don't believe in science. Science is an intellectual dead end. It's a lot of little guys in tweed suits getting up frauds on foundation grants.'

In Thomas Pynchon's grotesquely comic fantasy *Gravity's Rainbow* there are several hints that the truly great scientist passes beyond scientific 'reality' into the realm of intuition. Pointsman, one of the villains, who has sold himself to the system, reaches an age where he knows he will never be a great scientist, one who gets 'into It far enough to start talking about God', but will be 'left only with Cause and Effect, and the rest of his sterile armamentarium'. Elsewhere a lecturer in engineering (also, perhaps, a villain, but a more visionary one) tells his class: 'Whatever lip-service we may pay to Reason, . . . to moderation and compromise, nevertheless there remains the lion. A lion in each one of you. . . . The lion does not know subtleties and half-solutions. . . . You will never hear relativity from the lion. He wants the absolute. Life and death.' Fantasy, including comic fantasy, is as often as not a search for the absolute. It hints that the absolute, if attainable, is to be found in creativity, whether scientific, technological, or literary. It is not confined within the bounds of the 'real', since by definition our conception of reality at any given time concerns itself with what is, refusing what might be.

The examples we have considered show that it is possible for thoroughgoing fantasies, not merely works with incidental fantastic elements, to exist within the realm of comedy. Yet the relation of comedy to outright fantasy is by no means a close, much less an essential one. 'In contemporary French literary language', Calvino notes in his essay on fantasy in *The Literature Machine*, 'the term *fantastique* is used chiefly of horror stories.' If French writers and readers think first of horror stories when they hear the word 'fantasy' (a view which is borne out by Tzvetan Todorov's book on the fantastic, originally written in French), English ones probably think first of heroic-romantic epics such as Tolkien's *Lord of the Rings*. Neither group seems to make an immediate, intuitive connection between fantasy and comedy. And while it is easy for most people to name some outright comic fantasies when asked to do so, the instances which spring to mind are not very numerous. Of those which do, many are parodies of horror stories or romances: Mel Brooks's *Blazing Saddles* and *Young Frankenstein*; the Monty Python team's *Holy Grail* and *Life of Brian*; Roman Polanski's *The Fearless Vampire Killers*.

The examples of Jonson, Kleist, and Synge have already shown us that some of the best writers of comedy, including some who think of their art as rooted in everyday reality, admit non-realistic or fantastic elements into their work; the example of Calvino shows that comedy can at times become radically, not merely incidentally, fantastic. It seems, however, to be the case that outright fantasy is a byway in the development of comedy. In most comedies reality and fantasy are delicately blended: there is no clear predominance of one over the other.

11

Reflexive Comedy

Our last chapter discussed the relationships between reality and
fantasy, chiefly in relation to the content of novels and plays. We
shall now turn from content to form and methods of presentation. However, this topic is more closely connected with its prede-
cessor than it might at first appear. Certain ways of telling a
story, or presenting a play or film, seem rooted in relatively
simple and secure notions of the nature of reality. Representative
of these is the opening sentence of Jane Austen's *Emma*: 'Emma
Woodhouse, handsome, clever, and rich, with a comfortable
home and happy disposition seemed to unite some of the best
blessings of existence; and had lived nearly twenty-one years in
the world with very little to distress or vex her.' The appeal of this
style of narration lies partly in its air of confidence and control.
Austen does not demand passivity from her readers, or discour-
age their participation: from the first they are invited to make
decisions, such as whether a given statement is to be read innocently or ironically. And they are, in a sense, offered more than
one possible viewpoint, since different characters in the novel will
see things in different ways. But to questions such as, 'Is this
sentence ironical?' or 'Should I approve or disapprove of this
character?' there is generally a right and a wrong answer; we are
not expected to query the story-teller's implied ruling. The
author-narrator remains largely in control of the universe which
she has created. She also seems intent on creating a strong sense
of the reality of the characters, settings, and events which she
describes.

Jane Austen used this technique successfully in several comic
novels, and other authors have done so since her time. But earlier
writers of comic fiction, such as Fielding and Sterne, used a
different method. They used narrator-figures who, instead of
effacing themselves, addressed readers directly, teasing or
challenging them, arguing with them about interpretations of
motive and effect: they also reflected self-consciously, and at

length, on the art of story-telling. By coming into the open in this way the narrator loses his or her air of omniscience. And in the absence of a presiding figure who implicitly claims to know everything, readers are less inclined to take the nature of the fictional 'reality' for granted. Instead of fostering the illusion that the fictional world is real and self-contained, the narrator encourages us to stand back from the work, reflecting not only on the art and status of fiction but on the precarious nature of our grasp of reality.

Such techniques have come to be described as 'reflexive' or 'metafictional': their application to comedy is the subject of this chapter. Perhaps the first point which should be made about them is that they irritate some readers and auditors: Patricia Waugh acknowledges this when she heads one section of her book on metafiction with the query, 'Why are they saying such awful things about it?' One reason often assigned for the hostile comments is that they come from people who feel more secure with traditional objective narrative in which the self-effacing narrator exercises an unobtrusive control. Evidently some readers' sense of propriety and order is offended when characters in plays suddenly change places with members of the audience, when confusion arises in a novel between the main story and some inset narrative, when an author (or figure representing the author) makes a direct address to readers or audience, or when a character in a film within a film steps off the screen to join those in the outer film. Another common complaint is that the use of metafictional forms and techniques is a sign of narcissism on the part of the artist: writers, it is claimed, should not bore their readers with technical questions which are of interest chiefly to other writers.

It is not necessary, here, to offer answers to these objections which would apply to all varieties of reflexive writing. We are concerned with comedy, and it is clear that the comedy of many times and places has successfully exploited techniques for teasing, cajoling, or disorienting readers and auditors, for exchanging back-chat with them, and even for drawing them into the performance. It has played tricks based on illusion; it has made a joke out of the tenuousness of the grasp human beings have on reality. It has turned the world upside down. Meta-fictional techniques, which lend themselves to such procedures, are for that reason peculiarly suited to comedy. As for narcissism or self-consciousness, it is generally easier to accept when accompanied, as in comic forms of reflexive writing it often is, with a disarming self-mockery. Then, too, most of the wide range of metafictional situations (such as a writer or auditor drawn into a fiction, or a character from a film, play, or novel stepping out of it) are inherently incongruous, and thus full of comic potential. Finally, reflexive comedy is at least as successful as other forms of writing in encouraging readers to re-examine their ideas about life, art, history, and the relationships between them.

These last are explored in *Aunt Julia and the Scriptwriter* by the Peruvian novelist Mario Vargas Llosa, who approaches the problem of what happens when we write fiction by comparing it with what happens when we write 'news'. His main character, Mario, runs the news department of a small radio station, whose bulletins consist of rewritten versions of items selected from newspapers. This process would seem to leave little scope for creativity or for ideological squabbles. Yet when the work of Pascual, the assistant newscaster, is criticized, he behaves like any temperamental artist, protesting: 'The thing is, Don Mario, the two of us have entirely different conceptions of what news is.' Pascual's news bulletins are, indeed, as individual as works of art. His preference is for death, violence, and the grotesque: he has to be restrained from devoting 'a whole three o'clock bulletin to a battle between gravediggers and lepers in the exotic streets of Rawalpindi'. News, in his hands, comes to resemble sensational fiction.

In the second chapter Pascual is put in his place by Pedro Camacho, recently hired to write soap operas: Pedro, as he makes off with one of the news department's typewriters, informs Pascual loftily that art must take precedence over news. But what is Pedro's conception of art? Asked whether the noise of traffic will disturb his writing, he retorts: 'I write about life, and the impact of reality is crucial to my work.' What reality, though? Pedro has only just come to Lima from Bolivia, but instead of nosing about the streets to pick up material he uses a street map, classifying each district according to his conception (presumably derived from hearsay) of the types of people who live there. (One is marked 'Bums Fairies Hoodlums Hetaerae' and another 'Sailors Fishermen Sambos'.) Pedro does check with Mario to see if these labels strike him as more or less correct. But he shows little interest in Mario's answers, which are too sceptical for his liking: 'It's not *all* the people who live in each district', he objects, 'but only the flashiest, the most immediately noticeable, those who give each section of the city its particular flavour and colour.' Pedro's choices for his fictions are as slanted as Pascual's for his news broadcasts. Pascual's approach to the art of writing news and Pedro's approach to the art of fiction-writing are almost the same.

In *Aunt Julia and the Scriptwriter* the even-numbered chapters, apart from the last, are episodes from Camacho's serials. (Readers, however, are left to discover this for themselves: the distinction between the two levels of reality or fictionality is not immediately announced). Though the serials are highly coloured, we accept them as stories which might capture a large radio or (nowadays) television audience. Llosa's attitude towards such fiction, and towards the people who produce and consume it, is indulgent: elsewhere he has proclaimed, 'The greater the role that rebellion, violence, melodrama, and sex, expertly combined in a compact plot, have played in a novel, the greater its appeal has been to me.' The outer, framing fiction, with its affair between a teenage student and a relation-by-marriage who is in her thirties, is a little like a Camacho soap opera: the resemblance is commented on by Mario and Aunt Julia themselves. Mario, of course, is himself a writer, one who can never decide whether to put more realism or more fantasy into his stories. (His lover Aunt Julia and his friend Javier give him contradictory advice.) Where Mario and Javier are well-read, Camacho is a literary primitive: with him the history of fiction almost begins again. He is literate enough to write stories, but has read few by other authors: if at times he stumbles on methods, structures, and theoretical problems which have exercised earlier writers, that is (Llosa asks us to believe) only natural. So is the fact that his fictions take on a progressively more modern flavour: logical coherence gives way to the absurd. A young married woman whose Frenchness has been carefully established suddenly becomes Italian. A character who deals in pharmaceutical medicines becomes merged with another who sells rat poisons. The same individual dies by flood in one serial and by fire in another.

Public reactions to these developments are intriguing. The station-proprietors, father and son, both think Camacho is playing some abstruse literary game. The older man is worried, wishing that the scriptwriter would 'cut out these modernist gimmicks', but he fears that (unerring choice of the incongruously perfect word) it would not be 'realistic' to fire him. (Realism, this time, seems to denote whatever you think you can get away with.) The son, however, is elated by what he takes to be Pedro's daring adoption of modernist approaches, and feels vindicated when the confusions in the serials actually boost the ratings. But Camacho's confusions between characters are not in fact 'modernist gimmicks'; the fires, floods, and earthquakes in which he kills off the cast of one serial after another are due not to 'nerve' or 'realism' but to terror. The creator of these innumerable characters and multiple fictional worlds can no longer remember which characters belong in which serials: the final solution can only be a holocaust. Soon the creator and destroyer of all these fictional beings will be taken to an asylum. Readers are left to decide whether his disease is modernism or madness, or whether they are the same thing.

The fate of a man driven mad by prolonged immersion in his own fictions is not, on the face of it, very amusing. One reason for regarding *Aunt Julia and the Scriptwriter* as a genuinely comic novel is that the atmosphere established by the inventive humour is never dispelled by the death or incurable madness of any character in the outer story: Camacho emerges from his confinement, cured but much subdued, at the end of the book. Another important reason for the success of the novel as comedy is the narrator's skill in teasing his readers about the complexities of the relationships between life and fiction: he enjoys confronting his alter ego, the youthful Mario, with a problem which is so many-faceted that neither he nor any of his friends can solve it. The effect goes beyond incongruity to a wild, intoxicating confusion.

Confusion is also an important source of humour in Woody Allen's film *Stardust Memories*. Like Mario, the aspiring writer in Llosa's novel, the film-maker Sandy, a fictionalized version of Allen himself, is criticized by different people for opposite reasons. Discussing his new film with the female star, he finds that she thinks it sentimental ('There's good sentimental,' he protests) and unreal ('*Now* you're going to bring up realism!'). He has reason to be disconcerted, since the producers chided him for making things too real (by which they meant too preoccupied with the sadness of things). 'It's pretentious,' one of them complained, 'His insights are shallow and morbid. I've seen it all before. They try to document their private suffering and fob it off as art.'

Sandy's wish to abandon comedy for a cinema of commitment and significance will meet many such snubs. 'You want to do mankind a real service?' scoff the executives, 'Tell funnier jokes.' The same message lies behind an exchange with two disillusioned fans: 'We love your films.' 'I especially like the early, funny ones.' 'I don't want to make funny movies any more,' Sandy protests, 'They can't force me to. I don't feel funny. I look around the world and all I see is human suffering.' The producers retort that human suffering doesn't sell tickets in Kansas City. The only admirers of Sandy's serious work are a group of film buffs ('You're a master of despair!' 'What a touch of Kafka!'), but it is hard to value the admiration of people who can at times be so stupid and pretentious ('What do you think the significance of the Rolls-Royce was?' 'Er—I think it's meant to represent his car').

Stardust Memories, then, exemplifies that capacity for self-mockery which we have already identified as one of the chief virtues of reflexive comedy. Another virtue, which cannot be adequately illustrated by a single work, is that metafiction as a subspecies of comedy proves unexpectedly varied and adaptable. In *Stardust Memories*, for example, the focus is on the figure of the actor-director. But in another Allen film, *The Purple Rose of Cairo*, the anti-realistic, metafictional device is one by which a romantic character steps off the cinema screen into the life of a star-struck admirer. The effect here is a little like that of *Northanger Abbey*, where the lovably immature heroine has to learn not to confuse Gothic horror fiction with reality. (It is indicative of the lure exerted by metafictional devices that Jane Austen, too, should use them for comic effect.) Even if we read or see metafictional works by Llosa, Allen, and Stoppard in the same week, we are unlikely to experience a sense of repetition, since metafictional writing can work in many different ways: undermining certainties about the status of the audience; questioning the status of the author in relation to the work; exploring the changing roles of the actors or director. What nearly all of them have in common is the incongruity that arises from confusing different levels of fiction or reality which are usually thought to be distinct.

In sharp contrast to the reflexive pieces discussed so far is the recent British stage play *Noises Off* by Michael Frayn. It is a farce about a group of actors presenting a farce called *Nothing On*. One of the main reflexive gags is the technical brilliance needed to portray bad acting and disastrous theatrical mistakes. The fictional actors are portrayed as tired, neurotic, and second-rate; the real ones need to be energetic and talented, with an exceptional sense of timing. They must make out that they are floundering, drying, improvising, or blundering when they are really in total control. They must also represent, simultaneously, a behind-stage action, an on-stage action, and the relation between the two. For in the second act the set which the audience originally saw from the front is reversed and seen from the back: we are invited to watch what happens behind-stage while the 'inner' play is in progress, with its dialogue audible between, through, or over the dialogue of the 'outer' play. The first, second, and third acts all centre on presentations of the same farce: the first a last-minute rehearsal, the second a performance in the middle of the run, and the third a blessedly terminal presentation at the last staging-point of a provincial tour.

To analyse *Noises Off*, or to find 'meaning' in it, is to be haunted by the voice of Woody Allen's Sandy who, when asked an earnest question about the purpose behind his work, replied deflatingly that he just did it to make people laugh. Yet Allen's film explored, with sensitivity as well as humour, the theoretical and practical problems of film-making, and Frayn's play likewise explores the theoretical and practical problems of farce. At what is supposed to be the dress rehearsal of *Nothing On*, on the eve and early morning of the day when the play is due to open, the director is plagued by dim-witted actors raising questions which they should have had the sense to ask long ago or, alternatively, to suppress now:

FREDERICK. Lloyd, you know how stupid I am about moves. Sorry, Garry—sorry, Brooke—it's just my usual dimness. [*To Lloyd*] But why do I take the things into the study? Wouldn't it be more natural if I left them on? . . . I've never understood why he carries an overnight bag and a box of groceries into the study to look at the mail.

Freddie's query is at the same time very silly and very penetrating: it strikes at the heart of farce. It is stupid because it tries to apply Stanislavski's doctrine (the actor must live the part, understanding in the depth of his being the reasons for every action) to farce, a medium for which Stanislavski's method is entirely unsuitable. It is intelligent because it reveals farce's spasmodic reliance on certain aspects of realism (logic, causality, the world of everyday objects) and its simultaneous willingness to dispense, when necessary, with them. The true answer to Freddie's question is that in farce it is vital for objects to be in the right place at the right time. For the purposes of the inner farce, *Nothing On*, the right place for the bag and groceries is where the actor who is due to enter next will not fall over them. But for the outer farce, *Noises Off*, which makes fun of the incompetence of the actors in *Nothing On*, the right place for the props is precisely where the next person will fall over them. Alerted to the possibility of a pratfall, the audience has the pleasure of anticipating one later in the play.

Nothing On, in which the *Noises Off* characters are acting, uses all the most shop-worn devices of farce. Yet somehow the farcical jokes, old as they are, still work, assisted by the 'unintentional' humour of the actors' blunders. Farce thrives on deftly executed movements depending on props: clothes, bags, bottles, boxes, eatables, letters, wallets. These appear and disappear, pass mysteriously from one character to another, trip people over, betray the whereabouts of those who are pretending to be somewhere else, and infallibly end up in the bathroom or the bedroom when they are urgently needed in the kitchen. Frayn's characters manage to convey to us the jokes that would have sustained the inner play if the actors had got it right, while at the same time offering the different kind of amusement of a performance which goes disastrously wrong. Even more audaciously, the outer-play action itself develops into a farce, complete with ingenious variants of the same familiar gags. Flowers, whisky bottles, plates of sardines, and travelling-bags—some needed for the inner play, some not—are passed around in bewildering succession, usually to those who were not meant to get them. It is in the outer play, not the inner, that one character tips a plate of sardines over another, a third has to take his trousers down because he has sat on a cactus, and almost all are involved in tortuous love-affairs which they try to keep hidden from rivals or former partners.

Reflexive or metafictional techniques are, as we have seen, associated particularly closely with modern literature. Robert Scholes and other critics have traced their recent popularity to the decline of realism, positivism, and utilitarianism in the modern world and in modern thought: once we recognize that perfect objectivity is unattainable, we become more tolerant of the use by creative writers of mirror-effects, of Chinese-box effects, of multiple viewpoints, and in general of devices which place our grasp of reality in question. However, the main examples discussed here (a South American novel, a North American film, and a British play) do not suggest that appreciation of reflexive fiction need involve a headlong flight from reality or from that large proportion of the reading, play-going, or film-going public which is not made up of critics and philosophers. Reflexive comedy, in particular, need not be bleak or aridly intellectual: it can be amusing and beguiling. In some cases it may even provide an introduction to philosophical questions which might otherwise remain out of reach.

12

Absurd and Existential Comedy

Modern existentialist and absurdist theatre, to which we now turn, is haunted by the fear that human life may be trivial and meaningless. The characters often wonder whether a higher power may be watching them; generally they conclude that if there is such a power it is cynical, detached, or malignant. 'I believe', intones the heroine of Woody Allen's film *The Sleeper*, 'that there's someone out there who watches over us.' 'Unfortunately', sighs the hero, 'it's the government.' The joke is exhilarating but evasive. In true absurdist writing the threat of a brooding presence, or brooding absence, is both more powerful and more vague. To localize it, to ascribe it to something as finite and comprehensible as a government, is comforting but also facile. Our task in this chapter will be to decide whether a less facile, and more probing, consideration of the problem of the possible triviality or meaninglessness of existence can be made comic. We shall begin our investigation with a consideration of absurd drama.

In common usage, as Martin Esslin notes, the word 'absurd' means 'ridiculous'; but a more precise formulation is needed when discussing the literature of the absurd. With this in mind Esslin quotes Ionesco: 'Absurd is that which is devoid of purpose . . . Cut off from his religious, metaphysical, and transcendental roots, man is lost; all his actions become senseless, absurd, useless.' Purposelessness, rootlessness, and alienation from religion are indeed leading characteristics of absurdist writing. In Beckett's *Waiting for Godot* religious questions are debated, not because either main character has any religious belief, but in order to pass the time (which 'would have passed in any case'). Estragon's clearest childhood memories of the Bible relate not to any message of grace or redemption but to the cool, refreshing blue of the Dead Sea as illustrated in the maps. Godot, for whom Vladimir and Estragon are waiting, probably isn't God, probably won't come, probably doesn't exist. Nature offers no more hope than the supernatural. When an apparently dead tree puts forth a few leaves the characters respond with no more than a flicker of interest: they fear the pain of false hope. In the world of the play the landscape all looks the same. One character has been, he thinks, in the Macon country, but it could equally well have been the Cackon country. One of the few natural features mentioned is 'that bog'—but the bog in question is the theatre audience, towards whom the two tramps gesture derisively.

It is debatable, of course, whether such drama should be thought of as comedy at all. Morton Gurewitch describes it as 'the dark trollish buffoonery of the transcendental' in which 'comedy, confronting a void that tantalizingly and painfully refuses to be transformed into a cosmos,' drifts to the verge of its own destruction. However, even this guarded attempt to inscribe absurd drama under the rubric of comedy is slightly suspect. If we consider a dramatist like Harold Pinter, whose affinities with absurdism are only tenuous, we are liable to find that those elements in his work which are most absurd are also those which are least comic. Pinter has said that in *The Caretaker* he was chiefly interested in what lies beyond comedy. But the comedy of the play arises out of traditional ingredients such as the interaction of characters. What goes beyond comedy is the evocation of loneliness, rootlessness, and despair over the human condition.

In the work of Beckett and Ionesco, which is more resolutely 'absurdist' than Pinter's, these elements are much more prominent. Ionesco's plays are full of hints that reason and the use of language, instead of making human beings superior to animals, only make their condition more miserable by allowing them to perceive and express the futility and repetitiveness of the cycle of birth, reproduction, and death. In *Jacques, or Obedience* a young man asserts his individuality by refusing to eat the family's staple food of French fries and by rejecting Roberta, the young woman who is offered to him as a wife. ('She's not ugly enough. . . . I want one with three noses.') But when left alone with the second candidate for his hand, Roberta II, Jacques is seduced by her lyrical speeches in praise of horses (animal energy) and fire (passion). Once the two have pledged themselves to one another the family stealthily re-enters to bark, howl, and sniff around them, evidently satisfied that they have formed a new breeding couple within the pack. Jacques's gestures of independence were futile: the family has got its way. Even the exhilaration of Jacques's lyrical exchanges with Roberta has done no more than contribute to this inglorious end.

In the same playwright's *Rhinoceros* respectable people begin turning, one by one, into rhinoceroses, until only two human beings are left. The man, Bérenger, asks the woman, Daisy, to help him regenerate the human race by breeding children. But Daisy shows no interest in the project of regenerating humanity: she regards having children as 'a bore'. At last she slips away to join the rhinoceroses, whose snorts and bellows she is beginning to find more harmonious than human speech. Her lover is left alone. His last, forlorn cry is: 'I won't give in!' But there have been hints in the preceding speeches that in the last resort he would have joined the herd if he could. The conclusion is dark, and Ionesco does not disapprove of productions which make the play almost tragic. But he does not discount, either, those which play up its comic and grotesque elements; and, with a succession of ordinary, bourgeois characters turning into pachyderms during the course of the action, that is not hard to do.

This reminds us that, however remote they may seem from comedy in other ways, absurdist works often succeed in making people laugh. Ionesco professes to have been 'almost surprised to hear the laughter of the audience' at his first play *The Bald Prima Donna*: they 'took it all . . . quite happily, considering it a comedy . . . even a sort of rag . . . I imagined I had written something like the *tragedy of language*'. The play is certainly more than a 'rag', but to chide the audience for laughing is too harsh. Ionesco reduces the characters to a state close to that of automata. His Smith family possesses a clock which strikes seventeen at the beginning of the play, seven a few moments later, then three, then five, all in the course of the same short scene. In this same scene a longish conversation concerns a family whose members, male and female, are all called Bobby Watson. The attentions of a fireman who appears later in the play arouse the other characters' fears that he may bore them, though it is hard to see how their lives could be more boring than they are already. Narrative seems the sole source of excitement, sometimes provoking outbursts of violence or passion.

All this is undeniably suggestive of the decay of meaning and purpose in life, but it is also irresistibly incongruous: the characters' behaviour does not match their implied claim to belong to a purposeful, civilized order of beings. It is, indeed, the combination of inventive nonsense with threatening hints about the disintegration of humanity that is the distinctive feature of many of Ionesco's best plays. The very smallness and insignificance of human beings, with their pathetic muddles, their unfounded conviction of their own importance, and their occasional struggles to transcend the repetitive cycles of family and workplace, make them laughable.

In order to find the reason for this we must recall the three theories of laughter outlined in an earlier chapter. The theory of psychic release applies to very few absurdist plays. One play of Ionesco's, *Amédée or How to Get Rid of It*, does end with a fantasy of freedom: the central character leaves his repressive wife, and the city flat where a mysterious corpse grew and festered, then abruptly soars over the roof-tops and flies away. The sense of release which is experienced here is characteristic of comic endings, and justifies the description of *Amédée* as a comedy. But such celebratory conclusions are rare in absurdist drama and fiction, whereas laughter is common.

The theory that laughter is aroused by a feeling of superiority is a little more promising in approaching this body of work. The characters are usually made to appear small and helpless, and we are tempted to laugh at their puny struggles to achieve significance. But this vantage-point is hard to maintain. Discerning audiences are likely to alternate between a sense of superiority and a more uncomfortable feeling of kinship: at times we hear in the dialogue of the puppet-like figures, and see in their actions, an echo of our own voices and a mirror of our own behaviour.

It may, indeed, have been the tone of the laughter rather than laughter as such which really disturbed Ionesco at the first production of *The Bald Prima Donna*. If audiences enjoyed a feeling of carefree superiority as they laughed, they were missing an

important point. The 'tragedy of language', which Ionesco identified as one of the play's major themes, can arouse the laughter
of superiority only among those who assume complacently that
they are exempt from its effects. The same is true of humanity's
confusion in the face of an enigmatic universe, which is explored
in so many other absurdist works.

The most promising explanation for the element of comedy
found in so much absurdist fiction and drama lies in the theory
that laughter is stimulated by the perception of incongruity. The
specific incongruity in question is the gap between human
aspirations and human insignificance, between our image of ourselves and the reality. Beckett's plays, for example, are full of
striking images of stunted human lives. In *Endgame* Nagg and
Nell, two rather endearing old people, live out their declining
years in adjacent dustbins. *Happy Days* opens with a woman
embedded up to her waist in a mound: she evidently spends her
life there, turning over the contents of her huge black shopping
bag, chatting to herself and to her 'poor dear Willie', who lives in
a hole at the back of the mound. When the second act begins she
is embedded up to her neck; by this time the debilitated Willie is
taking longer and longer to respond to her conversational open-
ings, though he finally appears 'on all fours, dressed to kill—top
hat, morning coat, striped trousers, etc., white gloves in hand.
Very long Battle of Britain moustache.' If presented in realistic
terms the situations of Nagg, Nell, Winnie, and Willie would be
merely sordid and pathetic. But the extravagance of Beckett's
theatrical metaphors tempers the bleakness with an irresistible
incongruity.

To place such works in perspective we have only to recall that
there are absurdist plays which make no attempt to play on
incongruity and which offer their audiences little or no temptation to laugh. In Ionesco's *Tueur Sans Gages* (*The Motiveless
Killer*), for example, the absurd in the sense of that which is
purposeless or illogical is certainly present, since, as the title
indicates, there is no rational motive for the killer's crimes. But
here there is none of that sense of the ridiculous that characterizes
The Bald Prima Donna. In yet another Ionesco play, *Macbett*,
the only possible source of laughter is the incongruity between

Shakespeare's *Macbeth* and Ionesco's modernized version, which effects Bergsonian reduplications such as the balancing of Lady Macbeth against a new creation, Lady Duncan. As parody or travesty, then, *Macbett* can perhaps arouse laughter. However, readers who lay stress on the parody, as some English-speaking reviewers did when the play first appeared, may be guilty of the same kind of wrong emphasis as the audiences who regarded *The Bald Prima Donna* as a rag. Ionesco's chief aim in taking Shakespeare's play as a starting-point seems to have been to destroy the antithesis between good and bad characters, reducing all to the same state of ambition and ruthlessness. The laughter, if any, arises from the characters' pathetic self-absorption, from their unfounded belief that they are unique and privileged individuals when in fact they are hideous mirror-images of one another. To return from such a play to *The Bald Prima Donna* or even *Rhinoceros* is to be reminded that, when we austerely define the absurd in terms of what is purposeless rather than in terms of what is ridiculous, we have left something out. That which is purposeless can in some circumstances be made to look ridiculous. This effect is liable to be generated whenever blatant incongruities (human beings turning into rhinoceroses or taking up their abode in dustbins) are brought into play.

Rosette Lamont once remarked that, while both absurdism and existentialism sprang from a perception of the futility of modern humanity, the absurdists, unlike Sartre and his followers, offered no solution to despair. It would be worse than misleading to represent Sartre's existentialism as facilely optimistic: his philosophical work, and much of his drama, is full of harsh truths about the human condition and human relations. But Sartre, unlike Ionesco or Beckett, never abandons hope.

Existentialism's characteristic preoccupation is with individual freedom and authenticity. Mary Warnock writes,

Sartre wants, above all, to maintain the pure Existentialist dogma that we are what we choose to make ourselves, that we have no essences, no Human Nature, and no character that we did not confer upon ourselves. To believe that our characters are either given us from birth or formed inevitably by the events and circumstances of our early childhood is . . . to fall into Bad Faith . . . The function of Bad Faith . . . is to protect us

from the recognition of our own responsibility. If we are honest, . . . we
will recognize that nothing has formed our 'character', . . . except our
free choice.

The best-known example of Bad Faith in Sartre's work is his
portrait, in the second chapter of the first part of *Being and
Nothingness*, of the waiter who overacts his role. The waiter is a
little too deferential to the customers, a little too daring in his
manner of balancing his tray. He is playing at being a waiter. This
behaviour is dictated by the expectations of the public, who
require him, during working hours, to refrain from any action
which goes beyond what is demanded by his job.

What relates this example to our present concern is the comic
element in the exercise of bad faith. Sartre's language as he
describes the waiter ('inflexible rigour . . . automaton . . .
mechanism') is strongly reminiscent of Bergson's essay on the
comic, where rigidity and machine-like behaviour are identified
as prime causes of laughter. Bad faith, then, is always potentially
comical, absurd in the popular sense of ridiculous.

Sartre's most unambiguously comic work is *Kean*, based on
the life of the legendary English Regency actor. The original
Kean, by Alexandre Dumas Senior, was first performed in 1836.
Sartre, when questioned about his revision of Dumas's play, said
that in the course of it he had been led to 'reflect on the personality of what is called an actor'. His conclusion was that the actor
was 'the reverse of the player, who becomes a person like anyone
else when he has finished work, whereas the actor "plays himself" every second of his life'. The idea was expanded in Sartre's
essay on the comic actor. We may well conclude that, for Sartre,
the actor's bad faith is even more profound than that of the
waiter, since he acts even when he is not on stage. Sartre's Kean
makes himself king of the London stage but still does not feel
free. He is the creature of the London audience: he is even slave to
a dead man, William Shakespeare, whose scripts he follows and
whose reputation he keeps alive. The only way for him to assert
himself as a man is to stop being an actor. He does so (though
only briefly) in a richly comic scene where he breaks all the most
hallowed theatrical rules. He chooses to act opposite a pretty

amateur who forgets her lines; he steps out of his role and addresses insulting speeches to his patron, the Prince of Wales, who is in the audience.

Where the actor sacrifices freedom, the director aspires to an unattainable control. Control suggests godhead: the idea of the writer or director as the last quasi-divine figure in an otherwise godless universe pervades modern writing. Sandy, the film director in Woody Allen's *Stardust Memories*, longs to convince himself that art confers mastery. 'Only art you can control,' he cries, 'Only art and masturbation. Two areas in which I am an absolute expert.' The attempt to write, direct, and star in one's own films constitutes a more than usually thorough attempt to become God in one's own universe: in *Stardust Memories* the metaphor is omnipresent, but in every case it is manipulated in such a way as to subject Sandy's megalomania to ridicule. One sequence shows the child Sandy disrupting a religious play in which he has a part: he is jealous of the actor playing God, and looks down on Abraham for meekly agreeing to sacrifice his son Isaac at God's command. In adult life, reminded that it is odd for an atheist to be making an Easter film, Sandy replies that God accepts him as His loyal opposition. Elsewhere, when someone suggests that he is narcissistic, Sandy replies that if he associates himself with a mythological figure it is not Narcissus but Zeus.

God, then, is a figure whom Sandy successively yearns to replace, defy, deny, impersonate, and team up with. Towards the end he has a day-dream of being shot by a man who introduces himself as 'one of your greatest admirers': the sequence alludes transparently to the last meeting between Judas and Christ. In his day-dream, Sandy visualizes himself triumphing over death by winning a posthumous award for playing God in a film. But the triumph is spoiled by the admission that, since he did not have the right voice for God, the lines had to be dubbed with the voice of another actor. This despairing fantasy recalls Sandy's rage and frustration over the producers' decision to change the ending of his film without his authorization: somehow, godlike control over his creation keeps eluding him. The expectations of his audience and backers, not to speak of his own limitations, keep thrusting him back into comic roles, frustrating his longing to be taken seriously and to create more overtly 'significant' works. Perhaps the most powerful joke in *Stardust Memories* is the comic hubris which leads an energetic, talented, but irredeemably unheroic figure to entertain such titanic longings: to find the meaning of life, to halt entropic decay in the universe, to help others, to find true love, to achieve immortality, to stand in for God. What Sandy/Woody finds so hard to accept is that the diminutive, funny figure that he is is more lovable than the tragic colossus he would like to become. His small stature, like Cyrano de Bergerac's nose, stands forever between him and what he wants.

Doubt about the possibility of true freedom of action, of genuine emancipation from the role in which one is cast, haunts many modern comedies. In Stoppard's *Rosencrantz and Guildenstern are Dead*, for example, the two main characters seem ridiculous chiefly because of their inability or unwillingness to break out of their roles. Yet comfortable superiority to the ineffectual, articulate pair is hard to come by: their plight is too familiar. From the start, they are made to feel that some obscure destiny is manipulating them. In defiance of probability a tossed coin comes down heads ninety-eight times in sucession. Unnerved, the two offer a variety of explanations: 'Guilt. . . . Divine intervention. . . . Chance. . . . Fate. . . . We have no control.'

Such echoes of the language of tragedy reverberate through the early part of the play: the audience is constantly encouraged to compare Stoppard's travesty with its Shakespearian original. A question then arises as to why, when the fate of Hamlet was seen as tragic, those of Rosencrantz and Guildenstern are not. Part of what makes Stoppard's play comic rather than tragic is, no doubt, the high incidence of wit and jesting. But the participants' refusal to struggle, their resigned certainty of their own impotence and unimportance, their spineless acceptance of annihilation by forces greater than themselves, contributes just as strongly to the comic effect. Like the audience of classical tragedy, Rosencrantz and Guildenstern sometimes try to tell themselves that there is reason and purpose in existence, and that whatever power is controlling them will show them what to do: 'We have not been . . . picked out . . . simply to be abandoned

. . . set loose to find our own way . . . We are entitled to some direction.' 'Direction' here is what a theatrical director gives a company: Rosencrantz and Guildenstern often suspect that they are unconsciously acting out parts which have been written for them in advance. But 'direction' in a lived situation is precisely what existentialism warns us not to desire or expect; the first step to freedom is to accept the non-existence of any ordering force. The subtlest temptation to inaction is the fear that an act of defiance may be just what 'they' are counting on: as Guildenstern puts it, 'our spontaneity' might turn out to be 'part of their order'.

This deep paranoia, this sense that our lives are spent in gambols on the edge of an abyss where we may be, almost sadistically, allowed to play for a while also pervades Thomas Pynchon's nightmarish comic fantasy *Gravity's Rainbow*. Here again we meet characters pondering Rosencrantz and Guildenstern's problem: 'At the moment I'm involved with the "Nature of Freedom" drill you know, wondering if *any* action of mine is truly my own, or if I always do only what They want me to do . . . regardless of what I *believe*, you see.' The mysterious wielders of money and power will perhaps tolerate the swashbuckling dissidents for their own amusement:

The failed Counterforce, the glamorous ex-rebels, half-suspected but still enjoying official immunity and sly love, camera-worthy wherever they carry on . . . doomed pet freaks.

They will use us. We will help legitimize Them, though They don't need it really, it's another dividend for Them, nice but not crucial.

Here the rebel, the dissenter, becomes reduced in his own eyes to the status of a comic buffoon, whose criticisms of the social order, and harmless lashings out at it, are permitted and even enjoyed because they are harmless. For Slothrop, the dynamic, half-wise jester and escapee, rebellion against authority and the father will not apparently lead to mystic union with any figure or entity representing mother, wife, or nature of the kind that Charles Mauron leads us to expect in comedy. Slothrop's destiny, it is hinted, is 'a long and scuffling future', 'mediocrity', with no 'clear happiness or redeeming cataclysm'. This absence of consummation is characteristic of modern comedy: plays and novels end inconclusively or in a ridiculous, undignified death.

Once again we must ask how such fables can be called comic. Incongruity, which we have already used to account for the element of humour and comedy in some absurdist and existentialist fictions, is still powerfully present in such later works as *Gravity's Rainbow*, and the incongruities that Pynchon exploits are not unlike those that surrounded the dramatic characters of Stoppard, Ionesco, or Sartre. A small creature endowed with large aspirations, unable to control its universe or even to understand what forces do control it, is incongruous and thus potentially ridiculous. And the gradual reduction of the struggling hero to the status of a fool or buffoon, with all the undignified connotations carried by the role, confers on the fable a further affinity with comedy. But somewhere behind *Gravity's Rainbow*, as behind Beckett's *Waiting for Godot* and Stoppard's *Rosencrantz and Guildenstern are Dead*, lies another concept: even if we have no liberty to act, it should still be possible for us to play. In *Waiting for Godot*, Vladimir and Estragon pass the time with jokes and music-hall routines. In Stoppard's play, Rosencrantz and Guildenstern engage in brilliant and inventive word games. In *Gravity's Rainbow* Slothrop's role of buffoon likewise brings laughter and enjoyment to his life, whether he is currently disguised as a comic-strip hero or hidden beneath the costume of a pig-spirit from a provincial carnival.

Though Slothrop looks as if he may succumb to fatalism, there still exists the paradoxical possibility that his fatalism may give him his freedom. The case is analogous to that of Jacques the Fatalist in Diderot's eighteenth-century comic novel. Jacques is convinced that whatever he does will make no difference: he can exercise no significant influence on his environment or on his fate. The obvious response is to relax and follow his feelings: *fays ce que vouldras*, as Rabelais would say. And by following this maxim Jacques achieves an odd kind of liberty, a freeing from responsibility and guilt. The same seems to be true of the Player in *Rosencrantz and Guildenstern are Dead*, whose advice to the worried pair is: 'Relax. Respond. That's what people do. You can't go through life questioning your situation at every turn.' It is this insight that makes the Player the most assured of all the characters. He knows his way around in this stage-play world: 'I can come and go as I please. . . . I've been here before.' He has little influence over what happens to him, but some over his own responses to his fate.

As intimations of what may lie beyond existentialism and absurdism, or as new approaches to the problem of the relation between the human individual and any wider reality, the formulations arrived at by Pynchon's Slothrop, Diderot's Jacques, and Stoppard's player are not exactly encouraging. But the characters who utter them are more vigorous, less world-weary, more full of laughter and exhilaration than Vladimir and Estragon: like Kean they retain a sense of the worth, or at least the fun, of life, that shadowy comic performance, for its own theatrical sake.

13

Festivity

In the course of the twentieth century, comedy has increasingly been regarded as a manifestation of festivity or carnival. Among literary critics who have adopted this approach are F. M. Cornford, in his study of ancient Greek comedy, and C. L. Barber, in his book on Shakespearian comedy. The historian Peter Burke agrees, naming the performance of a play, usually a farce, as one of three recurrent elements in carnival. In this chapter we shall consider the relationship and its implications.

One of the most widespread characteristics of festivity is the temporary inversion of social order. Mircea Eliade describes an ancient Babylonian festival which represented dramatically 'the abolition of past time, the restoration of primordial chaos, and the repetition of the cosmogonic act'. There was 'enthronement of a "carnival" king, "humiliation" of the real sovereign. . . . The slaves became the masters.' Every feature suggested 'universal confusion, the abolition of order and hierarchy, "orgy", chaos'. Yet all this prepared for 'a new and regenerated human species'. Parallel instances of festive anarchy are found in many other cultures and in much later times. In carnival, as in farce and comedy, the reversal of order is often accompanied by mockery, victimization, and practical jokes. In some cultures, as Frazer shows, there have been human sacrifices. In early modern Europe, festivals often ended with a trial and mock-execution of the spirit of carnival. In carnival and other forms of festivity the authority-figure, the serious person, is mocked. But at the end of the festive period the tables are turned, authority is reasserted, and the representatives of riot and anarchy are subjected to a real or symbolic punishment. This raises disturbing questions about the nature and functions of festivity.

Some late twentieth-century writers, such as Barber, have argued that laughter and festive licence act as safety-valves: by releasing dangerous social pressures, they help to preserve the established order from destruction. Others, such as Victor

Turner, have argued that relaxation from seriousness and work may lead to creative questioning of established order and may bring about radical change. Turner holds that 'antistructural' activities can 'generate and store a plurality of alternative models for living, from utopias to programs, which are capable of influencing the behaviour of those in mainstream social and political roles . . . in the direction of radical change, just as much as they can serve as instruments of political control'. This is reminiscent of some suggestions made many years earlier by George Bernard Shaw. The hero of a Shaw novel saw humour and laughter, rather than sober reason, as productive of creative change: he saw advances in knowledge as brought 'by instalments in the form of fictions, hypotheses, or jokes'. One of Shaw's dramatic characters likewise proclaims: 'Every jest is an earnest in the womb of time.' Quoting this remark approvingly in *The Quintessence of Ibsenism*, Shaw adds, 'All very serious revolutionary propositions began as huge jokes. Otherwise they would be stamped out by the lynching of their first exponents.'

It would be pleasant to think of comedy and laughter contributing to the good of humanity in such a creative way. Let us see, though, what fate the Shaw/Turner theory meets at the hands of a more recent writer. In Kurt Vonnegut's comic fable *Galapagos* the most serious joke is that the big brains of humans are an evolutionary disadvantage. Mary, the most likeable character, believes that there is 'no harm, and possibly a lot of good, in people's playing with all sorts of ideas in their heads . . . Mental games played with even the trashiest ideas had led to many of the most significant scientific insights.' But the narrator's comment is discouraging:

Those old-time big brains . . . would tell their owners, in effect, 'Here is a crazy thing we could actually do, probably, but we would never do it, of course. It's just fun to think about.'

And then, as though in trances, the people would really do it—have slaves fight each other to death in the Collosseum, . . . or build factories whose only purpose was to kill people in industrial quantities.

This does not, of course, prove that the results of mental *bricolage* are always catastrophic, but it should give pause to those who would argue that they must necessarily be good.

Recent work in various disciplines displays a growing scepticism about the notion of comedy, play, and carnival as redemptive and liberating. 'Bakhtin', observes Umberto Eco, 'was right in seeing the manifestation of a profound drive towards liberation and subversion in Medieval carnival. The hyper-Bakhtinian ideology of carnival as *actual* liberation may, however, be wrong.' Peter Burke, Michael Bristol, and Terry Castle all offer historic examples of carnivals which helped bring about actual liberation, but all seem unhappily aware that they constitute exceptions rather than the basis for a rule. Turner, too, implicitly admits that festivity can be used as an instrument of political control: what he pleads for is a recognition that it need not always function in that way.

Among comedies there is at least one which, instead of reconciling audiences to their lot, seems to have strengthened their determination to change the system under which they lived. In Beaumarchais's *Marriage of Figaro* the professedly liberal Count begins to regret giving up the traditional right of the landowner to spend the first night with any bride whose marriage is celebrated within his domains. Figaro, learning from his betrothed that the Count has been paying her unwanted attentions, appears before him with a crowd of other servants to congratulate him on renouncing the old privilege. He even asks the Count to present to Suzanne, in public, the ceremonial head-dress made of white feathers and ribbons, emblem of bridal virginity. This ceremony, Figaro suggests, should be performed at all marriages on the estate, with a song to recall the Count's goodness in abolishing the bad old custom. Figaro's gesture amounts to more than a deft way of shaming the Count into sparing Suzanne. It appropriates a traditional festivity, the rustic wedding, to make it sanction the aspirations of servants and peasants while discrediting the nobility's exploitation of them. It reveals the servant Figaro as a bolder and cleverer man than his master.

The Marriage of Figaro was regarded in its own time as an incitement to revolution, and it still provides a convincing example of the revolutionary potential of both comedy and festivity. But parallels to it are rare. Overall there is little to suggest that festivity has much potential for revolutionary change. Much more plausible is the implication in Marquez's description of mulatto festivities in *Love in the Time of Cholera*:

On Saturdays the poor mulattoes . . . tumultuously abandoned their hovels of cardboard and tin on the edges of the swamps and in jubilant assault took over the rocky beaches of the colonial district . . . During the weekend they danced without mercy, drank themselves blind on home-brewed alcohol, made wild love among the icaco plants, and on Sunday at midnight broke up their own party with bloody free-for-alls.

This is exuberant and exhilarating, but not instinct with potential for creative change. In the same passage Marquez describes the land as standing 'unchanging on the edge of time'; nothing has happened there for four centuries except 'a slow ageing among withered laurels and putrefying swamps'. Mulatto festivities are conceived as part of an essentially unchanging cycle.

The idea that comedy, as a literary mode, has revolutionary potential may owe something to Schiller, who associated it with freedom. However, there is little to indicate that Schiller was referring specifically to political freedom. And when Northrop Frye, in the twentieth century, tries to improve on Schiller by arguing that the ending of a comedy celebrates a new social order, his argument suffers from the examples he cites. The endings in question are those where a young man achieves a desired marriage in the face of opposition from an older man: this is not a new order, but a readjustment of the old. In other comedies the indiscretions committed in festive settings do have lasting results (in Jonson's *Bartholomew Fair* the foolish Cokes is tricked out of his money and his intended wife) but once again these disruptions work at the level of individual rivalry, not that of social reform. In so far as comedy does stimulate change it is, as Calvino suggested, the comedy of fantasy that does so, not the comedy of festivity.

Where festivity is concerned, the safety-valve theory still seems more plausible than the theory of creative change. It certainly seems to have the support of creative writers, including many with a pronounced comic talent. The early chapters of Heller's

Catch-22 display a world of war which, though dedicated to the destruction of human beings, provides havens of carnival plenty and enjoyment: the hospital, the mess-hall, the bawdy-house. In the mess-hall there is

shish-kabob . . . huge savory hunks of spitted meat sizzling like the devil over charcoal after marinating for seventy-two hours in a secret mixture Milo had stolen from a crooked trader in the Levant, served with Iranian rice and asparagus tips Parmesan . . . Yossarian wondered awhile if it wasn't perhaps all worth it. But then he burped and remembered that they were trying to kill him, and he sprinted out of the mess hall and ran looking for Doc Daneeka to have himself taken off combat duty and sent home.

The hospital is much the same: inside there is plenty to eat and plenty to laugh at, but Yossarian cannot be happy because outside there is 'still nothing funny going on'.

Intrusions of the outside world on the world of laughter and feasting do not at first stir Yossarian to revolt. What finally achieves this is the authorities' progressive desecration of the festive locales that their own military machine has created. Milo, the catering officer, becomes so involved in the black market that he lets the standards of the mess-hall decline, and even tries to make the troops eat a consignment of Egyptian cotton which he has rashly bought. In the hospital, one of Yossarian's friends is kidnapped and never heard of again. In Rome, the idyllic bawdy-house is smashed by the military police and the women dispersed. Walking through the city, now an inferno rather than a carnival paradise, Yossarian longs for the consolation of a woman, but the impulse is short-lived: 'The girls were all gone . . . He had grown too old for fun, he no longer had the time.' The era of youth and festivity is over; the moment for resistance has come. The sequence is weirdly reminiscent of some passages in Peter Burke's book, suggesting that Lent (the period of abstinence) and not the preceding carnival (the time of festivity) is what begets revolutionary action. (Another valid inference from Burke's evidence, though it is one that Burke himself resists, is that the serious puritan reformers, not the carefree revellers, were the

initiators of revolutionary change.) In the early part of *Catch-22*
the men enjoy enough revelry to keep them docile. As the climate
changes, and the safety-valves begin to close, their resistance
stiffens.

A more recent novel, Milan Kundera's *The Book of Laughter
and Forgetting*, offers an antithesis between two kinds of laughter, the devil's and the angel's. (Kundera, after the manner of
Blake, implicitly invites his readers to take the devil's side.) The
devil's laughter came first; its target was the angel's world of total
order and meaning. The angel countered the devil's invention
with a new laughter, expressing delight in absolute order and
rationality. The archetypal image of angelic laughter and rejoic-
ing is that of losing oneself in a festive group with 'a single body
and a single soul, a single ring and a single dance'. The narrator
describes one such group which assembled for 'one or another of
those anniversaries of God knows what' in the streets of Prague
in 1950. It was 'the day after Milada Horakova had been hanged.
She had been a National Assembly representative of the Socialist
Party, and a Communist court had charged her with plotting to
overthrow the state.' The young Czechs at the celebration 'went
on dancing and dancing, and they danced all the more frantically
because their dance was the manifestation of their innocence, the
purity that shone forth so brilliantly against the black villainy of
the two public enemies'. Such official, collective celebrations
invite a submergence of individual personality and responsibility
in which the group first dissociates itself from the outsiders and
then forgets them. Hence Kundera's title *The Book of Laughter
and Forgetting*, a reminder that laughter and carnival can cease
to be, as in Bakhtin's vision, expressions of the spontaneous
impulses of the people, and can be appropriated by a government
which aspires to erase inconvenient memories from people's
minds.

Later in Kundera's book the narrator describes a speech delivered by President Husak, 'the President of forgetting' as he is
ironically called, to a group of schoolchildren. Husak likes to be
thought of as president of the eternal, not the ephemeral. (But
'history is a succession of ephemeral changes'. A preference for
the eternal may be made a pretext for ignoring history.) 'He is on

the side of children, and children are life, and life is "seeing, hearing, eating, drinking, urinating, defecating, diving into water and observing the firmament, laughing, and crying".' This summary of Husak's credo makes it sound rather like Bakhtin's, and in fact that is just what Kundera means by saying that the prim angel's laughter is a deceptive imitation of the genial devil's. (We recall Bakhtin's comments on the warmth and friendliness of devils and hell.) Husak reminds the children that they are the future. Behind this statement the narrator detects a sinister meaning, namely that 'mankind is moving more and more in the direction of infancy, and childhood is the image of the future'. Husak approves of this movement because children can easily be persuaded to turn against an undesirable outsider: the operation of punishing a scapegoat is carried on within the framework of a festivity or game. Elsewhere in Kundera's book a young woman dissenter is exiled to an island inhabited entirely by children. At first the children enjoy having an adult to join in their games, but later they turn on her and hound her to death.

This is only one of many instances in literature of the idea that a festive group defines itself in relation to the rejected or persecuted outsider. In W. H. Auden's 'The Sea and the Mirror' a figure based on Shakespeare's Caliban observes, 'Without a despised or dreaded Them to turn the back *on*, there could be no intimate affectionate Us to turn the eye *to* . . . Without these prohibitive frontiers we should never know who we were or what we wanted.' John Barth, in his fable of the universe as a university, credits a different kind of outsider with a similar insight. 'The way the campus works there's gotta be goats for the sheep to drive out, ja?' argues Max, the gentle educator and martyr, 'If they don't fail us they fail themselves, and then nobody passes.' The more closely we examine both comedy and carnival, the more deeply penetrated by scapegoating and victimization they seem to be. Even Bernard Shaw, whom we have seen putting forward an optimistic theory of the creativity of jokes and humour, could call 'booking seats to shout with laughter at a farcical comedy' a 'deliberate indulgence of that horrible, derisive joy in humiliation and suffering which is the beastliest element in human nature'. In the 1980s Umberto Eco goes further: 'Comic is always racist: only the others, the Barbarians, are supposed to pay.'

Eco, as we have seen, is inclined to reject the idea of comedy and carnival as bringing 'actual liberation'. Indeed, where Kundera sees laughter and carnival being appropriated by totalitarian governments for their own purposes, Eco sees it being exploited in the interests of commerce: 'To support the universe of business, there is no business like show business. Therefore, there is something wrong with [the] theory of cosmic carnivalization as global liberation. There is some diabolic trick in the appeal to the great cosmic/comic carnival.' Of the theory of comedy and carnival as creative transgression Eco writes, 'Such a transgressional theory has many opportunities to be popular, today . . . It sounds very aristocratic. There is but one suspicion to pollute our enthusiasm: the theory is unfortunately false.'

14

Laughter or Harmony?

Early in this book it was suggested that in comedy the potentially disruptive force of laughter was at odds with the movement of the comic fable towards reconciliation, harmony, and acceptance of the world. At the time, however, it seemed best to postpone detailed consideration of this problem until other aspects of comedy had been treated. Examination of these confirmed the original analysis. Among forces within comedy which were seen to work against harmony were jokes against marriage and the family; triumphant and admiring laughter at the exploits of rogues and tricksters; merriment in the face of death and decay; exploitation of the subversive and disruptive possibilities inherent in human language; a temptation to deride, as well as sympathize with, diminutive human beings faced with a cruel or indifferent universe; and mocking laughter against those considered worthy of expulsion from a festive group. We shall now explore the conflict between laughter and harmony a little further, principally through an analysis of two specific works. The first is a dramatic comedy, Shakespeare's *The Merchant of Venice*. The second is a philosophical essay, Bergson's 'Laughter'.

In the first scene of *The Merchant of Venice* Graziano rallies Antonio on his sad demeanour, and the two engage in a friendly argument about the relative merits of hilarity and gravity:

> ANTONIO. I hold the world but as the world, Graziano,
> A stage, where every man must play a part,
> And mine a sad one.
> GRAZIANO.   Let me play the fool.
> With mirth and laughter let old wrinkles come,
> And let my liver rather heat with wine
> Than my heart cool with mortifying groans.
> Why should a man whose blood is warm within
> Sit like his grandsire, cut in alabaster . . .?
> There are a sort of men whose visages

> Do cream and mantle like a standing pond,
> And do a wilful stillness entertain
> With purpose to be dressed in an opinion
> Of wisdom, gravity, profound conceit . . .

It is tempting to take Graziano's speech as a statement of the value-system of comedy, which often seems to celebrate foolery rather than wisdom, livers warmed with wine rather than faces that 'cream and mantle like a standing pond'. But that would be premature, for in the course of the play Graziano's doctrine is called in question. Graziano praises gaiety, and dismisses sobriety as a mask put on to delude others. But the other young people in the play do not go so far. Solanio is no fonder of those who 'will evermore peep through their eyes | And laugh like parrots at a bagpiper' than of their opposites, who will not 'show their teeth in way of smile | Though Nestor swear the jest be laughable'. And Bassanio thinks of the laughter-loving Graziano as someone who speaks 'an infinite deal of nothing'.

Graziano, in the first act of the play, sees refusal of laughter as a denial of life. But in the last act Lorenzo detects denial of life in 'the man that hath no music in himself', not in the man who never laughs. As he and Jessica gaze on the stars, they reflect that music and laughter are antipathetic to one another:

> JESSICA. I am never merry when I hear sweet music.
> LORENZO. The reason is your spirits are attentive,
> For do but note a wild and wanton herd
> Or race of youthful and unhandled colts,
> Fetching mad bounds, bellowing and neighing loud,
> Which is the hot condition of their blood,
> If they but hear perchance a trumpet sound,
> Or any air of music touch their ears,
> You shall perceive them make a mutual stand,
> Their savage eyes turned to a modest gaze
> By the sweet power of music.

When Lorenzo begins to speak of 'youthful and unhandled colts' being tamed by the power of music, we may recall that several of the exuberant young men of the opening scene are now, in the final act, preparing to submit themselves to the order and harmony of marriage. There are some jokes about marital infidelity in this last act, but they are of the kind that seem designed to ward off, or warn against, actual infidelities. Laughter is present, then, but it is subordinated to harmony. It is true that in the course of the earlier acts the festive group has defined itself by its opposition to Shylock, an outsider. But there have been few attempts to treat Shylock as an object of ridicule: he has even been given speeches which have aroused sympathy rather than laughter, such as the celebrated 'Hath not a Jew eyes? . . . If you prick us do we not bleed? If you tickle us do we not laugh?' I do not wish to suggest here that in *The Merchant of Venice* Shakespeare satisfactorily solves the problem of the scapegoat. What I do wish to show is that this play, a comedy from the point of view that it moves towards a harmonious ending, not only refrains from exalting laughter but also shows a strong consciousness of its dangers and limitations.

Such a consciousness is not as alien to comedy as we might think. Whereas an individual joke may deride an absent or fictional victim without thought for consequences, the comic fable cannot easily avoid the question of the likely effects of derision on the scapegoat or outsider, the target of laughter. At the end of Noel Coward's *Design for Living* Ernest, who has married Gilda in the hope of settling her down and keeping her to himself, has her stolen back from him by two of her former lovers. At the end of the play Ernest stamps off stage 'quite beside himself with fury', and falls over a package of canvases on the way out. 'This is too much for Gilda and Otto and Leo,' the stage direction continues, 'they break down utterly and roar with laughter. They groan and weep with laughter . . .' Some audiences found this ending unsettling because it seemed to be mocking the defeated Ernest. Coward's explanation in his preface ('I as author . . . prefer to think that Gilda and Otto and Leo were laughing at themselves') is unlikely to convince those who take the helpless laughter of the three scapegraces as mockery of Ernest. Comedy often takes the form of a contest in which some characters win while others lose: the impulse to laugh at the losers always conflicts to some degree with the wish to see them drawn back into the festive group to share the harmonious conclusion.

Let us turn now to Bergson's essay. Since his topic is laughter, not comedy, Bergson finds little occasion to consider comic form, the movement from discord or difficulty to a state of harmony or joy. In the last act of *The Merchant of Venice*, and to a lesser extent in many other comedies, the characters are overtaken by emotion, even rapture. But Bergson insists, in a now-famous phrase, that 'laughter has no greater foe than emotion'. 'I do not mean', he continues, 'that we could not laugh at a person who inspires us with pity, for instance, or even with affection, but in such a case we must, for the moment, put our affection out of court and impose silence on our pity.' We can think of comedies to which this applies, but they do not include Chaplin's or Shakespeare's.

In an earlier chapter we saw the philosopher Bernard Mandeville suggesting: 'If a man falls or hurts himself so slightly that it moves not [compassion], we laugh, and here our pity and malice shake us alternately.' This goes some way towards solving our problem. Mandeville does not suggest that the two feelings can blend, but he does seem to believe that they can succeed one another very rapidly. This, however, still leaves us with the notion of conflicting elements within comedy or within situations which generate laughter.

One possible way out of the difficulty is to argue that, where comedy is concerned, our laughter does no harm because we are laughing at fictional characters. Thus the English Romantic critic Charles Lamb, writing of English Restoration comedy, argued that its charm consisted precisely in 'the escape from life—the oblivion of consequences—the holiday barring out of the pedant Reflection'. The bane of comic drama in his own time, Lamb felt, was its infiltration by seriousness, in other words by compassion and morality; this in turn was due to the failure of audiences and actors to separate the fictional from the real. 'We substitute a real for a dramatic person, and judge him accordingly. . . . We cling to the painful necessities of shame and blame. We would indict our very dreams.' The Romantic actor mistakenly tries to elicit sympathy for the distresses of comic victims such as Sheridan's Sir Peter Teazle, but only succeeds in making the audience uncomfortable. He would do better, Lamb suggests, to play for laughs.

Lamb seems here to be implying, as Bergson was later to do, that feeling is fatal to laughter; in doing so he comes close to arguing that comedy offers us a respite from feeling. However, in another equally famous essay Lamb commends a spectacular breach of his own rule, an interpretation of Shakespeare's Malvolio which turned this comic victim into an object of compassion, a tragic figure. Laughter may at times be able to cut itself off from feeling: comedy, it seems, cannot.

There are differences as well as similarities between Bergson's view of laughter and Lamb's. Where Lamb, in his essay on Restoration comedy, accepts scornful laughter in the theatre because its targets are imaginary characters rather than real ones, Bergson largely ignores this distinction. He holds that scornful laughter affects actual living, helping to preserve the adaptability of people in society. Thus laughter, though harsh, is healthful: it acts as a check on tendencies that are harmful to life. Lamb experiences 'artificial comedy', with its laughter at fictional butts, as a relaxation from the stresses of the real world. But for Bergson it is sympathy that constitutes a relaxation from the task undertaken by laughter, namely that of protecting humankind from rigidity. The comic butt is someone who has lost elasticity, adaptability, a quality which has a species-preserving function. When the mind relaxes to admit sympathy for those who have succumbed to rigidity, it is shirking its obligation to preserve humanity from degeneration by means of ridicule. Laughter, for Bergson, is a duty which may only be abandoned during brief moments of self-indulgence.

The debate about scornful laughter was taken a stage further by Sartre. 'A cuckold', Sartre writes, 'is of course absolutely ludicrous; but if he is my brother and I know that he is suffering, I am very liable to display a suspect compassion for him.' Evidently Sartre, like Bergson, sees ridicule of the cuckold or other butt as a more authentic response than sympathy, which is 'suspect'. But he notes that in social life we are obliged to suppress derisive laughter; this means that, if we wish to enjoy it, we must go to the theatre. Here we may deride not only comic butts in general but, implicitly, our brothers along with the rest. This unrestrained laughter, which puts sympathy aside, confers a desired feeling of mastery and even racial superiority. But at whose expense? In Sartre's view, at the actor's. The actor arouses laughter by 'wallowing in sub-humanity in order to smear his own self with the stains that might tarnish the "human personage" and to display them as the taints of an inferior race vainly trying to approximate to ours'. He is 'more disquieting and guiltier than a drunkard or a cuckold' because he, unlike them, makes himself ridiculous voluntarily and knowingly. 'Laughter safeguards the serious,' Sartre writes, 'but how can anyone be serious if his job is to make himself a ridiculous object?' The actor is a 'helot', a slave to other people's need for laughter.

This last idea is reminiscent of a passage in Plato's *Laws* (VII. 816–17), where the point at issue is the regulation of those 'laughable amusements which are generally called comedy'. There it is conceded that 'serious things cannot be understood without laughable things'. A member of the governing élite needs to be acquainted with what is low and ridiculous as well as with what is serious, and so should be acquainted with comic performances. But he should 'never take any serious interest in them himself': the task of representing the ridiculous on stage should be left to 'slaves and hired strangers'. This passage anticipates Sartre's argument that the comic actor is somehow tainted by his role, and may well have suggested Sartre's description of the comic actor as a 'helot'. Umberto Eco may likewise have been thinking of Plato's assignment of comic roles to 'hired strangers' when he described the comic as racist, making 'the others, the Barbarians' pay. From these examples it will be seen that discussions of laughter, even those which fully take into account the fictionality of the comic fable, are haunted by the idea that laughter is somehow to be distrusted: in particular, that it always has a victim.

Laughter, according to Bergson, necessarily arises from within a group. Though aware of, and even inclined to emphasize, its harsh aspects, Bergson sees laughter as fulfilling a healthful function. A group, he argues, laughs scornfully at an individual who has become rigid, inelastic, unfit for social living: the group's laughter cures the victim's rigidity and makes him an acceptable member of society. But one of the examples given by Bergson works to undermine his argument: the ritual of initiation carried out on a young man entering a military academy. The initiation, Bergson suggests, is aimed at fitting the newcomer for his new life, at 'breaking him into harness'. But we can see that this 'breaking in', far from correcting rigidity, may simply subject the initiate to a new rigidity, the conservative tradition of the group. There is no a priori reason for concluding, when a group and an individual are in conflict, that it is the group which is flexible, innovative, and the dissenter who is rigid.

Bergson is aware of this difficulty. He even admits that 'it is the business of laughter to suppress any separatist tendency'. But the admission is more than damaging: it threatens Bergson's whole argument. In the closing pages of his essay, indeed, Bergson almost retracts his earlier positive evaluation of laughter. 'Laughter', he concludes,

cannot be absolutely just. Nor should it be kind-hearted either. . . . [It arises from] a spark of spitefulness or, at all events, of mischief. . . . Here, as elsewhere, nature has utilized evil with a view to good. It is more especially the good that has engaged our attention throughout this work. . . . [Laughter] is gaiety itself. But the philosopher who gathers a handful to taste may find that the substance is scanty, and the aftertaste bitter.

Having insisted throughout the essay that the comic butt is afflicted with a dangerous rigidity which laughter can and should cure, Bergson concedes in the closing section that scornful laughter may also turn at times on those who do not deserve to be derided, such as the lonely poetic genius or tragic hero.

Laughter and comedy are not uniformly cruel or harsh. The joviality of which comedy is capable is pleasingly evoked in Ian Donaldson's description of the fourth act of Congreve's *The Way of the World*: 'The mood is genial, expansive, a little heady; four proposals are made, a bottle or two is uncorked, a few songs are sung, some poetry absently recited; there is a dance.' Equally evocative is S. M. J. Minta's eulogy of Marquez's *Love in the Time of Cholera*: 'It is a novel in praise of spontaneity, sexual passion, disorder and vitality, a triumph of the uncertain, sprawling confusion of life over the comforting, dull precision of authority, a victory of the indigenous over the imported, old age over death, the popular over the learned.' However, the element of cruelty is not entirely absent either from Marquez's comic novel or from Congreve's comic play. Nor, as we have seen, is it entirely plausible to excuse such cruelty by arguing that the comic action has nothing to do with real actions: the similarity of many situations and patterns of response is too close. Thus it is that philosophers and critics from Plato to Sartre and Eco have found reasons for distrusting comedy, festivity, and laughter, whether on account of their psychological effects on actors and audiences or because of the ways in which they may be manipulated for sinister ends. Comic plays, films, and novels which seek to eliminate malicious or harsh laughter and rely only on laughter which is at least partly compassionate (on what Eco, following Pirandello, calls 'humour' as opposed to 'comic') are often too bland to satisfy their audiences, provoking comments like that of William Hazlitt on Steele's play *The Conscious Lovers*: 'Lackadaisical, whining, make-believe comedies . . . are enough to set one to sleep . . .' At the other extreme harsh farce, or what Baudelaire and Kern call 'absolute comedy', often goes too close for comfort to what Frye calls 'the condition of savagery', where laughter arises from the torturing of a helpless victim. An element of sympathy or compassion seems to be necessary to comedy if the term is to retain any of its warmer and more genial associations. If laughter is essential to comedy, the yearning for harmony and reconciliation is equally so. Yet the endings of comedies, especially modern comedies, seldom achieve what Pynchon would term 'clear happiness or redeeming cataclysm'. Perhaps, then, the most honest ending is that which simply returns us to the inadequacies of the world ('The rain it raineth every day', as Feste mourns in *Twelfth Night*), to the awareness that life is a struggle in which nobody can always be on the winning side, and where each of us will sometimes fill the role of victim, scapegoat, or fool.

Selected Further Reading

This list consists of secondary sources, such as critical, philosophical, and anthropological works. The volumes edited by Lauter, Morreal, and Sypher, and listed under their names, are collections of key writings on comedy: most significant theories are advanced or discussed in one or more of these three books.

M. H. Abrams, *A Glossary of Literary Terms* (New York, 1981); John Allen, introduction to *Four Continental Plays* (London, 1964); Mary Anderson, *The Festivals of Nepal* (London, 1971); Aristotle, *De Partibus Animalium*, in *Works*, ed. J. A. Smith and W. D. Ross, v (Oxford, 1912); *The Poetics*, in *Aristotle's Theory of Poetry and Fine Art*, trans. S. H. Butcher (New York, 1951); Roger Ascham, *The Schoolmaster*, in *Works*, ed. W. A. Wright (Cambridge, 1904); Stuart Baker, *Georges Feydeau and the Aesthetics of Farce* (Ann Arbor, 1981); Mikhail Bakhtin, *Rabelais and His World* (Cambridge, Mass., and London, 1968); C. L. Barber, *Shakespeare's Festive Comedy* (Princeton, 1959); Charles Baudelaire, 'Of Virtuous Plays and Novels' and 'Of the Essence of Laughter', in *Selected Writings on Art and Artists*, trans. P. E. Charvet (Harmondsworth, 1972); Simone de Beauvoir, *The Second Sex*, trans. H. M. Parshley (London, 1953); Eric Bentley, 'The Psychology of Farce', in *Let's Get a Divorce and Other Plays* (New York, 1958), and 'Varieties of Comic Experience', in *The Playwright as Thinker* (New York, 1946); Henri Bergson, 'Laughter': see below under Sypher; Geoffrey Borny, introduction to Jean Racine, *Petty Sessions*, trans. G. Borny (Armidale, 1988); M. D. Bristol, *Carnival and Theatre* (New York and London, 1985); Norman Brown, *Life Against Death: the Psychoanalytical Meaning of History* (Middletown, 1959); Anthony Burgess, *Joysprick* (London, 1973); Peter Burke, *Popular Culture in Early Modern Europe* (London, 1978); Deirdre Burton, *Dialogue and Discourse* (London, 1980); Olive Busby, *Studies in the Development of the Fool in Elizabethan Drama* (London, 1923); Italo Calvino, *The Literature Machine*, trans. Patrick Creagh (London, 1987); Susan Carlson, 'Women in Comedy: Problem, Promise, Paradox', *Themes in Drama*, 7 (1985), 159–71; Lodovico Castelvetro, *Commentary on Aristotle's 'Poetics'*, extracted in Lauter (see below); Baldesar Castiglione, *The Book of the Courtier*, trans. George Bull

(Harmondsworth, 1967); Terry Castle, *Masquerade and Civilization* (London, 1986); Nevill Coghill, 'The Basis of Shakespearian Comedy', *Essays and Studies*, NS 3 (1950), 1–28; Jeremy Collier, *A Short View of the Immorality and Profaneness of the English Stage* (London, 1698: repr. New York, 1972); Lane Cooper, *An Aristotelian Theory of Comedy* (New York, 1922); F. M. Cornford, *The Origins of Attic Comedy* (London, 1914); Peter Coveney, *Poor Monkey: the Child in Literature* (London, 1957); Noel Coward, *Autobiography*, ed. Sheridan Morley (London, 1987); Harvey Cox, *The Feast of Fools: a Theological Essay on Festivity and Fantasy* (Cambridge, Mass., 1969); Jonathan Culler (ed.), *On Puns* (Oxford, 1988); Jessica Davis, *Farce* (London, 1978); Lloyd deMause (ed.), *The History of Childhood* (New York, 1976); Ian Donaldson, *The World Upside Down* (Oxford, 1970); J. K. Dover, *Aristophanic Comedy* (Berkeley and Los Angeles, 1972); Bernard Dukore, *Harold Pinter* (London, 1982); Umberto Eco, 'The Frames of Comic "Freedom"', in *Carnival!*, ed. Thomas A. Sebeok (Berlin, 1984); Mircea Eliade, *The Myth of the Eternal Return* (Princeton, 1954); George Elliott, 'Afterword' to Mark Twain, *Huckleberry Finn* (New York, 1959); Martin Esslin, *The Theatre of the Absurd* (London, 1962); Willard Farnham, *The Shakespearian Grotesque* (Oxford, 1971); James Feibleman, *In Praise of Comedy: A Study of its Theory and Practice* (New York, 1970); Michel Foucault, *The History of Sexuality*, trans. Robert Hurley, pt. ii, *The Use of Pleasure* (Harmondsworth, 1986); Sir James Frazer, *The Golden Bough*, pt. vi, *The Scapegoat* (London, 1913); Sigmund Freud, *Jokes and their Relation to the Unconscious*, trans. James Strachey (London, 1960: reptd. 1983); Northrop Frye, *Anatomy of Criticism: Four Essays* (Princeton, 1957), 'The Argument of Comedy', *English Institute Essays* (1948), 58–73, and *A Natural Perspective: The Development of Shakespearean Comedy and Romance* (New York and London, 1965); Helen Gardner, '*As You Like It*', in *More Talking of Shakespeare*, ed. John Garrett (London, 1959); Robert Goldsmith, *Wise Fools in Shakespeare* (Liverpool, 1958); Morton Gurewitch, *Comedy: the Irrational Vision* (Ithaca and London, 1975); Charles Hayter, *Gilbert and Sullivan* (Basingstoke and London, 1987); William Hazlitt, *Lectures on the Comic Writers of Great Britain*, in *Complete Works*, ed. P.P. Howe, vi (New York, 1967); David Hirst, *Comedy of Manners* (London, 1979); Baruch Hochman, *The Test of Character* (New Jersey, 1983); Norman N. Holland, *Laughing: a Psychology of Humour* (Ithaca, 1982); Johan Huizinga, *Homo Ludens: A Study of the Play Element in Culture* (London, 1949); Kathryn Hume, *Fantasy and Mimesis: Responses to Reality in Western Literature* (New

York and London, 1984); Robert Hume, *The Development of English Drama in the Late Seventeenth Century* (Oxford, 1976); Francis Hutcheson, *Reflections upon Laughter, and Remarks upon the Fable of the Bees*, in *Collected Works*, vi (reptd. Hildesheim, 1971); Eugene Ionesco, *Notes and Counter-Notes*, trans. Donald Watson (London, 1964); Ludwig Jekels, 'On the Psychology of Comedy', extracted in Lauter (see below); C. G. Jung, 'On the Psychology of the Trickster Figure', in *Collected Works*, ix, pt. 1 (London, 1959); Edith Kern, *The Absolute Comic* (New York, 1980); Walter Kerr, *The Silent Clowns* (New York, 1975); L. C. Knights, 'Notes on Comedy' (see under Lauter) and 'Restoration Comedy: the Reality and the Myth', in *Explorations* (London, 1946); Leszek Kolakowski, 'The Priest and the Jester', *Dissent*, 9 (1962), 214–35; Ernst Kris, *Psychoanalytic Explorations in Art* (New York, 1952); Jacques Lacan and the École Freudienne, *Feminine Sexuality*, ed. Juliet Mitchell and Jacqueline Rose, trans. Jacqueline Rose (London, 1982); Charles Lamb, 'On Some of the Old Actors' and 'On the Artificial Comedy of the Last Century', in *Works*, ed. E. V. Lucas, ii (London, 1903); Rosette Lamont, 'The Metaphysical Farce', *French Review*, 3 (1959), 319–28; Susanne Langer, *Feeling and Form* (New York, 1953); J. Laplanche and J.-B. Pontalis, *The Language of Psycho-Analysis*, trans. Donald Nicholson-Smith (London, 1973); Paul Lauter (ed.), *Theories of Comedy* (New York, 1964); Harry Levin, *Playboys and Killjoys: an Essay on the Theory and Practice of Comedy* (New York and Oxford, 1987); Claude Lévi-Strauss, *Tristes Tropiques*, trans. John and Doreen Weightman (London, 1973); Douglas MacDowell, 'Clowning and Slapstick in Aristophanes', *Themes in Drama*, 10 (1988), 1–13; George McFadden, *Discovering the Comic* (Princeton, 1982); Bernard Mandeville, *The Fable of the Bees*, ed. Philip Harth (Harmondsworth, 1970); Charles Mauron, *Psychocritique du Genre Comique* (Paris, 1964); Moelwyn Merchant, *Comedy* (London, 1972); George Meredith, 'An Essay on Comedy': see under Sypher; John Modic, *The New Way: Sympathy in Comedy from Menander to Cumberland* (Ann Arbor, 1975); David Monro, *Argument of Laughter* (Melbourne, 1951); John Morreal (ed.), *The Philosophy of Laughter and Humour* (New York, 1987); Friedrich Nietzsche, *The Birth of Tragedy*, trans. Walter Kaufmann (New York, 1967) and *Thus Spoke Zarathustra*, trans. R. J. Hollingdale (Harmondsworth, 1961); Ronald Paulson, *Book and Painting . . . Literary Texts and the Emergence of English Painting* (Knoxville, 1982); Plato, *The Republic*, trans. Desmond Lee (Harmondsworth, 1955), and *Works*, trans. Benjamin Jowett, ed. Irwin Edman (New York, 1928); L. J. Potts, *Comedy*

(London, 1948); Victor Raskin, *Semantic Mechanisms of Humour* (Dordrecht, Boston, and Lancaster, 1984); Alice Rayner, *Comic Persuasion* (Berkeley, 1987); W. D. Redfern, *Queneau: Zazie dans le Métro* (London, 1980); Nigel Rees, *Graffiti Lives O. K.* (London, 1979) and *Graffiti 2* (London, 1980); E. C. Riley, *Don Quixote* (London, 1986); Jean-Paul Sartre, *Being and Nothingness*, trans. Hazel Barnes (New York, 1966), and 'The Comic Actor', in *Sartre on Theater* (New York, 1956); Friedrich Schiller, *On the Naïve and Sentimental in Literature*, trans. Helen Watanabe-O'Kelly (Manchester, 1981); Robert Scholes, *Fabulation and Metafiction* (Urbana, 1979); M. A. Screech, *The Rabelaisian Marriage: Aspects of Rabelais's Religion, Ethics, and Comic Philosophy* (London, 1958); Elizabeth Sewell, *The Field of Nonsense* (London, 1952); George Bernard Shaw, 'The Farcical Comedy', in *Selected Passages from the Works of George Bernard Shaw*, ed. Charlotte Shaw (London, 1912); Lee Siegel, *Laughing Matters: Comic Tradition in India* (Chicago and London, 1987); Ronald de Sousa, 'When is it Wrong to Laugh?' in Morreal (cited above); Wylie Sypher (ed.), *Comedy* (Baltimore and London, 1956: reptd. 1980). Contains essays by Meredith, Bergson, and Sypher; Tzvetan Todorov, *The Fantastic*, trans. Richard Howard (Cleveland, 1973), and *Grammaire du Décaméron* (The Hague, 1969); Victor Turner, *From Ritual to Theatre: The Human Seriousness of Play* (New York, 1982); Mary Warnock, *Existentialism* (Oxford, 1970); Patricia Waugh, *Metafiction* (London, 1984); David Willbern, 'Malvolio's Fall', *Shakespeare Quarterly*, 29 (1978), 85–90; William Willeford, *The Fool and His Sceptre* (Evanston, 1969); Ludwig Wittgenstein, *Philosophical Investigations*, trans. G. E. M. Anscombe (Oxford, 1978); Michael Wright, 'The Comic Elements in the Corpus Christi Drama' (unpublished thesis, University of New England, Armidale, 1968); Wayland Young, *Eros Denied* (London, 1968).

Index